D1172634

The Time Is Always Now

for Todd,

with Thanks, and continuing
hope for a better world.

Nick

THE TIME IS ALWAYS NOW

Black Thought and the Transformation of US Democracy

NICK BROMELL

OXFORD
UNIVERSITY PRESS

OXFORD
UNIVERSITY PRESS

Oxford University Press is a department of the University of Oxford.
It furthers the University's objective of excellence in research, scholarship,
and education by publishing worldwide.

Oxford   New York
Auckland   Cape Town   Dar es Salaam   Hong Kong   Karachi
Kuala Lumpur   Madrid   Melbourne   Mexico City   Nairobi
New Delhi   Shanghai   Taipei   Toronto

With offices in
Argentina   Austria   Brazil   Chile   Czech Republic   France   Greece
Guatemala   Hungary   Italy   Japan   Poland   Portugal   Singapore
South Korea   Switzerland   Thailand   Turkey   Ukraine   Vietnam

Oxford is a registered trademark of Oxford University Press
in the UK and certain other countries.

Published in the United States of America by
Oxford University Press
198 Madison Avenue, New York, NY 10016

© Oxford University Press 2013

All rights reserved. No part of this publication may be reproduced, stored in a
retrieval system, or transmitted, in any form or by any means, without the prior
permission in writing of Oxford University Press, or as expressly permitted by law,
by license, or under terms agreed with the appropriate reproduction rights organization.
Inquiries concerning reproduction outside the scope of the above should be sent to the Rights
Department, Oxford University Press, at the address above.

You must not circulate this work in any other form
and you must impose this same condition on any acquirer.

Library of Congress Cataloging-in-Publication Data
Nicholas Bromell.
The time is always now: black thought and the transformation of US democracy / Nick Bromell.
pages cm
Includes bibliographical references and index.
ISBN 978-0-19-997343-9 (hardback: alk. paper)   1. African Americans—Politics
and government—Philosophy.   2. African American intellectuals—Political activity—
History.   3. United States—Politics and government—Philosophy.   4. Liberalism—United
States—History.   5. Equality—United States—History.   6. Political culture—United
States—History.   I. Title.
E185.615.B727 2013
323.1196'073—dc23
2013011934

1 3 5 7 9 8 6 4 2
Printed in the United States of America
on acid-free paper

To the Stanford English Department 1978-'87,
kind, generous, and wise.
And especially to
Jay Fliegelman and Arnold Rampersad,
mentors and friends.

Contents

Acknowledgments

FOR ENCOURAGEMENT ALONG the way, I thank Danielle Allen, Susan Wallace Boehmer, David Bollier, Patrick Bressette, Kay Dodd, Ray LaRaja, Amy Kaplan, Dana Nelson, and John Tirman. For wise counsel, I thank Lawrie Balfour, Clark Dougan, Tom Dumm, Robert Gooding-Williams, Robert S. Levine, Daniel Rodgers, George Shulman, and Jason Frank. For research assistance and support with the manuscript, I thank Shelby Kinney-Lang, Daniel Fennell, Marissa Carrere, Sean Gordon, Casey Hayman, Nirmala Iswari, and Neelofer Qadir. For their care with all stages of the publication of this book, I thank David McBride, Alexandra Dauler, and Peter Ohlin of Oxford University Press.

At the University of Massachusetts: two Deans of the College of Humanities and Fine Arts (Joel Martin and Julie Hayes) have generously supported my interest in political theory; Stephen Clingman and my colleagues in the Interdisciplinary Studies Institute's seminar on "Engagement: The Challenge of Public Scholarship" helped me think through questions about my multiple audiences; and Mary Deane Sorcinelli and her colleagues at the Center for Teaching and Faculty Development helped me with a Mellon Mutual Mentoring Grant on "The New Meanings of Race."

Early versions of parts of this book have appeared in a number of journals, and I thank the editors for their support: Josh Cohen and Deb Chasman at *The Boston Review;* Robert Wilson at *The American Scholar;* Mary Dietz at *Political Theory;* Gordon Hutner at *American Literary History;* Jackson Lears at *Raritan;* and Priscilla Wald at *American Literature.*

Dr. Ronald Bleday at Brigham and Women's Hospital, and Jewel and Verena Johanna Smith brought me back to good health. I will always be grateful for the care they gave me.

My deepest thanks go to my partner and soulmate, Laura Doyle, who read almost every word of this book (suggesting more than a few of them!) and helped me find the path through a maze of revisions to the book you now hold in your hands.

Introduction

BLACK THOUGHT AND THE TRANSFORMATION OF US PUBLIC PHILOSOPHY

"JUST WHAT IS democracy?" a student asks his teacher in W. E. B. Du Bois's unfinished and unpublished novel, *A World Search for Democracy*. The novel's main character, Abraham Lincoln Jones, falters in response. He has answered this question confidently many times before, but now he is perplexed. And when his student presses him, asking, "Where is democracy to be found?" Jones reluctantly confesses, "I do not know. I used to know. I was quite certain. But today I am puzzled."[1]

Many Americans today are just as puzzled as Jones and Du Bois himself were some seventy years ago. Whether we are scholars who study democracy or citizens who observe and reflect upon it, many of us feel not only uncertainty but pessimism or despair amid the persistent crises, the spirit of acrimony, and the energies of resentment or greed that plague our own and so many other democracies today. *The Time Is Always Now* is addressed to all readers who share these feelings. It suggests that as we search to understand and practice our democracy better, we look beyond the predictable authorities we usually rely on (such as Madison, Hamilton, Tocqueville, Dewey, and more recent theorists like John Rawls and Sheldon Wolin) and seek guidance as well from a number of black Americans such as David Walker, Maria W. Stewart, Frederick Douglass, Anna Julia Cooper, W. E. B. Du Bois, Nella Larsen, James Baldwin, Malcolm X, and Toni Morrison. We might ask ourselves: How does the thinking of these writers and thinkers address our current crisis of democracy? How do their insights correct the blind spots of a tradition of white political theory that extends from Plato and Aristotle to Arendt and Agamben? What might we find if we thoroughly unpacked Du Bois's claim that there have been "no truer exponents of the pure human spirit of the Declaration of Independence" than black Americans?[2] *The Time Is Always Now* tries to answer these questions.

Black American thought about democracy has been too varied and complex to be reducible to a single program or philosophy. Still, within the ever-changing stream of black American political reflection, we can discern a strong current that has sought to achieve full citizenship for black Americans by transforming democracy for all Americans.[3] This current has drawn from both the assimilationist and separatist strains of black political thought, so it cannot be held within either term of this binary.[4] Its vision arises in large part from its critique of the racialized nature of US democracy, or what Charles Mills has called "racial liberalism,"[5] yet it does not abandon hope for democracy. Nor should it be identified with what cultural historian Richard Iton has called (perhaps unfairly) the Bayard Rustin legacy of "pragmatism, instrumentalism, and compromise" that renders black political ideas "acceptable [only] if they correspond to the patterns and practices prevalent in the American national context."[6] Many black American thinkers provide insights into democracy that disrupt established "patterns and practices" and propose fundamental transformations of "mainstream American norms" of democratic thought and citizenship.[7]

Their thinking originates in a standpoint, or perspective, profoundly different from that of white Americans and from much mainstream democratic theory, be it liberal, republican, Marxist, Straussian, communitarian, agonistic, or deliberative. As Mills and other black philosophers have emphasized, black American political thinkers have understood themselves to be embedded in the matrix of their historical moment, so that the distancing move on which so much history and philosophy depends was seldom available—or appealing—to them. They have been *activist* thinkers engaged in the politics of the moment. Their raced black bodies have made it doubly unthinkable to them that their theorizing could be occurring somewhere outside of time and space, in a realm of pure thought. This is why Leonard Harris has called black thought a "philosophy born of struggle," and why Patricia Hill Collins writes that "It is impossible to separate the structure and thematic content of thought from the historical and material conditions shaping the lives of its producers." Eschewing the stance of distance and the trope of spectatorship that are embedded in the word "theory" itself, black thought works, as George Yancy writes, "within the concrete muck and mire of *raced* embodied existence." From this place, from the mire of an unrealized democracy, black political thinkers have found that some of the concepts and keywords coined by the white mainstream are inadequate to the task at hand.[8]

For this reason, black American writers and thinkers have often invented vocabularies with a different accent—crafting images, stories, concepts, and keywords to name different stakes and values. We may have read them, but we may not have recognized their words *as* bearers of "political thought" if we have read them solely through the lens provided by the mainstream, white political tradition. "There are tongues in trees, sermons in stones, and books in the running brooks! Those laws did speak!"[9] Frederick Douglass declared in response to the Supreme Court's overturning of the 1875 Civil Rights laws. Douglass was plainly figuring those laws as things of nature that could speak. But why? If we read his words *only* as a metaphor and fail to take with complete seriousness the radical vision of democracy the metaphor points to, we miss most of what he, once considered a "thing" himself, had to say: things can sometimes speak what men know but cannot or will not say. Any effort to put black political thought into conversation with conventional political theory must register the ways black thought exceeds and radically supplements such theory.[10]

A small but growing number of scholars in the field of political theory have begun this work—and as shall become clear, I am deeply indebted to them. (They include, among others, Danielle S. Allen, Lawrie Balfour, Gregg Crane, Eddie S. Glaude, Robert Gooding-Williams, Michael Hanchard, Jason Frank, Richard H. King, Ross Posnock, Adolph Reed, George Shulman, Jack Turner, and Iris Marion Young.)[11] They have given me—as someone housed in an English department and trained to read literary texts—much of the conceptual vocabulary I use to articulate the ways literature thinks about the political in general and democracy in particular. I find common ground with many of these scholars also in believing that the imagination itself does important political work, providing what Wolin has called "a corrected fullness," a vision of political phenomena not only as they are, but as they might be.[12]

Bringing together political theory with my own training in literary and cultural studies, then, I hope to contribute to a vigorous conversation between these fields. Yet even as I work in both disciplines, I also depart from some conventions they share. This book is neither a history nor an elaborated theory of black American perspectives on democracy. Instead, following the orientation of the writers it treats, it put their ideas to work in the present and in response to a particular problem today, and it tries to do so in the most accessible way I can achieve while remaining faithful to my identity as a scholar. (For this reason I have relegated some important technical matters and detailed argumentation to the notes, which I hope my colleagues will turn to if and when they worry that I may be oversimplifying matters.) For *now* is the temporal frame within which these black American thinkers usually placed themselves. They lived in and shared Martin Luther King's "fierce urgency of now." They occupied with Frederick Douglass "the ever-present now" from which he declared, "we have to do with the past only as it is of use to the present."[13]

The Time Is Always Now has been written, then, at a particular moment and with an eye toward a specific problem: the disintegration of Americans' shared understanding of democracy. That shared understanding is sometimes referred to as *public philosophy*, which Michael Sandel defines as "the political theory implicit in our practice, the assumptions about citizenship and freedom that inform our public life."[14]

For the middle fifty years of the last century, such a public philosophy was provided by a broadly liberal tradition that held sway from Franklin Roosevelt through Jimmy Carter. (This distinctive political and cultural liberalism should not be confused with the more narrow economic liberalism known as Manchester liberalism and, more recently, as neoliberalism.) It held within its flexible framework both Republicans and Democrats. They disagreed on many points, of course; but they were willing to bargain with each other, and their bargaining pivoted on the central values and assumptions they held in common.

Since the late 1960s, however, liberalism has stopped making sense to many Americans from all walks of life, and it has failed in particular to command the interest and loyalty of most intellectuals anywhere on the political spectrum. Seizing the opportunity opened by this collapse of liberalism, a well-funded political movement of radical conservatism has worked strenuously to develop and disseminate its own version of public philosophy and thereby to occupy the pivotal center of democratic politics. Its success is evident today not so much in the strength of the Tea Party as in the acceptability of ideas that only a few decades ago would have been considered extremist by most Americans. Meanwhile, the efforts of progressive intellectuals to craft a competing version of postliberal public philosophy have been much less successful. Some have argued that liberalism might be bolstered by an infusion of the eighteenth-century republicanism of the founders; others have called for a strengthening of the nation's civic associations; some have urged a return to FDR liberalism's emphasis on economic fairness; and still others have suggested that the center-left renew itself by drawing upon populist and progressive thought of the late nineteenth and early twentieth centuries. Worthy as they all are, none of these visions of a new public philosophy has gained significant traction in contemporary American political culture.[15]

My proposal here is that some black American thinkers and activists point a way forward. Long familiar with the dangers of American social and political conservatism, yet just as aware of the shortcomings of mainstream liberalism, they offer powerful, alternative practices and visions; they present these as products of American history; and they model what I would call a radical engagement with the center that scholars and intellectuals on the left have much to learn from. In what follows, I focus on four issues I take to be critical in the battle for a new public philosophy—issues that a range of the writers I discuss consistently addressed, if sometimes implicitly. The book deals with these problems sequentially, then examines Barack Obama's ideas and policies in relation to this body of black democratic thought, arguing that he reflects the degree to which some of it—though by no means all—has already entered into and begun to change US public philosophy. I conclude with a brief coda that urges my colleagues in literary studies to reinvest in vision along with critique, and to recall that it is not just the unconscious that is political but the imagination.

The Present Crisis of Public Philosophy

The first challenge to democracy I address is anger. American politics are angrier today than they have been for many decades. The rise of Fox News on the right, and of competing programs on the left, raises a difficult question about anger: when is it a legitimate expression and means of engaged democratic citizenship, and when is it merely a self-defeating form of what Nietzsche called *ressentiment* (resentment)? Can we harness the democratic energies of anger without risking the destruction of democracy itself? These questions have only recently begun to engage political theorists, but as the founders knew, they are questions any public philosophy of democracy must ask and try to answer. What the black political thinkers in this book suggest is that some anger must be honored, but it must also be transformed in order to become productive. Here, for example, is civil rights activist James Bevel's handling of these questions in response to the bombing of the Sixteenth Street Baptist Church in Birmingham, Alabama, on September 15, 1963:

> My first reaction … was anger, rage. The bombing felt almost like a personal insult; the reactionary forces of the Klan, or whoever, were trying to teach us a lesson. Then I got information to the effect that some of the guys involved in it were from the sheriff's department, and then I was thinking about killing people. I had to do a lot of thinking

about that. That's when I started thinking about what would be the appropriate response to that kind of situation.

Clearly, when anger is checked and held as Bevel checks and holds it, it opens a path to reflection, analysis, and action. Yet as Bevel notes, the anger must also be felt and honored, not simply repressed: "I think it's natural for humans to get angry when there's an intense violation, and I think if a person doesn't have the capacity to get angry, they don't have the capacity to think through fully the implications of that which causes them to be angry."[16] As we shall see, the particular kind of anger Bevel is describing here—what I will call "democratic indignation"—promotes constructive reflection and action on behalf of democracy. It also reminds us of what the shared etymology of indignation and dignity implies: such indignation affirms one's dignity and helps recover the importance of dignity to democracy. It thus encourages us to place, alongside the traditional democratic values of freedom and equality, this third value, dignity. For all these reasons, I will argue, democratic indignation is an anger that citizens should respect and even nourish.[17]

The second problem I focus on is the loss of community many Americans are experiencing as they find themselves living in an increasingly multicultural polity. Since the 1960s, the United States has plainly become a more diverse nation: many Americans now reject pressures to conform to an idealized norm—be it ethnic, social, sexual, or religious—and they insist on their right to be themselves and to decide for themselves what they will value. Just as obviously, many Americans cannot accept such differences in others and feel threatened by them. The so-called "culture wars" are still being fought over this disagreement about the scope of legitimate difference in a democracy. Within political theory, this debate has generated a very rich body of thought, much of which centers on whether we should retain some form of universalism, Kantian or otherwise.

The black writers and activists I will be discussing profoundly change the terms in which this issue has usually been cast. Instead of assuming that a democratic community requires its citizens to share ideals and norms, they have imagined community as flowing from citizens being in relationships that mutually recognize and affirm each other's dignity. When the mulatta heroine of Charles Chesnutt's novel *The House behind the Cedars* is snubbed by her white lover after he discovers that she is "black," she says: "he left me without a word, and with a look that told me how much he hated and despised me. I would not have believed it—even of a white man."[18] Such a "look" appears in many works of fiction by black Americans, and their dramatizations of it implicitly argue that a functioning democracy cannot afford to allow its citizens to cast such looks. Further, these black thinkers suggest that white Americans' relentless attacks on the dignity of blacks actually mask a problem that has gone unnoticed by most political philosophers and strategists: most citizens are reluctant to admit that their dignity is not intrinsic to their innermost being but is in fact dependent upon relationships through which it is seen and confirmed. These writers suggest further that as Americans have sought to evade this truth about the vulnerability of their dignity, they have invested in manifest and seemingly incontrovertible signs of it—in their whiteness, above all, but also in manliness and heterosexuality. Thus, they channel their fear about the vulnerability of their own dignity into aggressive attacks on the dignity of persons they mark as "others" by differences of skin color, gender, religion, and sexuality. Racial prejudice, these writers indicate, serves not only to confer economic advantages to whites, as David Roediger and other historians have established, but also to enable their willed, collective blindness to the vulnerability of *every* citizen's dignity. For these reasons, then, US public philosophy should recognize what dignity is and accord it as much importance as freedom and equality.[19]

The third challenge I discuss is often called "globalization." Political theorists and cultural studies scholars have been deeply engaged with this issue in conversations that revolve around the meaning of terms like "cosmopolitanism," "patriotism," "nationalism," and "worldliness." Outside of the academy, many Americans need no such vocabulary, for they clearly see that their nation faces enormous, perhaps unprecedented, challenges to its accustomed autonomy. Many know that global capitalism and transnational financial and commercial institutions are eroding the nation's control over its own economy. They also see this loss of national sovereignty will bring new threats to national security: as *all* nations find their autonomy eroded, military conflict will take both its familiar form of nation fighting nation and also the relatively new shape of attacks by nonstate actors on transnational values and international institutions. This is why after 9/11 the French could proclaim, quite sincerely, that "We are all New Yorkers." But if the French are New Yorkers, are they also Americans? In such a world, who exactly are "We the People?" As political theorist Judith Shklar writes: "If 'we the people' are the sole source of public authority, who are the people? ... No question has been more vexing for modern democratic thought, because it arises not only when self-government is defined, but also whenever democratic governments have to consider their relations to aliens and to other states and peoples."[20]

The radical conservative response to this challenge has been to dig in and fortify the national position: to insist on US autonomy, sovereignty, and even dominance—all evidence to the contrary notwithstanding. Instead of giving Americans a *new* language of national identity that would help them adapt to global changes over which the United States has little or limited influence, it has encouraged them to cling to outdated fantasies of American exceptionalism and world leadership. Political theorists of democracy have been much more constructively engaged with this challenge, and I will be drawing on their work—at times leaning upon it.[21] Yet I shall also be showing that some black writers and artists provide new ways to think about this issue because many have possessed what several historians call "black worldliness": stemming from the black diasporic experience, this is a disposition that readily perceives linkages between the local and the global that many white Americans have ignored, such as the connection in the early twentieth century between Jim Crow in the United States and European and US colonial projects around the world.

We hear such worldliness in the cool reflectiveness of James Weldon Johnson's voice throughout his autobiography *Along this Way*. He recalls, for example, listening to a gang of working-class men talking with each other aboard a steamship sailing between Panama and New York City. In one paragraph, he lays out this sharp analysis of racism and labor in the making of the Atlantic world:

> One expression that they constantly used brought to me more vividly than anything else ever had a realization of the Negro's economic and industrial plight, of how lean a chance was his with his white brothers of the proletariat. The expression which I heard at least a hundred times was, "Never let a nigger pick up a tool." "Never let a nigger pick up a tool." "Never let a nigger pick up a tool." This expression echoed in my mind for a long time.... For no condition under which he struggles oppresses the Negro more than the refusal of a fair and equal chance to earn a living—to say nothing of earning it in ways in which he is able to prove himself well fitted.[22]

Additionally, numbers of black American artists, activists, and intellectuals traveled and lived abroad, where they adopted what Michelle Stephens has called "the perspective of a travelling black subject." This new angle of vision led at least some of them to embrace a conception of democratic citizenship thoroughly infused with worldliness. More specifically, it disposed them to perceive that while the principles on which the United States was founded are indeed distinctive, this nation has no legitimate proprietary claim to them; nor does it have a special responsibility to promote them throughout the world, nor does it even have an insider's superior understanding of them. These writers urge Americans to remember that the founders themselves considered the truths enunciated in the Declaration of Independence to belong to all who chose to acknowledge them. Indeed, they remind us that this document makes the United States an exemplary paradox: it is a nation founded on principles that are inherently and explicitly transnational. Their worldly understandings of US citizenship and identity, I suggest, lend themselves to the challenges of globalization much better than the myth that the United States is a "city on a hill" with a special message and a "mission" to help the rest of the world become American.[23]

The last of the challenges to US democracy I discuss in this book is that of reimagining the place of faith in democratic politics. Liberalism took a clear position on this issue: that there needs to be "a wall of separation" not just between church and state, but between religious and political speech. This view rests, of course, on liberalism's deep commitment to protecting free speech and freedom of worship. Liberalism maintains that we shouldn't care what other citizens say or think so long as those thoughts and words do not interfere with our personal freedom to think and believe and speak as we wish to. To protect and preserve such freedom of speech and worship, liberals ask that we all refrain from injecting our religious values into democratic policy debates.

Since the 1960s, however, increasing numbers of Americans all across the political spectrum have rejected the liberal position. Young citizens on the left became skeptical of liberalism's agnosticism about religious values when they saw how slow many liberals were to embrace the civil rights movement and how long liberals defended the war in Vietnam; to them, liberalism seemed more interested in technocratic efficiency than in basic questions of right and wrong. For Americans on the right, the liberal policies of banning prayer in public schools and eliminating tax-exempt status for denominational schools were likewise manifestations of a public philosophy that had no deep spiritual commitments, no abiding beliefs, no conception of universal truths— that even seemed hostile to them. For these Americans, a conception of democracy that makes room for *everyone's* deepest values seems to foster a democracy that has *no* values. They believe, intuitively in some cases and after much reflection in others, that democracy depends upon its citizens mutually affirming their loyalty to a particular conception of character with particular virtues. They also suspect that liberalism was craftily hypocritical because, while it insisted on value-neutrality from others, value-neutrality was in fact one of its own values.[24]

By and large, whatever their attitude to liberalism might be, most progressives today temperamentally resemble liberals insofar as they distrust religion and "faith talk" of all kinds. This is especially true, I suspect, of political theorists, scholars in literary and cultural studies, and most other academics. Their widely shared assumption is that as responsible intellectuals we must learn to "think without a banister" because there are no transcendent truths, or because "history goes all the way down." As we shall see, however, the reflections of a number of black writers profoundly challenge this assumption, and in ways that speak to both the needs of public philosophy and the lacunae of political theory. Cutting straight across the faith versus pluralism binary that tends to structure this question for both citizens and theorists of democracy in particular, they come at the problem from a different angle, one shaped by black American historical experience.

Living through more than two centuries of slavery and one of Jim Crow segregation, many black Americans turned to and depended on religious faith in order to survive and continue their struggle for full democratic citizenship. For these Americans, there could be no wall of separation between faith talk and democratic politics. Yet many were also aware that most of the established churches in the United States staunchly defended slavery and later the race-based hierarchies enforced by Jim Crow. This dual historical legacy of both needing religious faith and distrusting and doubting it explains why a number of black American thinkers and artists have been able to develop a political language that reconciles—albeit with much tension—their equal commitments to both faith and democratic pluralism.

Here, for example, is Anna Julia Cooper in her essay "The Gain from a Belief" (1892). Addressing skeptics who would urge an essentially secular understanding of life and of democratic citizenship, Cooper argues that what people who wish to *change* the order of things need most is "heroism, devotion, sacrifice; and there cannot be heroism, devotion, or sacrifice in a primarily skeptical spirit. At such times most of all, do men need to be anchored to what they *feel* to be eternal verities." Note, however, Cooper's careful emphasis on standpoint and contingency: what we *feel* to be eternal verities, not what *are*. She goes on to describe what her conception of "faith" consists of:

> I do not mean by faith the holding of correct views and unimpeachable opinions on mooted questions, merely; nor do I understand it to be the ability to forge cast-iron formulas and dub them TRUTH. For while I do not deny that absolute and eternal truth *is*,—still truth must be infinite, and as incapable as infinite space, of being encompassed and

confined by one age or nation, sect or country—much less by one little creature's finite brain.[25]

Cooper thus offers a powerful corrective to habitual secular hostility to faith in democracy without thereby succumbing to the temptations of theocracy, universalism, or tradition. As we shall see, she and other black writers and activists, including Martin Luther King and Malcolm X, understood religious faith as a powerful tension between belief and doubt. They encourage us to admit that there is not much difference between faith in a transcendent order and faith in the equality of all persons. Faith of both kinds requires belief in the evidence of things not seen. Cooper and the other thinkers I discuss point toward a transformed public philosophy that reimagines what faith is and how it might support rather than threaten a pluralistic democracy. They thereby add a valuable dimension to the efforts of those thinkers on the left who, like Jim Wallis, E. J. Dionne, Sally Steenland, and William Connolly, have been trying to reimagine a postliberal relation between faith and democracy.[26]

Certainly these are not the only problems facing Americans today and challenging us to radically rethink our public philosophy of democracy. Some readers may think that the most notable omission from my list is the question of economic fairness: how might Americans reconceive the principles and purposes of their democracy so as to narrow the gap between the nation's wealthiest and its poorest citizens and provide every citizen with the material conditions necessary to sustain human dignity and make freedom and equality meaningful? This is indeed a crucial question, and black American thinkers and activists have much to say about it. (Du Bois, to name just one, by 1933 had given up on democracy understood narrowly as a matter of social reform through electoral politics, and he urged what he and others called "industrial democracy.")[27] I had planned to include a chapter devoted to their thoughts on the subject, but in the end I chose not to for two reasons. First, as I write, a broad range of left-of-center intellectuals and activists are working to foreground the need for greater economic fairness, and a number are already developing arguments that make the pursuit of such fairness congruent with our understanding of democracy. Discussion of economic fairness is already on the agenda; the phrase "1 percenters" means something to almost every American today. Second, and more importantly, I believe that these arguments on behalf of economic fairness can be most effectively advanced if they are framed as corollaries to the arguments I focus on in this book—arguments that place dignity, human relationships, and faith at the center of a progressive vision of democracy. That is, in order to argue effectively for greater economic fairness today, we need to *begin* from a rather different conception of what our democracy is all about—a conception we can derive in considerable part from the insights and experiences of the black Americans I discuss in this book.

Political theorist Michael Hanchard has argued that "black political thought contains within its traditions the possibility of enriching and complicating discussions in political theory about the relationship between theory and history, theory and politics, and the conceptualization of the political."[28] I would go one step further and suggest that black political thought can do more than enrich and complicate: it can fundamentally *transform* conventional political theory and public philosophy with a perspective that has hitherto been largely excluded from them. It is time to take seriously Du Bois's claim that "there have been no truer exponents of the pure human spirit of the Declaration of Independence" than black Americans, and Patricia William's claim that while "blacks never fully believed in rights" they "believed in them so much and so hard that they gave them life where there was none before." It is time to heed Thurgood Marshall's sardonic observation that "'We the People' [are] no longer enslaved, but the credit does not belong to the framers. It belongs to those who refused to acquiesce in outdated notions of 'liberty,' 'justice,' and 'equality,' and who strived to better them." Or as Alain Locke bluntly stated: "It is 'the man farthest down' who is most active in getting up."[29]

Of course, not every white American is ready to give up the fantasy that US democracy is essentially white, but many are. James Baldwin and Toni Morrison and countless other black writers and artists have demolished the notion that a purely white American experience exists somewhere untouched and unshaped by the experience of black Americans.[30] Black American thought, art, language, and attitudes are already woven into US history and culture. These are resources all Americans can draw on as they try to rethink the meaning of their national identity and democracy. If as Reverend Joseph Lowry declared, "It's time for whites to embrace what's right," then it is also time for whites to embrace black insight—perspective, knowledge, and theory.[31] Why should the political thought of white Europeans and Americans remain the only theory to which Americans of all ethnicities turn when constructing and reconstructing their public philosophy? Must we remain locked in this apartheid of experience and perception even after whites have become a minority population in this nation? Hasn't the 2012 presidential election made clear that the time has come to build not just on the votes of citizens of color, but on the varieties of democratic thought their experience has engendered?

I

From Indignation to Dignity

WHAT ANGER DOES FOR DEMOCRACY

*My response to racism is anger. I have lived with that anger,
on that anger, beneath that anger, ignoring that anger,
feeding upon that anger, learning to use that anger before
it laid my visions to waste, for most of my life. . . . My fear of
that anger taught me nothing. Your fear of that anger will
teach you nothing, also.*

—AUDRE LORDE, "The Uses of Anger"[1]

OLIVIA CHERRY, a black woman who lived in Virginia in the early twentieth century, sometimes found temporary work as a field hand at harvest time. At one such job, her white employer kept forgetting her name and calling her "Susie." Finally, she lost her temper.

"Olivia!" she exclaimed. "My name is Olivia. Can you say that?"[2]

A rich political theory of democracy is packed into Olivia Cherry's plainly indignant outburst, but to discern it we will have to place her words in the context of numerous examples of black indignation at white racism and other forms of injustice. Taken as a whole, these indicate first that indignation can have powerful intellectual consequences: it can set one's mind on fire and provoke an inquiry into the *causes* of one's anger. But some black Americans also suggest that for indignation to take this creative turn, one must check and channel it. That is, while they knew that blunt expression of their indignation could be dangerous, they also knew that they would be mistaken to simply repress that upwelling of legitimate rage. Their challenge, then, was to transform it into a productive political emotion—one that encourages an expression of democracy's failures (*I am not being treated fairly*), a strengthening of democratic practice (*recognize my dignity and that of other citizens*), and an enriching of democratic theory (*what exactly is dignity? why do citizens not recognize its importance to each other and to the polity?*).

More than one black American writer, thinker, or activist has believed also that an upsurge of indignation, precisely because it feels involuntary, gives powerful proof of our dignity—to others and to ourselves. They thus perceived the crucial connection between indignation and dignity that is implied by their shared etymology: both words derive from the Latin *dignus*, meaning "worthy," and from the Indo-European root *dek*, "to take, accept." By reminding us that what's at stake in indignation is often *dignity*, these black Americans point us toward a profound revision of American public philosophy—one that places as much emphasis on human dignity as on liberty and equality.

Finally, these black writers, activists, and ordinary citizens suggest that indignation has a third relevance for the theory and practice of democracy. Political theorist Martha Nussbaum has pointed out that because "Indignation involves the idea of a wrong or harm," it is conducive to "reasoning that can be publicly articulated and publicly shaped."[3] This is true. But the figures I will be discussing remind us that indignation also marks the moment when reasoning seems to have run its course, when there is nothing left to discuss. Indignation declares, against all odds and in defiance of what might seem reasonable, that enough is enough. "What!" exclaims Frederick Douglass in one of his antislavery speeches, "am I to argue that it is wrong to make men brutes, to rob them of their liberty, to work them without wages, to keep them ignorant of their relations with their fellow-men, to beat them with sticks, to flay them with the lash, to load their limbs with irons, to hunt them with dogs, to sell them at auction, to burn their flesh, to starve them into submission to their masters? No; I will not. I have better employment for my time and strength."[4] Indignation is thus absolute and unwavering. It tolerates no objection or even qualification: *No, I will not.*

And yet, it is also more dialectical than that. Notice how Douglass himself does in fact argue and reason even as he is indignantly refusing to do either. He melds obdurate indignation with deliberative reasoning, and he thus walks the fine line along which indignation turns into what I will be calling *democratic* indignation. Likewise, Olivia Cherry's shrewd choice of words—calling out her employer with "Can you say that?"—made a reasoned appeal to him even as she vented her rage. She too, in her own way, was walking that line. Democratic indignation is thus a powerful yet self-opposing energy: it risks conflict, yet in checking itself and turning back upon itself, it becomes a cold anger that analyzes and deliberates. To describe it in terms familiar to political theorists: democratic indignation is a dynamic field on which deliberative and agonistic (conflictual) models of democracy find common ground, or blend into one another. It has special pertinence today for anyone who wishes to bring his or her anger into democratic politics, yet who fears that doing so might undermine democracy itself.

"That's When I Started Thinking": Indignation and Political Reflection

In his autobiography, *Along This Way*, James Weldon Johnson writes that as a young man living in Jacksonville, Florida, early in the twentieth century, he would enjoy stopping at a local bicycle shop. "In those days," Johnson recalls, "the bicycle shop rivaled the barber shop as a place for the exchange of masculine talk and information. I used to talk freely about race and racial injustices with white men in town that I knew; perhaps more freely than cautious judgment would have warranted." One afternoon, he found about a half-dozen white men he wasn't familiar with standing around. As he expressed himself with his usual frankness, he was interrupted suddenly by one of them, "who remarked with a superb sneer, 'What wouldn't you give to be a white man?'"

Johnson was stunned by the insult. "The remark hit me between the eyes. The sheer insolence of it rocked me." He felt an instant rush of fury: "The hot retort surged up for utterance." Then, "with great effort I collected and held myself and replied in as measured and level a tone as I could command, 'I don't know just how much I would give. I would have to think it over. But, at any rate, I am sure that I wouldn't give anything to be the kind of white man you are. No, I am sure I wouldn't; I'd lose too much by the change.'" The man "went livid, then purple. The titter died." For a moment, violence threatened to explode. But the young white man "seemed to realize that to beat me up would not improve his position in the eyes of the witnesses to the incident. He was spiritually licked."

Johnson mounted his bicycle and rode away feeling quite satisfied with his reply, but after a while he realized that he was still disturbed by the man's insolent words. They challenged him in a way he had to face. "I thought: I must go over this question frankly with myself; I must go down to its roots; drag it up out of my subconsciousness, if possible, and give myself the absolutely true answer." Did he, somewhere in his being, wish he were a white man? The answer he eventually arrived at was negative: "To conceive of myself as someone else is impossible, and the effort is repugnant."[5] Thus, Johnson's reflections—prompted by controlled indignation—went down to the "roots" of his psyche and discovered there a dignity—dignity understood as a powerfully visceral unwillingness to "conceive" of oneself "as someone else."

We have already seen James Bevel's account of his reaction to the September 15, 1963, bombing of the Sixteenth Street Baptist Church in Birmingham. Here is Pauli Murray, the first black female Episcopal minister and a cofounder of the National Organization of Women, describing a similar moment. Murray goes one step further in identifying what happens in this moment when indignation is transformed into *democratic* indignation; what Bevel calls "the capacity to think through" she describes as "the problem of transforming psychic violence into creative energy":

> It took many years for me to get over the shock of my father's murder....And while I could not always suppress the violent thoughts that raged inside me, I would nevertheless dedicate my life to seeking alternatives to physical violence and would wrestle continually with the problem of transforming psychic violence into creative energy.[6]

The narratives written by former slaves attest that this challenge of holding and transforming indignation is as old as African American experience itself. Henry Bibb recalls the deep indignity of being "compelled to stand and see my wife shamefully scourged and abused by her master," and he writes, "The circumstances in which I was then placed, gave me a longing desire to be free. It kindled *a fire of liberty* within my breast which has never yet been quenched."[7] William Craft describes the day when he and his beloved sister were auctioned off to different owners; he implored the auctioneer to allow him to say goodbye to her, but he was callously rebuffed. Craft writes: "the thought of the harsh auctioneer not allowing me to bid my dear sister farewell, sent *red-hot indignation* darting like lightning through every vein. It quenched my tears, and appeared to *set my brain on fire*, and made me crave for power to avenge our wrongs!"[8]

This rhetoric of heat and fire, which I have italicized, appears frequently in descriptions by former slaves of their reaction to willful and seemingly capricious slights to their dignity. Their narratives testify that they experienced this intensely visceral emotion as a cognitive awakening—a sudden enlargement of thought or activity of mind, a setting of "the brain on fire." J. W. C. Pennington writes that after his father was whipped for no good reason by their master, "each member felt the deep insult that had been inflicted upon our head; the spirit of the whole family was roused; we *talked of it in our nightly gatherings*, and showed it in our daily melancholy aspect....Although it was some time after this event before I took the decisive step, yet *in my mind and spirit*, I never was a *Slave* after it."[9] Perhaps the most eloquent account of the way indignation could be transformed into political reflection and action is James McCune Smith's description of Frederick Douglass: "blows and insults he bore, at the moment, without resentment; deep but suppressed emotion rendered him insensible to their sting; but it was afterward, when the memory of them went seething through his brain, breeding a fiery indignation at his injured self-hood, that the resolve came to resist, and the time fixed when to resist, and the plot laid how to resist."[10]

James Baldwin's phrase for this "fiery indignation" is "the rage of the disesteemed," which he describes as follows:

> The rage of the disesteemed is personally fruitless, but it is also absolutely inevitable; this rage, so generally discounted, so little understood even among the people whose daily bread it is, is one of the things that makes history. Rage can only with difficulty, and never entirely, be brought under the domination of the intelligence and is therefore not susceptible to any arguments whatever. This is a fact which ordinary representatives of the *Herrenvolk*, having never quite felt this rage and being unable to imagine it, quite fail to understand.[11]

Like Johnson, Bevel and Murray, Baldwin describes the painful tension of both feeling one's anger and checking it. Baldwin also tells us that such rage "can only with difficulty, and never entirely, be brought under the domination of the intelligence." In other words, while the intelligence must seek to dominate in order to transform anger into reflective and creative thought and action, that control can never become absolute, since intelligence alone can neither bring dignity into existence nor reason it away. Indignation, as he puts it, "is not susceptible to any arguments whatever." Baldwin also calls attention to two other features of such rage. One is that those who have never experienced it cannot imagine it or understand it.[12] A second is that even those who have experienced it "daily" often fail to honor and understand it; too often, he implies, they feel slights to their dignity as so wounding and so threatening that they choose to repress rather than to reflect upon and rebut them.

"The Stable Equilibrium of Opposition": The Dialectics of Democratic Indignation

If indignation is not susceptible to argument, usually impossible for others to imagine, and often repressed even by those who experience it, it does not obviously recommend itself to theories of democracy that stress communication and deliberation. Yet as we have seen, Murray, Bevel, Johnson, and Baldwin all indicate that indignation can be *transformed* into a creative political disposition if it is turned back upon itself, so that it becomes a self-critical, self-opposing energy.

When indignation does in this way check itself and then turn into political thought and calculation, it seeks to understand why dignity has been denied, and how and when to resist such injury to selfhood. It also becomes a self-opposing as well as an other-opposing emotion; as it critiques the forces that have caused the slighting of one's dignity, it also continuously monitors and appraises one's own response to that slighting. Within African American political discourse, this simultaneously critical and self-critical dynamic has often taken the form of a contentious discussion about when to resist and how to resist, as well as a heated debate about whether black Americans can reasonably hope to secure a dignified place for themselves in a plainly racist US polity. We can hear this appreciation for self-criticism, for example, when Du Bois states that "earnest and honest criticism . . . is the soul of democracy," and when Malcolm X declares about black American political leaders of the 1960s, "I think all of us should be critics of each other. Whenever you can't stand criticism you can't grow."[13]

One early instance of this simultaneously other-opposing and self-opposing quality of black democratic indignation is David Walker's *Appeal to the Colored Citizens of the World*(1829), considered by many to be the first work of black American political philosophy. Walker argues that the "insupportable insult" of denying dignity to the enslaved is precisely what has made the American system of slavery worse than any other form of tyranny known to history.[14] While both the Egyptian enslavement of the Jews and US enslavement of blacks had in common a willingness to exploit and injure the enslaved, only in the United States has insult been added to injury. Whites have blacks in their power, or "under their feet," says Walker, and they take advantage of this to gratuitously insult them. The capriciousness of such insult—that it often seems to serve no practical purpose—points toward its political function, which is to disqualify the enslaved from citizenship in humanity.[15] To such insult, Walker insists, one *must* respond with indignation: "O! My God! I appeal to every man of feeling—is this not insupportable? Is it not heaping the most gross insult upon our miseries, because they have got us under their feet and we cannot help ourselves?" (12).

Walker's *Address* then becomes *self*-oppositional as he turns from criticizing white slaveholders and white citizens to chastising those of his black readers who have failed to respond indignantly to the denial of their dignity—thereby seeming to prove what white men have asserted: that blacks lack a sense of intrinsic worth or dignity. For just as indignation's spontaneous combustion is the indisputable outward sign of one's inner dignity, for oneself and for others, so too the failure to become indignant can be read as a sign of dignity's absence. The stakes are especially high, Walker knows, because when it comes to recognition of their dignity, the black community and the black individual rise or fall together; white racism has joined their fates inextricably.[16] Thus, in his Preamble, Walker addresses those black Americans who "will rise up and call me cursed" and who will argue that "we are well situated, and there is no use in trying to better our condition, for we cannot." To these, writes Walker, he will reply with just a question: "Can our condition be any worse?—Can it be any more mean and abject?" The first step in improving these conditions, he implies, is to see them for what they are and then to react, to become indignant instead of "mean and abject." Walker rails against those of his "coloured brethren, all over the world" who refuse to "rise from death-like apathy" who are "ignorant, abject, servile and mean" (Article Four). Indeed, Walker hopes that his own indignation "will awaken in the breasts of my afflicted, degraded and slumbering brethren a spirit of inquiry and investigation respecting our miseries and wretchedness in this *Republican Land of Liberty!!!!!*" (Preamble). He hopes, in short, that aroused indignation will encourage political reflection (and theory) that might lead to a reformation—or an overthrow—of the Republic.

Maria W. Stewart, a black Bostonian inspired by Walker's writings, makes these self-oppositional energies of transformed indignation even more explicit. In "An Address Delivered at the African Masonic Hall, Boston, Feb. 27, 1833," she points out that "They [whites] boldly assert that did we possess a natural independence of soul, and feel a love of liberty within our breasts, some one of our sable race, long before this, would have testified it, notwithstanding the disadvantages under which we labor."

> We have made ourselves appear altogether unqualified to speak in our own defence, and are therefore looked upon as objects of pity and commiseration. We have been imposed upon, insulted and derided on every side; and now, if we complain, it is considered as the height of impertinence. We have suffered ourselves to be considered as dastards, cowards, mean, faint-hearted wretches; and on this account (not because of our complexion) many despise us, and would gladly spurn us from their presence.... These things have fired my soul with a holy indignation, and compelled me to thus come forward.[17]

Clearly, Stewart's indignation is both a response to white denial of black dignity and then a "holy indignation" at those black Americans who refuse to feel such indignation and thereby invite whites to regard them as "dastards, cowards, mean, faint-hearted wretches."

As a "creative energy" responding to the denial of dignity, then, black democratic indignation has helped produce political reflection that is both practical and theoretical, both other-opposing and self-opposing. Melding critique of the demos with self-criticism, it has contested oppression, deplored quiescence, and debated the forms resistance to oppression should take. It is thus imbued with an intensely dialectical spirit and a deep appreciation for conflict. Anna Julia Cooper both typifies and describes this spirit when she writes, in *A Voice from the South*, "Progressive peace in a nation is the result of conflict; and conflict, such as is healthy, stimulating, and progressive, is produced through the co-existence of radically opposing or racially different elements." She calls this coexistence "the stable equilibrium of opposition."[18] Similarly, as historian Manisha Sinha has argued, black abolitionist thought was never "thoroughly integrated into the dominant political and intellectual discourses" of the antebellum period. Rather, it used "the metaphor of revolution" in ways that "contested the notion and legacy of revolution in the United States." In short, it sought to revolutionize the American Revolution. At the same time, this view of black political thought in the antebellum period must be held in tension with another. As William Andrews says of black autobiography in that period, "the black autobiographer usually rests his case for personhood and justice on proof that he was no stranger to, but in all essential ways the personification of, the principles of the New Testament and the Declaration of Independence."[19] Ralph Ellison often expressed an appreciation of this subtle, self-opposing understanding of the value of conflict. "American democracy is a most dramatic form of social organization, and in that drama each of us enacts his role by asserting his own and his group's values and traditions against those of his fellow citizens. Indeed, a battle-royal conflict of interests appears to be basic to our conception of freedom."[20] His account of jazz as "antagonistic cooperation" at once epitomizes this understanding of the close relation between conflict and freedom and aptly describes a process of transforming "psychic violence" into "creative energy"—a transformation that fuses opposition *and* self-opposition.[21]

In *The Souls of Black Folk*, W. E. B. Du Bois famously asserted that because of their enforced marginalization in white American society, African Americans possessed what he called "the gift of second sight."[22] This perspective has allowed them to see much that white Americans hide from themselves and remain unaware of. What I am calling black democratic indignation is a complementary disposition, but one that is more outcome-oriented and self-reflexive. It is not "political" in the sense that it always or necessarily leads to political action, but it does produce what I am calling political "reflection" that is by nature *driven* toward a goal, for in essence it is always a form of anger seeking relief. In this latter respect, it resembles the democratic "ethical strategy" political theorist Mark. E. Button recommends, one that is informed by Nietzsche's "pathos of distance" and thus "provides a critical reflexive relation to ourselves that affords unavoidably limited and partial beings the opportunity to reflect upon the propensity and price of denying, forgetting, or avoiding moral blind spots."[23] Yet here, too, there are crucial differences. When indignation turns upon itself and becomes a "thinking through" of what caused it, and when it then ponders what might or must be done to eliminate this cause, the individual mind is immediately placed in self-questioning dialogue with itself. Democratic indignation is not so much about "distance"—a stepping back or away—as it is about having to remain within certain conditions and therefore having to check, redirect, and transform the powerful energies of anger. This difference points to a second: democratic indignation certainly is concerned with one's own "denying, forgetting, or avoiding" (as Maria Stewart chastised those of her readers who refused to admit the abjection of their condition); yet democratic indignation is first and foremost a response to the "denying, forgetting, or avoiding moral blind spots" practiced by those who have denied or slighted one's dignity. Simultaneously self-opposing and oppositional, it is an intrinsically *relational* democratic ethics.

What Is "The Essential Dignity of Humanity?"

If indignation bears powerful witness to one's dignity and prompts reflection that analyzes the reasons why one's dignity has been denied or challenged, what exactly *is* the dignity that it both reveals and protects? Within the slave-narrative tradition, the best-known answer to this question is Frederick Douglass's, which he gives as he concludes his account of his wrestling match with the slave-breaker Edward Covey:

> This battle with Covey was…the turning point in my "life as a slave."
> It rekindled in my breast the smouldering embers of liberty. It brought
> up my Baltimore dreams and revived a sense of my own manhood.
> I was a changed being after that. I was nothing before: I was a man
> now. It recalled to life my crushed self-respect, and inspired me with

renewed determination to be a free man. A man without force is without the essential dignity of humanity. Human nature is so constituted,
that it cannot honor a helpless man, though it can pity him, and even
this it cannot do long if signs of power do not arise.[24]

A man without force is without the essential dignity of humanity: following on the heels of his description of his physical struggle against Covey,
Douglass's words have the ring of immediate, intuitive truth. But in fact they
are saturated with ideology. They share the founders' republican conception
of manhood, one epitomized by Patrick Henry's "Give me liberty or give me
death." They also lay claim to the "freedom-loving" character many whites in
the 1850s wished to restrict to the Anglo-Saxon "race," or to the "Germanic"
tribes described by Tacitus in his *Germania*. Finally, Douglass's words refute
the slaveholders' claim to a monopoly of honor and assert that the enslaved,
too, have honor they can defend. Therefore, although Douglass seems to be
asserting a natural fact, he knows very well that he is weaving a sophisticated
rhetorical argument when he lays claim to such dignity for enslaved blacks.
These words are no more an objective description of the outcome of his wrestling match than, say, his Christological rhetoric in the very next paragraph,
where he writes, "It was a resurrection from the dark and pestiferous tomb of
slavery, to the heaven of comparative freedom."

So *is* Douglass correct? *Is* "the essential dignity of humanity" a form of
force or power? Although as Paul Giles has suggested, power was "the central criterion and reference point within Douglass's world…the one thing
he can never forget" (785),[25] the testimony of slave narratives is mixed on
this question; indeed, Douglass's *Narrative* is anomalous because it is one
of the very few to recount an act of successful *physical* resistance to a slave
master. Most other narratives throw into relief how contingent Douglass's
decision was on his unusual circumstances—his personal size and strength,
the happenstance of his being put out to hire with Covey (who had a repu-
tation to protect), and the unwillingness of his fellow slaves to intercede
and help Covey.

Dignity and indignation are represented differently—and more typically—in Harriet Jacobs's *Incidents in the Life of a Slave Girl*. Unlike Douglass,
who tends to present himself as a heroically self-made individual, Jacobs
locates herself within a network of relationships and makes clear that she has
learned about her dignity by observing others and modeling her behavior on
theirs.[26] She tells us that as a girl she was influenced by the stubborn dignity
modeled by her father and by her brother William. She also carefully points

out that her father's dignity seemed to have two sources—one inherent and natural, the other produced socially through his work: he "by his nature, as well as by the habit of transacting business as a skillful mechanic, had more of the feelings of a freeman than is common among slaves."[27] She tells us too that her brother William likewise derived his sense of self-worth both from his own nature ("my brother was a spirited boy") and from his relationship with their father ("being brought up under such influences, he early detested the name of master and mistress") (9). In short, she describes dignity as a quality that confounds the distinction between nature and nurture: somehow, it feels intrinsic to one's being, yet it is produced through social relationships.

One day her brother was called simultaneously by his father and his mistress. He hesitated, uncertain as to who "had the strongest claim upon his obedience," and then went to his mistress. His father was greatly displeased, and instructed him: "You are my child,…and when I call you, you should come immediately, if you have to pass through fire and water" (9). The lesson was clear: by honoring his father's dignity he would also fortify his own.

William absorbed the lesson, and thereafter he encouraged his sister to adopt the same attitude. One particular scene between them is notable in this respect. Linda (as Jacobs calls herself in the narrative) had just been pressured by her master Dr. Flint to submit to his lust, and his "stinging, scorching words" still "scathed ear and brain like fire." She is filled with indignation—"O, how I despised him!"—that is both the sign and the source of her sense of dignity: "When he told me that I was made for his use, made to obey his command in every thing; that I was nothing but a slave, whose will must and should surrender to his, never had my puny arm felt half so strong." Following this scene, she is "absorbed in painful reflections" of the sort that we have already seen such indignation spark when William appears. In the conversation that follows, she at first adopts their grandmother's line and urges William to "not expect to be happy," to try to be "good," and to hope that that eventually such submission will bring him "contentment." William replies that he does try to be good, but that his master troubles him nonetheless. He also says that "he did not mind the smart of the whip, but he did not like the idea of being whipped"—that is, the indignity implied and enforced by such humiliation—and so his involuntary indignation triumphs over his will "to be good." Jacobs confesses, "While I advised him to be good and forgiving I was not unconscious of the beam in my own eye. It was the very knowledge of my own shortcomings that urged me to retain, if possible, some spark of my brother's God-given nature.… The war of my life had begun; and although one of God's most *powerless* creatures, I resolved never to be conquered" (19; emphasis added).

Because Jacobs was a woman subject to the constant threat of rape, and for that reason even more "powerless" than Douglass, she might have seen more clearly than he that dignity seldom can be reduced to a matter of one's personal "force." Continually harassed and bullied by Dr. Flint, she feels his lascivious advances as threats to her "self-respect" and "pride," words that at first express her fidelity to what she calls the "pure principles" of Christian womanhood instilled by her first mistress and her grandmother. However, when she realizes that Flint will never cease trying to seduce and threatening to rape her, she enters into a liaison with another white man whom she calls "Mr. Sands." Narrating this part of her life story, she is painfully conscious that she risks alienating or offending her nineteenth-century readers, most of whom were white, middle-class abolitionist women in the North. In what may be the most-discussed chapter of her book, Jacobs addresses their misgivings directly: "And now, reader, I come to a period in my unhappy life, which I would gladly forget if I could. The remembrance fills me with sorrow and shame. It pains me to tell you of it; but I have promised to tell you the truth, and I will do it honestly, let it cost me what it may."

Jacobs confesses that her "calculation" to have an affair with Sands was "deliberate." Her motives were complex, but the one she emphasizes has to do with asserting her "pride," which I take to mean not her vanity but her personal sense of dignity and self-worth: "to be an object of interest to a man who is not married, and who is not her master, is agreeable to the pride and feelings of a slave, if her miserable situation has left her any pride or sentiment. It seems less degrading to give one's self, than to submit to compulsion. There is something akin to freedom in having a lover who has no control over you, except that which he gains by kindness and attachment" (54–55). Later, to be sure, Jacobs gives a more conventional reason for her affair: knowing that she will perforce bear the children of whichever man she has sexual relations with, she prefers to bear the children of Sands. For Flint was known to sell slaves with whom he had affairs, "especially if they had children." But Jacobs then reverts to the first version of her motives, explaining that she wanted to anger Flint: "I knew nothing would enrage Dr. Flint so much as to know that I favored another; and it was something to triumph over my tyrant even in that small way." Clearly she wants to get revenge on Flint; she feels she can shore up her own dignity through a sally at his, since by preferring another man, she can cast doubt on Flint's manhood.

We can, I think, infer two things about the nature of dignity from Jacobs's *Narrative*. The first is that it is not reducible to or dependent on "force." The second is that, while dignity thrives in conditions of personal and political freedom, it is not to be identified with them. As Jacobs put it, her dignity is something "akin to freedom." Nor is it to be confused with agency.[28] As we have seen, slave narratives suggest that the feeling of possessing dignity is rarely something one can will or exercise agency about; nor does a sense of one's dignity always lead to or take the form of resistance. Dignity occupies a middle space between these terms. It refers to the always-present possibility that a person might recover, remember, or reclaim her sense of intrinsic self-worth through intersubjective exchanges in which that very thing is being slighted or affirmed. Involuntary indignation is often the sensation that catalyzes this possibility, and indignation is always a social emotion, totally embedded in a matrix of intersubjective relations between persons. (We can be angry with things and animals, but not indignant with them. Nor can we willfully display our dignity without looking pompous.) Thus, our dignity is something we cannot ever be the sole creators or possessors of; we need relations with others in which they recognize it; by its nature, dignity is something socially produced and affirmed (or denied).[29] For these reasons, any analysis that simply opposes dominance to resistance and power to agency cannot adequately describe the nature of dignity nor give a complete account of indignation's effects on what Orlando Patterson has called "the battlefront of the political psychology of [the slave's] relation with the slaveholder."[30] Dignity flourishes or suffers in a world in which persons are dependent on one another for an affirmation of one another's worth.

Jacobs's account of dignity as a quality "akin" to freedom but not entirely identical with it can help us perceive an overlooked aspect of Douglass's very masculinist account of dignity as "force." For when Douglass comes to the end of his celebration of his recovery of his dignity, he seems to find that he has not quite exhausted the matter. He writes that his violent resistance to Covey has radically transformed his disposition because it has rendered him "unafraid to die." "I was no longer a servile coward," Douglass writes, "trembling under the frown of a brother worm of the dust, but my long-cowed spirit was roused to an attitude of independence. I had reached the point at which I was not afraid to die. This spirit made me a freeman in fact, though I still remained a slave in form. When a slave cannot be flogged, he is more than half free. He has a domain as broad as his own manly heart to defend, and he is really 'a power on earth.' "[31]

Robert Gooding-Williams has argued that Douglass describes this fearlessness as being a *consequence* of his willingness to use physical force. And it is true that he does. But once again, his words may not be representative of black American experience. As Martin Luther King's strategy of "militant nonviolence" indicates, such a willingness to die in defense of one's dignity is in a very real sense the *opposite* of "force": one can become unafraid of death without lifting a finger, since attitude, not action, is the key. Indeed, Douglass himself describes his inner state as one in which he has fully accepted that he is just a "worm" living among other human worms; he narrates, that is, his acceptance of the absolute nullity of human life, of its meaninglessness, and of the absurdity, therefore, of his ego's terror of extinction. Paradoxically, then, it may have been his radical acceptance of his (and all persons') wormlike *lack* of importance, as much as his force and physical resistance, that enabled him to claim and repossess his dignity. In other words, even his account suggests that dignity can sometimes consist not in defying or resisting the conditions of existence but in snapping one's fingers at them. If this is so, then a full recognition of the unimportance of one's life can become the catalyst of a willingness to die in defense of one's dignity, a willingness that in itself turns out to be the very sign and substance of one's dignity. Such an attitude can predispose one to be ready to use force (though it need not do so), and it can also serve notice to others that one is not to be lightly dealt with. (I believe Malcolm X was threading all these implications together in his phrase "by any means necessary"—the precise meaning of which he consistently refused to specify.) This complex entwining of acceptance and agency, of passivity and power, is voiced in Jacobs's phrase "akin to freedom" and in Douglass's dual explanations of how his wrestling with Covey restored his dignity—and of what that dignity was.[32]

For a mind that reasons only from the presumption of its own freedom, this entwining is difficult to grasp. A mind that presumes itself to be free tends not to see that it is in fact always conditioned by an ineluctable situatedness. It is disposed to carve existence into two distinct realms, the free and the unfree. By contrast, living as they do within conditions of radical *un*freedom, Jacobs and Douglass produce "philosophical reflective thought" that knows its own starting point to be "within the concrete muck and mire of *raced* embodied existence."[33] For this reason, their standpoints and their experience don't quite line up with the conceptual language they must employ to express these ideas. Indeed, the freedom/unfreedom binary itself doesn't quite map onto their life as they experience it nor the world as they know it. Within conditions of enslavement, they can know something "akin to freedom" but not freedom itself. Consequently, their words offer a perspective on freedom and dignity that the conceptual vocabulary derived from classic political theory tends to occlude: We repossess our freedom in part through a recognition of our ontological situatedness; we repossess our dignity in part through a recognition of our individual unimportance; we repossess our power in part through our acceptance of our vulnerability. A person (like Jacobs) who reasons from within conditions that make the *presupposition* of freedom unreasonable does not say only, "I am indignant because you have deprived me of an ontological state of freedom"; for she has experienced possessing dignity when she is *not* free, and she undergoes a loss of dignity when gratuitous insult is added to deprivation of freedom. She understands that dignity has to do with recognition and regard, not just liberty; this is why her relationship with Sands helps her repossess her "pride," or dignity, even though it takes place within conditions of radical unfreedom and therefore requires "compromises" that her audience of "free" readers will censure. She sees that while dignity does indeed refer to the feeling of having "intrinsic human worth," this very feeling arises within—and is dependent upon—a social matrix of interpersonal relations.[34]

The vulnerability of one's dignity—its dependence upon the regard of others—may reveal itself quite strikingly when the tables are turned. Often an enslaved person's mildest acts of self-assertion—or her unconscious presumption of personal dignity—were taken by whites to be personal attacks on their own dignity. That whites' sense of their dignity depended upon its being recognized and affirmed by blacks was something no white person wanted to admit. They asserted (and believed) that their dignity was intrinsic, and the manifest sign of its inward existence was the outward fact of their skin color. Not the look or glance of another, but the whiteness of their skin is what they wished to believe gave them dignity. But in fact, many found that they needed something more—they needed a respectful look from the men and women they enslaved. Yet such a look could have real value only if the person casting or bestowing it was likewise a person with some dignity. So slave masters entrapped themselves in an intersubjective nightmare. Not wanting their dignity to be vulnerable to its denial by, say, the knowing ("insolent") look of an enslaved person, they sought to protect themselves by identifying dignity with whiteness. This logic might have worked if, in fact, the enslaved were not persons themselves (no matter how hard slave masters tried to reduce them to the status of "beasts" or "tools"). Inevitably, however, enslaved persons often consciously or unconsciously acted as the persons they were, and in those moments the racial logic of dignity collapsed. Paradoxical and absurd as it may seem, in such moments the slave master often felt insulted and reacted with his or her own fiery indignation. Indeed, much of the seemingly gratuitous insult heaped upon the enslaved might have sprung from whites' sense of the vulnerability of their own dignity and from their desperate need to place it beyond the reach, so to speak, of those whom they enslaved—by reducing them to nonpersons whose regard or disregard meant nothing. Take this dramatic scene from J. W. C. Pennington's *The Fugitive Blacksmith*:

> I was one day shoeing a horse in the shop yard. I had been stooping for some time under the weight of the horse, which was large, and was very tired; meanwhile, my master had taken his place on a little hill just in front of me, and stood leaning on his cane, with his hat drawn over his eyes. I put down the horse's foot, and straightened myself to rest a moment, and without knowing that he was there, my eye caught his. This threw him into a panic of rage; he would have it that I was watching him. "What are you rolling your white eyes at me for, you lazy rascal?" He came down upon me with his cane, and laid over my shoulders, arms, and legs, about a dozen severe blows, so that my limbs and flesh were sore for several weeks; and then after several other offensive epithets, left me.[35]

Why did his master fly into a "panic of rage" when Pennington's eyes accidentally met his own? "He would have it that I was watching him," writes Pennington: the master interpreted this casual glance as an act of surveillance. But why would he leap to such a paranoid inference? And why would it provoke him to such violent, *panicked* anger? The answer is that by being so absorbed in the craft of his own work, Pennington had existentially stepped out of slavery—not into freedom, of course, but into a state "akin to freedom." When he happened to look up, his eyes were those of a man who had dignity and was expressing it in his very attitude. Not knowing that his master was nearby, he hadn't veiled his eyes or assumed a submissive posture to protect himself and his master from the explosive collision of their two personhoods. His master *panicked* because the truth had suddenly burst into plain view: the truth, so threatening to a slavery system based upon the presumption of innate black inferiority, was that an enslaved black man was a *person* with as much dignity as a free white man. But this was impossible according to the racial logic that identified dignity with whiteness. The master's rage was *panicked* because for an instant this logic had broken down. He could not deny the evidence that his own eyes had involuntarily absorbed by meeting Pennington's glance: that he was seeing and being seen by a *person*. And this was profoundly threatening not just to the slavery system, but to his own personhood and sense of self-worth.

"The Price of the Ticket": The Pain of Nonrecognition

The question of how to transform justifiable indignation into creative political consciousness lies at the center of James Baldwin's essays "Everybody's Protest Novel" and "Many Thousands Gone," which together form a devastating critique of Richard Wright's novel *Native Son* for having failed to effect such transformation. Baldwin begins by situating *Native Son* in a particular historical moment: it was "one of the last of those angry productions, encountered in the late twenties and all through the thirties, dealing with the inequities of the social structure of America." The climate of the 1930s and '40s "promised for a time to shape his [Wright's] work and give it purpose" but actually had the effect of fixing it "in an ever more unrewarding rage."[36] Bigger Thomas's rage, which Baldwin takes to be Wright's as well, is "unrewarding" not because it is an unreal or surreal fantasy; on the contrary, Baldwin declares that "there is...no Negro living in America who has not felt, briefly or for long periods,...simple, naked, and unanswerable hatred; who has not wanted to smash any white face he might encounter in a day." The reason why Wright's rage is "unrewarding," Baldwin argues, is that it remains unanalyzed and uncontrolled; it is no more than a stereotype of African American life, as Bigger's anger merely reproduces the familiar "image" of the "nigger":

> The "nigger," black, benighted, brutal, consumed with hatred as we are consumed with guilt, cannot be blotted out. He stands at our shoulders when we give our maid her wages, it is his hand which we fear we are taking when we are struggling to communicate with the current "intelligent Negro," his stench, as it were, which fills our mouths with salt as the monument is unveiled in honor of the latest Negro leader.... He is indeed the "native son," he is the "nigger." Let us refrain from inquiring at the moment whether or not he actually exists; for we believe that he exists. (28–29)

What the Bigger image erases, writes Baldwin, is the fact that every black American has had to make an "adjustment to the 'nigger' who surrounds him and to the 'nigger' in himself" (29). The image does express a truth, the flaring of his inner rage; but it also obscures a truth—that most black Americans adjust to the image by seeing that it is incomplete. Most black Americans realize, according to Baldwin, that identifying completely with such rage amounts to surrendering one's complex personhood to the stereotype of the "nigger" that white Americans would like to reduce one to. This is why the "adjustment must be made—rather, it must be attempted, the tension perpetually sustained—for without this he has surrendered his birthright as a man no less than his birthright as a black man" (29–30).

The "tension" that "must be perpetually sustained" is precisely the struggle to honor indignation by acknowledging yet also transforming it into an energy that isn't self-destructive or self-limiting. Because *Native Son* neither invokes nor sustains this tension, Baldwin argues, it actually fails to do justice to the "anger which is, on the one hand, exhibited and, on the other hand, denied" (31). Again, Baldwin insists that he is not advocating an Uncle Tom-ish acquiescence or forbearance, for his point is that blacks in America are "compelled to accept the fact that this dark and dangerous and unloved stranger [the nigger/Bigger] is part of" them forever. And they must accept this part, recognizing at the same time that it is not the whole of who they are. "Only this recognition sets him [the Negro] in any wise free and it is this, this necessary ability to contain and even, in the most honorable sense of the word, to exploit 'the nigger,' which lends to Negro life its high element of the ironic" (33).

In the last analysis, Baldwin provocatively continues, Wright's seemingly radical work inadvertently reproduces the old and innocent liberal dream unwittingly articulated by the radical lawyer Max, who defends Bigger. "Max's long and bitter summing up," writes Baldwin, "is addressed to those among us of good will and it seems to say that, though there are whites and blacks among us who hate each other, we will not; there are those who are betrayed by greed, by guilt, by blood lust, but not we; we will set our faces against them and join hands and walk together into that dazzling future when there will be no white or black. This is the dream of all liberal men, a dream not at all dishonorable, but, nevertheless, a dream" (34). It is a dream because it does not face what Baldwin calls "reality." It does not come to grips with the reality of human suffering, and it fails to understand that human beings are indelibly marked by "greed and guilt and blood lust."

It is worth noting here that, as they sought to transform their rage into "creative energy," both Baldwin and Ellison committed themselves to what we might call a radical engagement with the center. Their critique of liberalism was an effort to critique and transform US public philosophy—since at that time liberalism was its dominant understanding of democracy. Ellison, himself deeply liberal in some respects, was especially concerned with the tendency of establishment liberals to maintain their power by avoiding conflict, mollifying southern racists, and counseling black intellectuals and activists to remain "patient." Directly engaging with liberalism as an interpretation of democracy, Ellison frequently argued that democracy is based on conflict—not, as most midcentury liberals would have it, on the disinterest of educated experts and the political consensus they brokered. Conflict has to be tolerated so it can express itself in the give-and-take of political competition and debate that is indispensable to a democracy; at the same time, however, such conflict has to be constrained and transformed so that it remains cooperative and never becomes violent. Ellison borrowed Kenneth Burke's concept of "symbolic action" to describe this transformation:

> the drama of democracy proceeds through a warfare of words and symbolic actions by which we seek to advance our private interests while resolving our political differences. Since the Civil War this form of symbolic action has served as a moral substitute for armed warfare, and we have managed to restrain ourselves to debate which we carry on in the not always justified faith that the outcome will serve the larger interests of democracy.[37]

Although Baldwin believed that the indignant person must try to "sustain the tension" in order to transform "unrewarding rage" into democratic indignation, he also made clear that such personal effort alone was not enough. Precisely because indignation is an emotion that expresses betrayal in a relationship, the person or persons who sparked that indignation also must shoulder responsibility for its transformation. A good deal of Baldwin's work expresses his bitter disappointment with whites because even the best of them refused to accept this responsibility. He frequently describes what happens to black rage when it encounters the blank, innocent defensiveness of the white man or woman who lacks the moral courage to understand and respond to it. Such unrecognized indignation "cannot be hidden," Baldwin says; "it can only be dissembled":

> This dissembling deludes the thoughtless, and strengthens the rage and adds, to rage, contempt. There are, no doubt, as many ways of coping with the resulting complex of tensions as there are black men in the world, but no black man can hope ever to be entirely liberated from this internal warfare—rage, dissembling, and contempt having inevitably accompanied his first realization of the power of white men. (122)

In short, when black indignation goes unrecognized by those white persons to whom it responds, it turns quickly into contempt. This contempt does little good for the person who harbors it, and it dangerously mirrors the white denial of black humanity that democratic indignation itself contests. Everyone concerned—the entire democratic community—falls into a vicious circle from which there seems to be no escape.[38]

We are now in position to understand what Baldwin meant when he wrote that "the concepts contained in words like 'freedom,' 'justice,' 'democracy' are not common concepts; on the contrary, they are rare. People are not born knowing what these are. It takes enormous and, above all, individual effort to arrive at the respect for other people that these words imply" (609). Baldwin's claim that "people are not born knowing" the meaning of these concepts is his way of saying that they are not born knowing what democracy is or how to practice democratic citizenship. Democracy requires them to make an "individual effort" to arrive at the "respect for other people" they do not naturally or conventionally feel. It requires them to understand that democracy and freedom and justice mean very little without dignity. In a later chapter, we will see Baldwin trying to dramatize in a work of fiction what such individual effort might look like—what pitfalls it must skirt and what risks it must be willing to take. Here we can gain a preliminary understanding from a published dialogue between Womanist Katie Cannon and (white) Episcopal theologian Carter Heyward. Both are making the kind of effort Baldwin called for.

"Black women writers have a never-ending commitment to present the anger and rage of the sisters of Yam," says Cannon, "to make whole the brokenness, to heal the bent-overness, so that we can stand tall, claiming the heritage 'from which we sprang when the birds of Eden sang.'" The question she poses to Heyward is, *Can you hold the anger?* This is the question all the black writers I have discussed in this chapter implicitly pose to their white readers:

> So if white sisters and others who cast their lot with us cannot or will not deal with black women's anger on the printed pages, how can they/you live in solidarity with our anger off the page, in real life? My anger, and my sisters' anger, this collective intense anger, is troubling the waters, and the question I pose with piercing X-ray vision inherent from the beginning [is]—Can you hold the anger? Do you know how? Will you ask why? If we understand the power of anger in the work of love, where is the power? Where is the love?[39]

Cannon's point is that the responsibility for transforming anger into the vital energy of democratic indignation falls equally upon two persons: the one who feels it, and the one who has provoked it. As Audre Lorde emphasizes in "The Uses of Anger," we must learn not just to express our own indignation but to hear and hold that of others: "We cannot allow our fear of anger to deflect us nor seduce us into settling for anything less than the hard work of excavating honesty.... Anger is a source of empowerment we must not fear to tap.... When we turn from anger we turn from insight, saying we will accept only the designs already known, those deadly and safely familiar" (8–9).

The holder of anger, or the antidote to contempt, is respect. Only respect for our own and each other's dignity is what gives us the strength to express and hear each other's anger. But when the trigger of that anger is, precisely, a failure to accord that respect to others, indignation must be the force that can catalyze such recognition. Yet, all too often, the response to such indignation is defensive denial, guilt, and fear. This vicious circularity explains, I believe, why James Weldon Johnson ruminated (in two unpublished notebook entries): "Is it really necessary for us to love each other? Is it possible? Is, after all, any more than respect for each other necessary and desirable?" And again: "It isn't so much love that is needed among the peoples of the world as mutual respect. We can get along with less love—but we need more respect. If it came to a choice between Love and Respect, I'd prefer to be respected. We sometimes hurt very badly the persons we love." This is also why Baldwin believed that "It takes enormous...effort to arrive at the respect for other people" that words like "freedom," "justice," and "democracy" imply. Lorde calls this effort "the painful process of translation" and "the hard work of excavating honesty." Painful and difficult, but not impossible. For as Cannon suggests in her phrase "the power of anger in the work of love," these seeming opposites can be held in tension, showing us that when indignation is understood and recognized as the vulnerable thing that it is, it can build the "beloved" democratic community. Conversely, as I shall now suggest, indignation that is not transformed or translated is all too likely to become a self-destructive *ressentiment*.

"Indignez-vous": From Ressentiment to Indignation

The words of black Americans who have experienced and reflected on indignation and dignity shed revealing light on the present moment. Today, in this country, many citizens who are perfectly at liberty to go where they choose and say what they think nonetheless find that their freedom in itself is not enough. They need as well a token or talisman, a visible sign of their dignity. For those citizens who have taken their whiteness to be such a talisman, the very idea of a black president is profoundly threatening, since it renders absurd their investment in whiteness as the sign and substance of their dignity. Feeling this injury to their selfhood, they respond with indignation; but it is not the self-checking indignation that transforms itself into a reflective and creative energy, it is a righteous and sometimes nihilistic fury. This is the rage James Weldon Johnson's young white interlocutor felt when he was faced with a black man more accomplished than he. It is the rage of those who feel disesteemed because the specious value of their whiteness is no longer readily available to them as a substitute for dignity.

Yet these black writers' insights into indignation do more than illuminate the nature and function of racism in a democracy; they also address the anxiety that helps produce racism in the first place. This is the worry that *every* citizen feels at times—the fear that he or she lacks dignity, that he or she will not be "seen." This fear circulates independently of racism and haunts citizens of all races, ethnicities, and classes. The perspective of the black figures I have been discussing indicates that while most citizens pay lip service to the idea of "intrinsic human dignity," very few wish to explore its meaning because doing so would bring them face to face with the truth that their dignity, while it might feel intrinsic, is actually a product of social interaction.

Today, thanks to the unceasing efforts of elites and other concentrations of power in the United States, these fears are being exacerbated. Increasing millions of citizens are living in or near poverty and are less and less able to secure the basic conditions that would enable them to live confidently with self-respect. Because, as Martha Nussbaum writes, they lack the "social bases of self-respect and nonhumiliation," they feel they are not being "treated as a dignified human being whose worth is equal to that of others."[40] Even those citizens who do not suffer these material deprivations are bombarded by a steady stream of untruths, equivocations, and euphemisms that constitute a running insult to the intelligence, and to the dignity, of the demos collectively and of each citizen individually. To be sure, these insults are usually less obvious and less immediately harmful than the words "We don't serve Negroes here," but cumulatively they take a heavy toll, enlisting citizens to join in mockery of their own stupidity and powerlessness.

Political theorist Wendy Brown has gone so far as to suggest that such failures of US democracy are inevitable. Because liberal democracy paradoxically espouses both liberty and equality, it ignores that these two ideals inevitably conflict with one another; if it delivers on its promise of liberty, it reneges on its promise of equality, and vice versa. And because US democracy also holds out to citizens the impossible promise of a self-mastering autonomy and full self-actualization few can actually achieve, millions of Americans are set up to "fail." Baffled and resentful, they look for someone or something to blame. Since blaming themselves would only intensify their pain, they blame and cause pain to others.[41]

This hard logic is Brown's version of Nietzsche's *ressentiment*, and it obviously has something in common with indignation: both terms describe an emotional response to the experience of being hurt or wronged by a political and social order, and both point toward the political consequences of this emotion. Nietzsche's and Brown's account is largely theoretical, a chain of inferences from their psychological understanding of how an individual tends to react to (what feels like) personal failure that (in fact) has been caused by a political and/or social domination and its ideology. My account is largely historical, derived from the first-person testimony of some persons who have experienced such emotion and who have then sought, successfully, to direct or control its political consequences. This testimony bears witness, first and foremost, that individuals do not always or necessarily respond to hurt with the *ressentiment* that worries Brown; on the contrary, they can—with the self-consciousness Johnson, Murray, Bevel, and Baldwin have exhibited—transform their initial pain into a productive political emotion rather than a corrosive one.

The question arises then: could *all* citizens—including white citizens—ever acknowledge that their dignity is vulnerable because it depends upon affirmation by others? Could they then understand that much of the pain they are feeling stems from assaults upon their dignity and from their own (repressed) fear of their dignity being denied or destroyed? And could they then respond to such assaults with democratic indignation rather than *ressentiment*? That is, absent the coercive forces that have *compelled* many black Americans to transform indignation into democratic indignation, could citizens today turn their anger into political reflection and, potentially, political action? Could the words Malcolm X spoke in 1964 to a mainly black audience ever have resonance for *all* Americans?

> When they [people] get angry, they bring about a change. When they get angry, they aren't interested in logic, they aren't interested in odds, they aren't interested in consequences. When they get angry, they realize the condition that they're in—that their suffering is unjust, immoral, and illegal, and that anything they do to correct it or eliminate it they're justified. When you and I develop that type of anger and speak in that voice, then we'll get some kind of respect and recognition,

and some changes from these people who have been promising us falsely already for too long.[42]

The answer to these questions depends a great deal on what Americans take to be their public philosophy of democracy. It depends, I would argue, on their reconstructing that public philosophy on the basis of three values, not two: liberty, equality, and *dignity*. Surely both the Tea Party and the Occupy Wall Street movements are expressions of anger, but it remains to be seen whether either will be able to "sustain the tension" for very long and thereby transform its anger into what Pauli Murray called "creative energy." The black writers I have discussed here would suggest that the moment for such transformation is always now. The question they would pose to those who have mistakenly imagined that they could take their dignity for granted is whether they can recognize their anger for what it is: a response to the denial of their dignity, that precious yet vulnerable sense of self-worth they neither hold by nature nor produce independently of one other. These black writers and thinkers would also ask whether Americans of all races and ethnicities can commit to protecting each others' dignity not by excluding "others" to whom they have denied it, but by recognizing and nurturing the real thing among themselves. These questions, which are surely political theory questions, are packed into Olivia Cherry's plain and indignant words to her employer: "Olivia. My name is Olivia. Can you say that?"

2

"*This Is Personal*"

THE POLITICS OF RELATIONSHIP IN
JIM CROW AMERICA

*Race relations, in an ultimate sense, are personal relations,
and changes in relations may be expected to follow changes
in personal experiences.*[1]
—CHARLES S. JOHNSON

"THIS IS PERSONAL," begins J. Saunders Redding's *On Being Negro in America* (published in 1951). What he meant by that sentence are two things deeply characteristic of the constellation of black thought that is the subject of this book. The first is skepticism toward representation—toward the idea that any one thing or person can accurately stand for others. As Redding goes on to say, "I have been clothed with no authority to speak for others, and what I have to say can be final only for myself."[2] Redding's second point is only implied: that democratic citizenship depends upon democratic *relationships* among persons, so that democratic politics are always, in this sense, "personal." We hear such sensitivity to the relational dimension of citizenship more explicitly when black congressman John Lewis urges Americans today "to begin turning back toward one another, to humanize one another.... We cannot afford to keep going this way. If we are to survive as a society, as a nation, we must turn toward one another and reach out in every way we can. It is not a choice; it is a necessity. We need to listen to one another, to look, to open our minds as well as our hearts."[3]

Before looking further into the historical roots of this disposition, I want to touch briefly on its significance for US public philosophy. The belief that we should imagine "We the People" as being in relationship with one another can be seen as occupying a middle space between liberalism and republicanism, public philosophies which have long competed with each other and which have tended to dominate current discussion of the subject.[4] Liberalism conceives of democracy as a collectivity of citizens bound only by a minimal agreement: they have given up certain freedoms in order to gain safety in numbers and secure their rights collectively; each of them may pursue a distinctive vision of personal happiness so long as he or she does not interfere with the rights of other citizens to do likewise. Liberal political theory is thus averse to the very idea of imagining citizens as bound together in a relationship of any kind. It tends to envision the demos as an aggregation of individual wills, like so many marbles filling a jar or so many individuals crowded into an elevator; no one is obliged to share values with, or even to speak to or make eye contact with anyone else. Republicanism, by contrast, asserts that the project of self-government can succeed only if those involved prepare and train themselves for the task. This requires them to share certain values, in the light of which they educate their children and themselves to become good citizens. In the eighteenth and early nineteenth century, US republicans believed in such "core values" as tolerance, reasonableness, patriotism, and prudence. More recently, some have argued that Americans must share "traditional family values," including obedience to the father and husband, and abomination of homosexuality. Advocates of republicanism as a public philosophy believe that before citizens set foot in the elevator, they should first agree upon a shared code of values and principles; and if they later come to dissent from these, they should be chastised and even punished.

Certain black American writers would steer a middle course. They would agree with civic republicans that a democracy needs powerful affective bonds holding citizens together in the collaborative enterprise of self-government, but they would also be resistant to any prescriptive basis for democratic citizenship—to any requirements or tests citizens would have to meet in order to belong to the demos. After all, for the nearly four hundred years that African Americans have lived on the North American continent, they have been excluded from such full participation in the demos on the basis of their alleged failure to live by its core values. They have seen firsthand the danger of permitting any one version of citizenship, or one set of values, or one vision of the truth, to represent the varied standpoints of the democratic polity as a whole. Their long history of being excluded has disposed them, therefore, to adopt *both* a more pluralistic conception of democracy than civic republicans espouse *and* a deeper appreciation of civic life and mutuality than most liberals find appealing.

As we have already begun to see, another reason some black Americans have been disposed to occupy this space between liberalism and republicanism is that they understand the importance of dignity to democracy. They have experienced how vulnerable our dignity is, and they have known that we produce and sustain it through relationships with one another. In recognizing the importance of dignity, they share with civic republicans the belief that citizens must have something "in common" with each other. But because dignity resembles a state of being more than it does a principle or value, it does not entail the kinds of substantive commitments that rightly worry pluralists—such as, for example, that citizens must all believe in God or must all possess particular virtues. Similarly, the conviction that citizens are obliged to nurture and recognize each other's dignity shares with civic republicanism the belief that democracy implies obligations, not just rights. But the obligation to recognize another person's dignity turns out to be less constraining than many of the kinds of obligations favored by civic republicans. As we shall see, to recognize each other's dignity is not so much to share a substantive quality called "dignity" as it is to relate to fellow citizens in accordance with certain protocols that guide us all.

To perceive this "in between" position more clearly, we might draw upon political theorist Bonnie Honig's distinction between virtue and *virtù* theories of politics. Writing in the early 1990s, Honig was worried that a broad range of political theories were formulating models of ideal democratic politics that worked to minimize the possibility of anything going wrong within them. Honig argued that these theories tend to exclude as "remainders" anything that might throw sand in their models or elude the boundaries of their definitions; they thereby inadvertently "displace" politics insofar as the political itself comes into being when and where contestation of such ideal systems occurs. Honig goes on to brilliantly elaborate an alternative way of doing political theory, one she calls "*virtù*" theory: it aims to disrupt rather than consolidate, to explore fissures rather than to seek closure, and to promote contestation rather than reconciliation. In so doing, it keeps politics alive within political theory and democracy.[5]

The black thinkers I discuss share the orientation of Honig's *virtù* thinkers insofar as they locate a radical indeterminacy at the heart of their politics of dignity. This indeterminacy resides in the fact that our dignity (as they see it) is inextricably bound up with our distinctive individual personhood, and this can never be fully known or shared by any other person. This unknowable personhood, and respect for it, is what safeguards their vision from hardening into a virtue theory; by placing such a mystery at the heart of the demos and its public philosophy, they keep these radically open to revision and enlargement. Yet, these black thinkers have an attitude toward the unknowable that is crucially different from Honig's position vis-à-vis what she calls the *performative* (the "let us say that it is so" statement). Honig wishes us to use reason, or reasoned arguments, to protect the performative from the despotism of the *constative* (the "this is what is" statement) because every time we claim to say that such-and-such *is* so, we shut down the very possibility that other things might be so, and that other perspectives might be valid. As we shall see in a later chapter, the thinkers I discuss would suggest that, if an indeterminacy is what allows free play and flexibility in both democracy and *virtù* theory, then we should offer it not just the protection of our reasoned arguments but our reverence. (As when Du Bois said: "We need, then, first, the strengthening of ideals of life and living; of *reverent faith* in the ultimate triumph of the good and of hope in human justice and growth.")[6] They are skeptical, that is, of reason's ability to keep its own tendency toward despotism in check. To be sure, any check we impose upon our reasoning must be exerted by our reason; yet for reason to have the strength to oppose itself in this manner, it must have a profound awareness of its *limits*—an awareness that opens itself to a sense of its own vulnerability. In turn, awareness of our vulnerability can call us to imagine having not just a custodial relation to that which destabilizes and disrupts but a relation characterized as well by humility. The "self-overcoming" Honig celebrates may require the self to acknowledge an unknowable that surpasses it. Such an attitude is just as incompatible with liberalism's emphasis on the self setting the terms for its own happiness as it is with republicanism's emphasis on the citizen having an identity that overlaps with others insofar as they all share certain values.

The Politics of Relationship and Dignity: From Slavery to Jim Crow

The inclination to understand both the importance of dignity and its dependence on relationships had its origin in the condition of enslavement. "Slavery, for the slave, was truly a 'trial by death,'" according to Orlando Patterson. "Out of this trial the slave emerged, if he survived at all, as a person afire with the *knowledge of* and the need for dignity and honor.... Confronted with the master's outrageous effort to deny him all dignity, the slave even more than the master came to *know* and to desire passionately this very attribute. For dignity, like love, is one of those human qualities that are most intensely felt and *understood* when they are absent—or unrequited."[7] I have emphasized Patterson's words *knowledge, know,* and *understood* because we are engaged here in a recovery of what enslaved persons might have known and even theorized about dignity, not just what they might have experienced without reflection. We can reasonably suppose that they knew their dignity to be exceedingly vulnerable to denial by others and therefore dependent upon recognition by others. They certainly understood as well the crucial role a community plays not just in affirming one's dignity through a casual look or word but in nurturing and sustaining one's dignity when it is under assault from others. These insights into the relational nature of dignity led them to understand in turn that relationships are sites of intense political struggle as persons assert dominance over, or resist submitting to, the power of others. The enslaved would have understood these things because, as Patterson makes clear, the slavery system waged unremitting war upon their dignity; it was not just incidentally or collaterally damaged by the master's exploitation of their labor; rather, their dignity was itself the citadel to be captured and razed, day after day, year after year, because the very system of slavery as it existed in the United States rested on the claim that the enslaved were not even persons. There could hardly have been an enslaved man or woman who did not know, by the time he or she had reached a certain age, that dignity was the precious possession over which the enslaved and the master fought—and that relationships were the terrain across which this struggle was waged. As historian Steven Hahn has argued, "Slavery...was a system of extreme personal domination in which a slave had no relationship that achieved legal sanction or recognition other than with the master, or with someone specifically designated by the master.... Consequently, the slaves' struggles to form relations among themselves and to give those relations customary standing in the eyes of masters and slaves alike was the most basic and the most profound of political acts in which they engaged."[8]

Relationships became contested political grounds both as enslaved blacks and then the freedmen after Emancipation struggled to preserve and promote relationships among themselves, and also as whites and blacks struggled to control the nature and the meaning of their relationships with each other. In *Incidents*, as we have seen, Jacob describes in detail her long, pitched battle with her master, Dr. Flint, who sought by all means short of brute force to make her his concubine—that is, to structure the master/slave relationship as a master/concubine relationship. Flint clearly wished to have at least the *semblance* of an authentic, reciprocal relationship with her. Jacobs never tells us so, but we can infer from Flint's words and actions that he did not wish her to be merely an inhuman object of his physical desire; he did not want to put himself in a position where sexual relations with her would have consisted of repeated rapes. In short, it wasn't just her body that he desired but her person, her personhood. However, as Jacobs makes clear, the very fact that he, who held her enslaved, could imagine having an authentic relationship with her, only intensified her repulsion and disdain—and her determination to resist. For what his fantasy expressed was the ugly hypocrisy lurking at all times in the attitude slave masters took toward the persons they had enslaved. If they had consistently treated them simply as "living tools" or "brutes," they would have been evil enough. But even worse was that they tried to form and benefit from relationships with their slaves—relationships predicated implicitly in word and glance and touch on their recognition of their slaves' humanity—while at the same time formally denying their slaves' personhood in order to continue benefiting from their unpaid labor.

Against this manifest hypocrisy, the political objective of many slaves was both "to form relationships with other slaves" (as Hahn argues) *and* to deny or transform their relationships with their masters. Since the master was trying to benefit from relationship even while formally and legally denying it, an enslaved person's political resistance could take the form of spurning such relationship (as Jacobs did) or of insisting that this relationship be acknowledged and honored. William Wells Brown writes that after being hired out to various persons by his master, he returned "home" to discover that all the rest of his family had been sold away. His master approached him "very politely," which immediately suggested to Brown "that something was the matter." Sure enough, his master informed Brown that, since he had sold all the rest of Brown's family, he thought it best to sell him now as well. In response, Brown tells us, "I raised up my head, and looked him full in the face. When my eyes caught his he immediately looked to the ground" (27). Clearly, Brown's master was deeply ashamed. He knew that he had a relationship with Brown and his family, and he knew that he had denied that relationship by selling them and by now intending to sell Brown. When Brown looked him "full in the face," he had to look away both to conceal his shame and to deny the relationship both men knew was there. But in doing so, of course, he implicitly acknowledged the very facts he was seeking to deny.

Both former masters and former slaves carried this knowledge about the politics of relationship and the contest over dignity into the radically different conditions that followed the Emancipation Proclamation and then the South's defeat in the Civil War. To be sure, most of the free black Americans living in the North also were aware of these dynamics; they had experienced a white racism as hostile to their dignity as anything experienced by the former slaves. But it was in the South that the importance of dignity and dignity-conferring relationships to democratic citizenship became most dramatically visible. Soon after the defeat of Reconstruction, southern states began passing laws that sought to prohibit absolutely any relations (other than employer and employee) between whites and blacks. It is astonishing how quickly and purposefully whites realized that striking at relationality was the surest way to perpetuate the slave system's denial of blacks' personhood. True, they also curtailed the freedom of blacks, and they dominated them economically, but these measures were deemed insufficient. Now that blacks could claim to be free and equal, those crucial criteria of democratic life had to be robbed of all meaning. And the surest way to do so had already been learned and practiced within the slavery system: do everything possible to destroy and deny their sense of their own dignity. Relationships between blacks and whites thus became a terrain of intense struggle over the very possibility of meaningful black democratic citizenship.

Whites were motivated mainly by political and economic self-interest: just as the slavery system had depended upon the denial of black personhood by whites, so too did the peonage system of sharecropping that quickly emerged to take its place after the Civil War. Moreover, the ideology of innate white superiority rendered almost impossible any cross-racial alliance between white and black workers and farmers.[9] But consistently obscuring (to themselves and to others) these self-serving motives, white southerners insisted that they had a principled, constitutional *right* to choose to avoid the company of blacks. While ceding (or feigning to cede) political equality to blacks, whites argued that they were under no legal or moral obligation to extend what they called "social equality" as well. They took their stand on the grounds of a particular understanding of the meaning of US democracy and the nature of democratic citizenship.

In itself, the phrase "social equality" had no precise meaning; indeed, its elasticity was what made it so useful. At one extreme, it connoted intermarriage and sexual relations between whites and blacks; at the other, it meant whites and blacks sharing public and private facilities like coaches and theaters. Advocates of segregation typically emphasized the "horrors of miscegenation" because they knew that they could thereby win the sympathies of most whites, north and south. No matter how many times black Americans asserted that they had no intention of seeking "social equality" understood as interracial sexual relations, white supremacists renewed the accusation. But they always had in mind as well their right, as they saw it, to create an absolute wall of separation between themselves and the black freedmen in their midst. They opposed not just interracial marriage but *any* form of interracial relations that assumed or expressed an equality of worth, or dignity. As Saunders

Redding would later observe of all laws prohibiting "mixed marriages": "Such [anti-mixed-marriage] statutes seem to me to be the most fundamental expression of the human inequality to which the Negro is subjected. They strike at the deepest roots of personal dignity and self-respect. It is one thing, and a very good thing, to be acknowledged as a first-class citizen: it is another and a better thing to be acknowledged a first-class human being."[10]

At first, many advocates for black civil and political equality conceded white southerners this right. In the congressional debates over the 1874 Civil Rights Act, for example, black representative Joseph H. Rainey from South Carolina replied to white southern opponents of the bill,

> [T]he negro is not asking for social equality. We do not ask…that the two races should intermarry one with the other. God knows we are perfectly content. I can say for myself that I am contented to marry one of my own complexion, and do not seek intercourse with any other race, because I believe that the race of people I represent…are just as virtuous and hold just as many high characteristics as any class in the country.…Sir, we are not seeking to be put on a footing of social equality. I prefer to choose my own associates, and all my colleagues here and the whole race I belong to prefer to make that choice. We do not ask the passage of any law forcing us upon anybody who does not want to receive us.[11]

Representative Alonzo J. Ransier, also black and also from South Carolina, pointed out that whether granted or not, "social equality" was just a distraction and a screen meant to conceal the political and economic motives of the bill's opponents:

> The bugbear of "social equality" is used by the enemies of political and civil equality for the colored man in place of argument. There is not an intelligent white man or black man who does not know that it is the sheerest nonsense; and I would have it distinctly understood that I would most certainly oppose the passage of the pending bill or any similar measure if I believed that its operation would be to force upon me the company of the [white] member from Kentucky [Mr. Beck], for instance, or anyone else. (16)

And Representative Benjamin Butler, a white man from Massachusetts, tried to make perfectly clear that the purpose of the bill was to ensure the freedmen's *political*, not social, equality:

"Equality!" We do not propose to legislate to establish any equality. I am not one of those who believe that all men were created equal, if equality is to be used in its broadest sense. I believe that "equal" in the Declaration of Independence is a political word, used in a political sense, and means equality of political rights.... But this is our doctrine: Equality...is not that all men are equal, *but that every man has the right to be the equal of every other man if he can.* (18)

The problem with all three of these arguments in favor of the bill is that they were incorrect: black Americans and their supporters in Congress *were* in fact demanding social equality of a kind that would foster social *relations*. Representative Milton J. Durham of Kentucky, an opponent of the bill, pointed this out quite bluntly:

The poorest and humblest white person in my district feels and knows that he or she belongs to a superior race morally and intellectually, and nothing is so revolting to them as social equality with this inferior race.... You may say that these are not social relations provided for in this bill; but, sir, if I am compelled to sit side by side with him in the theater, the stage coach, and the railroad car, to eat with him at the same table at the hotels, and my child to be educated at the same schools with his child—if these are not social relations I do not understand them. (17)

Representative James B. Beck, also a southern enemy of the bill, made the point in a different way. If the bill's sponsors wanted nothing more than blacks' political equality, then they should have no objection to an amendment to the bill specifying that "nothing herein be construed as to require hotel-keepers to put whites and blacks into the same rooms, or beds or feed them at the same table, nor to require that whites and blacks shall be put into the same rooms or classes at schools" (16). Of course such an amendment would have been radically inconsistent with both the spirit and the letter of the proposed legislation.[12]

As Representative Rainey's speech indicates, the reason black citizens were willing to concede to white southerners the right to feel aversion and to choose their own company is that their own years of enslavement in which they had no such rights had made these freedoms especially precious. Representative Rainey was perfectly sincere when he stated, "Sir, we are not seeking to be put on a footing of social equality. I prefer to choose my own associates, and all my colleagues here and the whole race I belong to prefer to make that choice." His colleague Congressman Ransier went even further, making a veiled but nonetheless pointed allusion to the ways white masters had *forced* social relations upon enslaved black women. "Yet they [whites] have found agreeable associations with them [blacks] under other circumstances which at once suggest themselves to us; nor has the result of this contact proved injurious to either race so far as I know, except that the moral responsibility rests upon the more refined and cultivated" (16).

Advocates of political and civil rights for the freedmen were thus caught in a double bind. They could not contest the right of white southerners to choose their own company if they wanted this right themselves, but they could not affirm that southern whites had such a right if they wished blacks to have access to public spaces and to public and private services such as schools, transportation, and so on. For all of these, as Representative Durham argued, would necessarily involve blacks and whites in "social relations." And to make matter worse, by arguing for "social equality" they would have found themselves accused of asserting the right of a black man to marry a consenting white woman—a politically suicidal move at that time. For a while, these complications and contradictions obscured what was most deeply at stake: whites were establishing a regime of segregation with the deliberate purpose of institutionalizing their right not to *see* their black fellow citizens.

Such a right seemed to be sanctioned even by a liberal interpretation of democracy. If casually read, John Stuart Mill could be understood as asserting it when he writes (in *On Liberty*), "We have a right, also, in various ways," to act upon our unfavorable opinion of anyone, not in the oppression of his individuality, but in the exercise of ours. We are not bound, for example, to seek his society; we have a right to avoid it (though not to parade the avoidance), for we have a right to choose the society most acceptable to us."[13] Do we indeed have such a right, and is it truly democratic?

Charles Chesnutt and the "Discipline of Unseeing"

Most Americans today believe strongly that as citizens of a democracy they have certain inalienable rights, among them the right to assemble, to worship as they choose, and to speak freely. Do these inalienable rights include as well the right to determine their own "social relations?" It would seem obvious that we all have the right to choose the company we keep. But does this right also imply that we have the right to turn away from others and to withhold the look that would recognize their dignity? If not, does US democracy include among its inalienable rights the right *to be seen* in the sense of having one's dignity recognized and thus affirmed by others? If so, what exactly does such a right require of other citizens?

Let us approach these questions through an account of what it *feels* like not to be seen. "Each morning," writes Pauli Murray in *Proud Shoes: The Story of An American Family*, "I passed white children as poor as I was going in the opposite direction on their way to school. We never had fights; I don't recall their ever having called me a single insulting name. It was worse than that. They passed me as if I weren't there! They looked through me and beyond me with unseeing eyes."[14] The white children were not interfering with Murray; they weren't insulting her, much less were they blocking her path toward her own school and education. In what sense, then, were they responsible for the harm their "unseeing" inflicted on Murray and on her sense of her own dignity?

Black philosopher Lewis Gordon has argued that such unseeing is a carefully constructed and deliberate act that does not so much *avoid* relationship as seek to *impose* a particular kind of relationship on someone (in this case Murray). Such aversion is not mere neutrality, much less is it indifference; it is insult and aggression. Although the white children might have considered their behavior to be natural or unexceptional, it was in fact the outcome of what Gordon calls a "discipline":

> Racism…is a denial of the humanity of another human being by virtue of his or her racial membership. This denial, properly executed, requires denying the presence of another human being in such relations. It makes the Other a form of presence that is an absence, an absence of human presence. That being so, the Other falls below the category of otherness, for an Other is a human being. Forced into the realm of property, even linguistic appeals—cries for recognition—are muffled, unheard; waving hands, gestures for acknowledgment are invisible. It is not that they do not trigger impulses between the eye and the brain. It is that there has been a carefully crafted discipline of unseeing.[15]

Gordon calls attention here to the fact that withholding relationship is itself a form of relationship, and an aggressive one at that. When an "Other" comes into our range of vision, we cannot help but "see" the person in a strictly objective fashion. But with practice we can learn to feign very successfully that we have not seen, and that the other occupies no space whatsoever in our visual field. We pretend that the person is invisible, and that we see through him or her. Eventually, with repetition, this pretense becomes a habit so deep that it feels natural—as natural as our not seeing the light switch our fingers can find without help from our eyes, as routine as our not noticing something as important as the color of our beloved's eyes. But there is an awful difference between these kinds of unseeing. One is learned and requires training and discipline; the other occurs simply because we have come to take something for granted. When we have learned to fail to see an Other, we must at first have *refused* to see that person many times. And this refusal means not merely keeping a human being in the category of the unknown other, like a stranger we have not yet met, but actually keeping him or her from even stepping into that category. We pen individuals into a realm in which they are stripped even of their Otherness as strangers to us. This is what Gordon means by saying that we turn them into "a form of presence that is an absence, an absence of human presence." This absence is not merely an absence; it remains a "form of *presence*" because we produce it in an intersubjective moment of exchange with the Other. What we exchange, on our part, is not mere indifference or blindness, but refusal. Yet we cannot refuse to recognize except insofar as we have first felt, however subtly and fleetingly, an impulse to recognize. We cannot refuse to recognize someone whom we literally do not see, only someone whom we know perfectly well is actually there before us. Our unseeing is palpable, like a withheld handshake. We cannot perform or transact it alone; we need the presence of the Other so that we can turn it into an absence.

Charles Chesnutt was one of the first black American writers to analyze these interpersonal dynamics and their implications for democracy. Although most literary criticism of his work focuses on issues of identity—on Chesnutt's representations of race and on his ambivalent feelings about his own racial identity—we can discern in his writings an interest also in intersubjective *activity*. In other words, his writings are probing dramatizations not just of static identity categories (e.g., of being "black" or "mulatto") but of the ways persons actively communicate within, through, and around these categories.

As we have seen, in the years following the collapse of Radical Reconstruction and leading up to the Supreme Court's 1896 *Plessy v. Ferguson* decision, political contestation of these relational dynamics took the form of debate over the meaning and validity of what was called "social equality." Like a number of other black intellectuals and politicians, Chesnutt believed at first that social equality was not a political right that could be legislated but a social condition to be achieved only through demonstration of one's fitness for it. In 1882, for example, he argued that "social equality is something that cannot be forced. The law can give us our political and civil rights and protect us in the exercise of them. But no man can compel us to associate with those we do not like. I am no socialist, no social equality theorist. I can think of nothing more disagreeable than for all men to be equal, unless indeed all men could be equally good."[16] Four years later, he made the same point more carefully, this time specifically defining what "social equality" meant:

> The Negro does not ask for social equality with white people; that is to say, he does not ask for admission into private white society. The fear of intimate personal contact with the Negro on terms of equality seems the greatest bugbear to the Southern people in the discussion of the Negro question.... Absurd fear, if it really exists at all! No right is more zealously guarded by our constitution and laws than the right of a man to be supreme within the walls of his own house.[17]

However, as the years passed and the nation marched steadily toward *Plessy v. Ferguson*, Chesnutt became increasingly impatient with the social equality debate. If racial hatred was being encouraged in order to keep black Americans from exercising their democratic rights and privileges, then surely it could not be regarded as the kind of personal preference that democratic citizens were entitled to hold. Regarded politically, race prejudice was at root a denial of a person's dignity, and as such it was totally incompatible with democratic principles. In 1891, sounding a good deal like Frederick Douglass before him and Malcolm X after, he urged black Americans to understand prejudice as an insult and to respond to it with indignation and even with force if necessary:

> The colored people will instigate no race war. But when they are attacked, they should defend themselves. When the Southern Negro reaches that high conception of liberty that would make him rather die than submit to the lash, when he will meet force with force, there will be an end of Southern outrages. The man who will offer a personal *indignity* to another who has not injured him, is a tyrant and a coward, and will not continue a conflict with no odds in his favor.[18]

Soon thereafter, Chesnutt began linking the fate of black Americans to a fundamental reimagining of US democracy and its founding texts. "The Declaration of Independence," he wrote, "was not the cool utterance of a nation secure in its position; it was the *indignant* remonstrance of an outraged, disorganized people; and coming from the heart it went to the heart, and not only inspired Americans to heroic effort, but enlisted the sympathy and admiration of lovers of liberty the world over" (83; emphasis added). With these words, Chesnutt was clearly shifting the issue of social equality away from "private society" and onto the grounds where the nature of democracy itself is in question. Eight years later, and three years after *Plessy v. Ferguson*, Chesnutt bluntly charged that "race prejudice" posed a powerful threat to US democracy and its principles: "The question of paramount importance at present is whether or not the results of the Civil War shall be nullified by race prejudice, embodied in the form of laws and judicial decisions *which are contrary to the Constitution and principles of our Government*, or whether these principles shall be steadily adhered to until, under their beneficent operation this vexed question shall be finally and correctly solved."[19]

Not surprisingly, then, Chesnutt decided that one of his main purposes as a writer should be to solve this "vexed question" by encouraging "a total revolution of Southern sentiment toward the Negro":

> The Negro is by reason of his color denied these things which come to others as a matter of course.... When every Negro has learned to read and write...some other means will be sought to preserve intact the power and prestige of the white race. There must be a total revolution of Southern sentiment toward the Negro before equality of learning, intelligence, or ability, will make the Southerner content to share equally with his darker fellow-citizens the benefits of citizenship. (163–64)

More specifically, Chesnutt hoped to destroy race prejudice by exposing it to a rigorous analysis, demonstrating that white "power" depended on white "prestige," which in turn depended on whites' denial of black dignity. His fiction certainly contributed to the larger project of African American literature, which was, as Kenneth Warren has underscored, to advance the progress of the race—as an instrument of such progress, or as an index of such progress, or in both ways. And the bulk of recent criticism of Chesnutt's work has read it as such an affirmation—staunch according to some, ambivalent according to others—of race pride and the value of black American culture. Yet we should not assume that these aims fully account for the ambitions or the achievements of Chesnutt and other black writers, for many intended their work to be, in Barack Obama's words, "black and more than black." Chesnutt's works of fiction are always a critique of white racism and a defense of black dignity, but as they pursue these objectives, they also yield deep insights into the theory and practice of democracy—insights that Chesnutt knew to be pertinent to *all* citizens.[20]

In *The House behind the Cedars* (1900), a novel set in the decade following the Civil War, Chesnutt's mulatta heroine Rena Johnson faces an excruciating decision. She is to all appearances white. She has recently left her mother and come to live with her brother John, who has passed as white for years and become a prominent lawyer and a respected citizen of Clarence in South Carolina. Predictably, a young client of John's, George Tryon, falls in love with Rena and proposes marriage. Rena falls deeply in love him. But exactly because she loves George so passionately, she feels obliged to tell him the truth about her origins. She wants a relationship based on honesty and trust. She wants to know that he loves her for *herself*—that he would love her even if he knew her to be legally "black." Yet she also knows that if she tells her secret to George, he is likely to break off their engagement. They would both be heartbroken, and her brother's standing in society would certainly be destroyed. What, then, should she do? Tell George or keep her secret?

Rena's dilemma is made even more intense by a deep irony Chesnutt has woven into his tale: she doesn't feel that she is actually "black" in any sense other than that prescribed by the southern "one drop" law. She looks white, and she wants to live as a white person among other whites. Her inner self, as she experiences it, *is* white. As critic William L. Andrews has observed, Chesnutt's novel poses the discomfiting question, "Why...should people who look as white as 'whites' and whose cultural affinities and socioeconomic goals mirror those of 'whites' be automatically condemned as racial imposters for simple being what to all appearances they actually are—white men and women?"[21] In other words, what would Polonius's advice to Hamlet—"To thine own self be true"—mean for Rena? After all, her "own self" as she experiences it *is* "white," so she is not being "false to" George by allowing him to think that she is so. And yet she would be false to him by concealing the identity that white southern law and custom have forced upon her. In short, the whole question of George recognizing and loving her for "who she really is" becomes incoherent—for who, really, is she?

By placing his heroine in a situation where she is forced to lie in order to love, and to be false in order to be true, Chesnutt was certainly aiming to expose the perverse moral consequences of racist laws and customs. He explicitly flung this challenge in the face of his early twentieth-century readers: "if there be a dainty reader of this tale who scorns a lie, and who writes the story of his life upon his sleeve for all the world to read, let him uncurl his scornful lip and come down from the pedestal of moral superiority, to which assured position and wide opportunity have lifted him, and put himself in the place of Rena and her brother."[22]

In challenging his white readers imagine themselves "in the place of Rena and her brother," Chesnutt could be quite sure that they shared the crucial assumptions on which Rena's dilemma was based. Like her, they would have believed that they had a "real" self, and that this self inhabited an "inner" realm that was "private" in the sense of deserving protection from the regulations and demands of the "public" or social world. When Rena asks her brother John for advice about what she should do, he instantly appeals to this set of beliefs: "What a poor soul it is," he declares, "that has not some secret chamber, sacred to itself; where one can file away the things others have no right to know, as well as the things one himself would fain forget! We are under no moral obligation to inflict upon others the history of our past mistakes, our wayward thoughts, our secret sins, our desperate hopes, or our heartbreaking disappointments" (321).

To claim that "others have no right to know" certain things about us is to claim that we have a right to keep them secret. It is to claim that we have a right to a certain kind of privacy, one that forbids others from intruding uninvited into the "sacred chamber" of our innermost being. With this argument, John (or Chesnutt—both of them being lawyers) cleverly turns the tables on white readers who might insist that Tryon has a right to know about Rena's past, since the principle John invokes here clearly shares a good deal of ground with the right invoked by white southern opponents of social equality: the right to chose and control their "social relations"—whom they will speak to, whom they will sit next to, whom they will *see*. But Rena is not quite satisfied by this answer, and nor (I will suppose) are most of Chesnutt's readers today. Like Rena, we feel that a relationship dependent on a deception would be fatally flawed. Like Rena, we want Tryon to know her for who she "really" is. But then again, who *is* she really? What does her legally imposed racial identity have to do with her own sense of who she is? Chesnutt's novel is a complex machine designed to keep these questions burning, and by their light we begin to feel that Rena's dilemma does more than indict the race codes of the Jim Crow South. It also calls into question both John's and our own assumptions about the very nature of the self. We get our first hint of these complications in the brief explanation Chesnutt's narrator gives of Rena's dilemma: "Rena's shrinking from the irrevocable step of marriage was due to a simple yet complex cause," he begins. "Stated baldly, it was the consciousness of her secret." So far, so good: we are still on the familiar ground of a sharp distinction between the private realm of inner identity and the public realm of custom and law. But the narrator goes on to say that "the complexity arose out of the various ways in which it seemed to bear upon her future. *Our lives are so bound up with those of our fellow men that the slightest departure from the beaten path involves a multiplicity of small adjustments.*" The narrator, whom we can reasonably take to represent Chesnutt's views, reinforces this point later: "For *connected* with our kind we must be; if not by our virtues, then by our vices,—if not by our services, at least by our needs" (317; emphases added). For Chesnutt, then, it is the *inevitability* of connection and relationship that causes Rena's dilemma, not merely the invasion of her inner self by intrusive law. If Rena and George had lived in a world unto themselves, the act of revealing who she "really" is to George would be a very different thing than it is in the world they actually inhabit, a world of custom, law, and myriad complex social relations with others. Thus, Chesnutt's novel asks its readers to understand themselves not just as a collection of autonomous individuals possessing certain inalienable rights, among them the right to feel aversion for others and to keep secrets from them, but also as citizens "bound up with" other citizens in relationships.

The novel's climactic recognition scene—actually a scene of *non-recognition*—dramatically shows that because we are so interconnected, a mere look can have devastating consequences for the vulnerable "inner" self of others. George Tryon has been told that a black woman is in the town pharmacy. When Rena emerges from that pharmacy a moment later, he realizes that she is the woman he has been told about. Therefore, she must be black. He is outraged. And when Rena turns and sees Tryon, she finds herself looking into a void of humiliating non-recognition: "he left me without a word," she later tells her brother, "and with a look that told me how much he hated and despised me. I would not have believed it—even of a white man." The effects of this "look" only increase as time passes. Rena tells John that Tryon's "expression in that awful moment grew upon me, haunted me day and night, until I shuddered at the thought that I might ever see him again. He *looked* at me as though I were *not even a human being.*... He did not love me—or he would have acted differently. He might have loved me and left me—he could not have loved me and *looked* at me so!" (386; emphases added).

White southerners like Tryon believed that democracy gave them the right to hold whatever private view of black persons they might choose to hold. Chesnutt replied by showing that when racial hatred hardens to the point that a white person sees nothing to honor in the eyes of a black person whom he has loved, more than the right to choose one's social company is at stake. What is being asserted, however unconsciously, is a right to refuse to acknowledge the dignity of that other person. Such a right cannot be asserted as a defense of one's own privacy because, as Chesnutt's novel shows, it so painfully invades the "sacred" inner space of another person—in this case, one who is undeniably a person to Tryon because he has known himself to be in love with her. To put the matter somewhat differently: it is the actual fact of their connection, that they are already in a relationship with each other, that renders Tryon's exercise of his right to feel aversion both despicable and absurd.

Some of Chesnutt's white readers might have argued, in reply, that the strength and visibility of Tryon's and Rena's relationship make it inappropriate as an analogüe for relations between blacks and whites more generally. They could have pointed out that the connective relationality of democratic citizenship that Chesnutt invokes did not *yet* exist between white citizens and black ones—and that, moreover, the prevention of interracial relationality was the very purpose of Jim Crow laws. Some readers might also have objected that personal, intimate relations between actual persons are never a helpful analogue for relations among citizens. To all of these objections, Chesnutt had a one-word answer: *mulatto*. Countless men and women of mixed blood lived in the United States, and many of them were so fair-skinned that they could and did pass for "white." Whites did have relationships with them, just as George had a relationship with Rena.

To this answer, some whites would have replied, "Yes, but we do not knowingly have such relationships. We have such relationships only when we are deceived because they do not tell us that they are black." But to this objection Chesnutt already has an answer: *are* these mixed-blood persons "black?" Says who? Those who have invented and seek to enforce the "one drop" rule have conspired to create the conditions in which merely being oneself, as Rena does, *becomes* an act of deception. If you claim to be able to "know" that a person is "black" because she is one-quarter or one-eighth or one-sixteenth black, do not now complain that you did *not* know because she doesn't "look" black and didn't tell you! (As Stacey Margolis has put it: "Chesnutt challenges the system of racial segregation not by refuting but rather by fulfilling its logic. If legalized segregation organizes the world according to color, characters like John and Rena reveal what it would mean to obey the letter of the law.")[23] As for whether Rena and Tryon's relationship is at all analogous to what we would optimally find among citizens of the demos, his novel's point is that we cannot theorize any kind of relationship into being. We have to start with relationships as we know them and proceed from there; this work is the form political philosophy must sometimes assume when it is undertaken in the "muck and mire of human existence." Chesnutt's mulatto figure is the literal embodiment of that which is present but rendered absent, of that which is here and must be reckoned with.

Let me summarize, briefly, this reading of *The House behind the Cedars*. The moral logic used by defenders of Jim Crow was straightforward: the democratic rights of citizens surely include the right to choose one's own company, which in turn implies the right to be averse to others whom one prefers to avoid. Chesnutt's response, as I have tried to show, is that we cannot have a "right" to be averse to others and avoid them because we *share* our rights with them; as democratic citizens, we stand in relationship with each other whether we wish to or not because in fact our rights are coproduced through mutual assertion and recognition. This codependency is made dramatically clear by the fact that exercising the so-called right to aversion has the effect of *invading* the self of an Other. What feels like a mere withholding to one person is felt as an attack by the Other, and this asymmetry can be explained only by the nature of dignity itself: it might feel at times like the pulse of our inmost being, but in fact it is always dependent upon recognition by others.

To see the importance of dignity to democracy is to take account of something that is not entirely subsumable under the category of "rights." If the experiment of collective self-government that we call "democracy" is to have any value, it surely rests on the worth of those selves who are citizens. Our very claim to certain rights presupposes that we each have value, have worth; conversely, a person so abject as to lack any sense of dignity or self-respect would feel no impulse to claim rights or equality with other citizens. It follows, then, that democratic citizens should imagine themselves not as individual and autonomous bearers of rights but as interconnected persons cooperatively producing and recognizing their dignity and their rights. This is what critic Terrence Johnson means when he argues that "Antiblack racism creates a form of spiritual isolation" the redress of which carries us beyond "rights talk" to other considerations of what is essential to democracy. As I do here, Johnson calls on "pundits, preachers, scholars, and the general public" to "consider expanding the themes and vocabularies that are employed in conversations dealing with race, religion, and democracy."[24]

"A Man of Imagination"

Writing in his journal in 1880, Chesnutt surmised that the "moral revolution" of southern sentiment would have to be undertaken subtly and indirectly:

> Not a fierce indiscriminate onset, not an appeal to force, for this is something that force can but slightly affect, but a moral revolution

must be brought about by a different manner. The subtle, almost inde-
finable feeling of repulsion toward the negro, which is common to
most Americans—cannot be stormed and taken by assault; the garrison will not capitulate, so their position must be mined, and we will
find ourselves in their midst before they think it.[25]

The history of the reception of Chesnutt's work—and of *The House behind
the Cedars* in particular—indicates the difficulty of achieving such a "moral
revolution." What Chesnutt's professional readers (critics and reviewers)
repeatedly praised was his control, restraint, and fairness. In so doing, they
were responding, I believe, to Chesnutt's method of presenting a dilemma in
which tension is sustained through poised and balanced oppositions. "Mr.
Chesnutt has a firmer grasp than any preceding author has shown in handling
the delicate relations between the white man and the negro from the point
of view of the mingling of the races" (29), wrote an anonymous reviewer in
Bookman on August 7, 1898. A reviewer for the *Boston Evening Transcript* of
March 22, 1899, praised Chesnutt's "control": "he seems endowed with judgment of a poise so happy that he may be trusted to be fair to both [races]."
Florence H. Morgan praised *The Conjure Woman* in *Bookman* in June
1899: "All the wrongs of the race are in these simple tales unfolded, but never
with a complaint, a strict justice being displayed in the drawing of the good
and bad master, the good and bad slave, each having a fair showing." Hamilton
Wright Mabie, dean of the genteel critics, praised Chesnutt's "The Wife of
His Youth" as "a story which, in keenness of perception, in restraint and balance,...must take its place among the best short stories in American literature." Elisabeth L[uther] Cary, writing for *Book Buyer* (August 1901) even
found some fault in this balance:

> Mr. Chesnutt has a keen, a subtle, and at the same time a curiously
> impartial appreciation of the insidious forces fighting for mastery in
> this battle between old and new conditions. A remarkable poise of
> mind saves him from exaggerating the painful aspect of unequal com-
> bat, and even prevents him perhaps, from laying sufficient stress upon
> it poignant and pitiful interest.[26]

Yet while most reviewers praised Chesnutt's fair and careful approach,
some were disturbed by and rejected his implied argument. An anonymous
critic for the *Nation* (in New York City) wrote in February 1901:

The tragedy of *The House behind the Cedars* is one for which the strongest literary presentation would fail to excite unquestioning sympathetic horror. A great many persons of kind and generous sentiment believe that a white man breaking his engagement to marry a women who has left him to discover by accident that she has a strain of negro blood, is morally and rationally justified and without dishonor. Such an opinion does not necessarily shield itself behind law or custom, but may be rooted in natural antipathies and a belief that, for the happiness of the individuals and the good of society, such an engagement is better broken than kept.

A reviewer for *Chicago Banker* (December 1900) tersely agreed: "Against the girl's deliberate deception the author says nothing."[27]

Both critics clearly failed to see that Rena herself is tormented by her "deception"; they also failed to notice that deception would have been unnecessary if her society had believed that we all hold our rights connectedly, not separately. Above all, they failed to understand that the novel's purpose is certainly *not* "to excite unquestioning sympathetic horror." It is to use the balance and poise so many reviewers praised in order to lure readers into the complex dilemma Rena faces so they can experience with her the difficulties that this dilemma poses.

In *The House behind the Cedars*, the word Chesnutt himself uses repeatedly to name the faculty he hopes his readers will bring to his book is "imagination." He tells us, for example, that despite the differences between Rena and John Warwick, "Warwick's imagination…enabled him to put himself in touch with her mood and recognize its bearings upon her conduct" (321). Judge Strait, the courtly white gentleman who has helped Warwick get his start in the law, is described as "a man of imagination; he had read many books and had personally outlived some prejudices" (347). Even George Tryon is somewhat redeemed by this faculty. "He tried to be angry with her," Chesnutt writes, "but after the first hour he found it impossible. He was a man of too much imagination not to be able to put himself, in some measure at least, in her place,—to perceive that for her the step which had placed her in [his white] world was the working out of nature's great law of self-preservation, for which he could not blame her" (363). No doubt Chesnutt believed that the most important work he could do to advance the cause of black Americans and renew US democracy was to stimulate and educate the imaginations of his white readers, urging them to understand that democratic citizenship is fundamentally relational in nature because dignity, which is indispensable to democracy, is either fostered or denied through interpersonal relationships. For such relationships to flourish, citizens must understand that we have no right to withhold a dignity-conferring look of recognition from our fellow citizens, not even by so mild a gesture as deliberately forgetting her name. As Chesnutt knew, and as the reception of his novel confirmed, the indispensable precondition for such understanding is strenuous use of our imagination.

Such effort is exactly what the novels we'll be reading in the next chapter also ask of their characters—and of us. Like Chesnutt's work, they underscore the importance of human relationships in democracy, and like *The House behind the Cedars*, they organize their narratives around moments of recognition and nonrecognition. They probe more deeply than his, however, into the complex dynamics through which persons think they know and on that basis recognize others. That is, they unpack recognition itself, showing their readers this paradox: that in order to know people well, we must understand that we cannot know them completely. They thus provide a pedagogy for the democratic imagination that is similar to, but also crucially different from, liberalism's injunction that we must "try to stand in the other person's shoes." They affirm the political importance of imagination by dramatizing both its necessity and its limits.

3

The Art of Citizenship

NELLA LARSEN, JAMES BALDWIN, AND THE
DIFFICULTY OF KNOWING OTHERS

WHEN A CHRISTIAN exchanges looks with a Hassidic Jew, when a straight man meets the eyes of a lesbian woman, when a black man meets an Asian man, how should they handle the presence of the very obvious differences between them? Should they ignore those differences and try to see through them to a universal human dignity they are confirming? Or is each person's dignity inextricably linked to such differences, so that ignoring or seeing through such a difference would be tantamount to disrespecting the person?

Works of fiction sometimes have greater power than philosophy to bring forth the complex textures of the intersubjective dynamics implied by such questions. Fiction can trace the minute folds and contours of what happens when persons encounter each other, recognize each other, and come to know each other. The "recognition scene," as literary critics call it, has been a staple of storytelling for a very long time. From the fire-lit reunion of cautious Penelope and crafty Ulysses in the *Odyssey* to the searching conversations of Fielding and Aziz in *A Passage to India*, works of fiction have been representing and analyzing acts of recognition for centuries. I don't want to claim that black American writers have handled this theme in a special or distinctive way, for that case could only be made through extensive comparison of works by both white and black writers, and that would carry us far from our purpose here. But I do suggest that we may read some black American writers as expressing an especially keen awareness—derived from the history sketched in the preceding chapter—that relationships and acts of recognition are often *political* activities with powerful implications for a democratic polity.

I will begin with Nella Larsen's *Passing*, which takes up the question of how (and whether) a look of recognition deals with difference and takes account of what seems unfamiliar and unknown in another person. Then I will show how James Baldwin's work unpacks the complex and subtle dynamics of recognition and relationship in ways that emphasizes the necessity of vulnerability and therefore of trust. Taken together, these two novels have much to teach us about what political philosopher Danielle S. Allen calls "the art of citizenship."[1]

Recognizing the Limits of Democratic Recognition: Nella Larsen's Passing

Literary historian George Hutchinson has argued that a number of black writers connected with the Harlem Renaissance sought to forge an aesthetic that would serve as a kind of democratic pedagogy for their readers, both black and white. They believed that "The exploration of otherness in novels of social analysis trains self-understanding and expands the range of human solidarity."[2] I would put the point more emphatically: it isn't just "otherness" that such novels explore, but the manner in which persons in relationships seek to make sense of otherness. The distinction is subtle but important because it moves us beyond an approach that focuses on the rather static notions of individual or group identity to a more fluid field in which persons are encountering each other in a democratic world and citizens must meet the challenge of recognizing and knowing each other.

No African American of the twentieth century plumbed the question of what it means to recognize and know an "other" person more deeply than Nella Larsen in her novel *Passing*. Critics writing about the novel since the 1970s have tended to agree that it is about the nature of identity—racial identity, sexual identity, class identity, or the interlocking interdependence of all of these. Many critics have concurred as well that the novel is hardly straightforward in its treatment of identity, and that it uses the theme of passing to suggest how complex identity formation is. All of these readings can be turned around, so to speak, so that the topic of *having* identity (what the self is to itself and to others, how power imposes a self on oneself) becomes the topic of *knowing* identity (what seeing, knowing, recognizing, and mistaking identity—and other selves—might be). The first ways of reading the novel stress what we might call substantives and nouns (black, female, lesbian, heterosexual, bourgeois, and so on), while the second focuses on movements and action. (Larsen's title elegantly anticipates both ways of reading, since the word *Passing* is a participle that can read as both a noun and a verb.) So while it is true that, as Elaine Ginsberg writes, "passing is about identities: their creation or imposition, their adoption or rejection, their accompanying rewards or penalties,"[3] it is also true that the act of passing is an intersubjective exchange in which the having or performing of identity cannot be extricated from the perceiving and affirming of such identity. In other words, the novel dramatizes not just what happens when a person with a given identity, or with the desire to perform a certain identity, decides to pass, or masquerade, as having a different identity; it is also about the complex processes of seeing, hypothesizing, sorting, testing, and revising that compose the activities of knowing and recognizing others. Moreover, the novel does not merely represent this process as it is being undertaken by its characters; as well, it puts us, its readers, in the position of having to engage in—and reflect upon—the process ourselves.[4]

Passing begins by placing us in the consciousness of a woman named Irene who has escaped from the swelter of a summer day in Chicago to take tea in the cool and luxurious Drayton Hotel. Once seated and served, she notices a remarkably beautiful woman sitting at a nearby table—and then she finds herself being observed by this woman in turn. Her curiosity chills to fear under the stranger's gaze:

> Did that woman, could that woman, somehow know that here before her very eyes on the roof of the Drayton sat a Negro?
>
> Absurd! Impossible! White people were so stupid about such things for all that they usually asserted that they were able to tell; and by the most ridiculous means, finger-nails, palms of hands, shapes of ears, teeth, and other equally silly rot....No, the woman sitting there couldn't possibly know.[5]

This moment is as explosive for many readers as it is for the characters they are reading about, since it is only now that we learn that Irene is black—and that by seeing through her eyes we have been inhabiting and identifying with a black person's consciousness. If we had assumed that Irene was white (and I believe that, by withholding until now any indications of Irene's race, Larsen intended at least her white readers to make this assumption), then we experience this moment as a shock of recognition—not just of Irene, but also of our own assumption that a certain kind of middle-class woman engaged in certain activities and thinking certain kinds of thoughts must be "white." And while thus teasing white readers for their racist assumptions, Larsen also mocks Irene for hers. Irene has simply assumed that she is looking at a white woman whom she instantly categorizes as being "stupid" in the ways white folks always are: arrogantly believing they can know blacks through certain reliable categories of physical differences such as skin color and fingernails. But in this case

Irene is the one who is being "stupid," for she herself has misidentified the other woman as "white" by relying on precisely those markers of physical difference.[6] In a moment she will learn that the beautiful stranger is black.

The woman now plays her own game with Irene, calling her by her old nickname "Rene" and forcing her to guess who she could be. Gazing back at her, "Irene felt that she was just about to remember her. For about the woman was some quality, an intangible something, too vague to define, too remote to seize, but which was, to Irene Redfield, very familiar."

Here we are placed on the threshold of a moment of recognition. To more fully understand Irene's state of consciousness as she tries to recall the beautiful woman's name, we would do well to turn to William James (who, along with other pragmatist philosophers, exerted a strong influence on the Harlem Renaissance movement of which Larsen was a part). James believed that consciousness was a continuous flow, or "stream," without interruptions or breaks. There is no "on/off" switch in the brain, and there is no absolute distinction between knowing and not knowing something or someone. Knowing, like consciousness, is a continuum. James gives many vivid examples of this mental continuity, one of which is the state we're in when we try to remember a name. "There is a gap therein," he writes; "but no mere gap. It is a gap that is intensely active. A sort of wraith of the name is in it, beckoning us in a given direction, making us at moments tingle with the sense of our closeness, and then letting us sink back without the longed-for term."[7] This "wraith" is precisely what Irene is searching for. It is "too vague to define, too remote to seize," but it is nonetheless "familiar." She cannot put a name to this "intangible something," but that does not mean that it is a void. There is a name in the "gap," though she cannot remember it. She knows this person though she does not yet know who she is.

Larsen repeatedly puts the characters of *Passing* and us its readers in this peculiar state of consciousness in which the seeming opposites of knowing and not-knowing melt into each other. Her purpose is to make us experience consciously the continuity across "gaps" that James was trying to describe. She wants us to feel that knowing another person often blends knowing and *not*-knowing them. Indeed, her novel will eventually show us that if we wish to know another person in the best way possible, we must always be aware that we can never know that person completely. This sense of our own limits is especially important when we are using certain conventional markers of difference—for example, skin color—to help us place the person and thereby suppose that we know who she is.

Larsen humorously dramatizes these points in the novel's second tea party, at which three women must read and reread each other through the subtle apertures that open where their differences and similarities overlap. All three are black and fair-skinned. All three pass for white, though in different ways: Clare as a deception practiced round the clock and in order to survive; Irene as an occasional matter of convenience; Gertrude only insofar as she has married a white man (whom she has not deceived) and must circulate in his world as well as her own. Two of the women (Clare and Irene) are beautiful; Gertrude is emphatically plain. Two of the women (Clare and Gertrude) share a prejudice against dark skin, though perhaps for different reasons; Irene is proud of her racial identity and claims to have no such prejudice. Two of the women (Clare and Irene) communicate quickly and easily through nuance and innuendo; Gertrude simply can't keep up with them. But two of the women (Irene and Gertrude) share a profound discomfort with the inexplicable risks that the third (Clare) has chosen to take. The tea party's comedy of manners bubbles up from the way the characters communicate with each other through the rapidly shifting alliances these differences and similarities create.

That a great deal is at stake in this witty drama becomes shockingly clear when Clare's white husband, John Bellew, enters the room and immediately addresses his wife as "Nig." Abruptly, all three women are united in their knowledge that they are all three black women who are (suddenly) passing. Bellew is an outsider to this knowledge, and much more obviously an outsider as he begins to display his unabashed racism. Yet in the instant the three women form their circle, Irene and Gertrude form their own, more inner ring, one that excludes Clare because it is a circle formed by two women who cannot imagine what "gain" could be worth the humiliation of living with such a man. Bellew crashes around in these delicate arrangements, oblivious that they are there and that they are placing *him*; his words suddenly make the drama of knowing others ugly, not comical. "I know you're no nigger," he declares to Clare, "so it's all right. You can get as black as you please as far as I'm concerned, since I know you're no nigger" (171).

Readers like myself who had assumed in the novel's opening pages that the point of view we were sharing was that of a white woman will wince here as we realize that we have been as stupid as Bellew. We will recognize, too, that Bellew's stupidity is a neat replication of Irene's since she, too, has gazed upon Clare and assumed that she was "no nigger." This deliberate sequencing of stupidities that rhyme with each other has a humbling effect: as readers, we start to become much more cautious about our assumptions and much more aware of the complexities and dangers involved when we meet and try to know one another.

Moreover, by arranging these blunders as she has, and by implicating us in the inadequate modes of knowing her characters employ, Larsen suggests that these dangers arise whenever the process of knowing is arrested or terminated—prevented from moving on through cycles of revision and reconstruction. When as readers we are required to "fill in" the "gap" in the identity of Irene, we at first use the term "white": she is white, we unconsciously assume. But when we learn that she is passing in the Hotel Drayton, we quickly revise what we thought we knew and we label her as "black." When Irene likewise learns that the vaguely familiar person in her memory is her childhood friend Clare, she does so even though she has to drastically revise the theory she has just constructed about the beautiful "white" woman sitting opposite her. But when John Bellew is confronted by evidence that would trouble the theory *he* has constructed about blacks, he stubbornly rejects it in order to maintain his theory intact. His resistance to revision drives him into multiple absurdities— affirming that he hates blacks even though he doesn't know (that he knows) any, insisting that he can know blacks "better than" blacks know themselves:

> Had Bellew, Irene inquired, ever known any Negroes?...
>   Bellew answered: "Thank the Lord, no! And never expect to! But I know people who've known them, better than they know their black selves." (172)

Larsen thus mockingly suggests that Bellew's absurd belief that he can know others "better" than they know themselves is the certain fate of *anyone* who fails to grasp that knowing others also means acknowledging that there's something about the person they cannot know. A person who looks at a different "other" through the prism of a fixed conception of what that difference is cannot adapt or change his views. When confronted with the inevitable contradictions between conception and actuality, he assumes that the fault cannot lie with his conception and must reside therefore in the other person. This is why he believes that he knows the other person better than that person knows himself.[8]

Crucially, Larsen insists that this twisted logic is not the special possession of racists like Bellew. Toward the end of the novel, we discover that Irene herself, the person whose viewpoint we have been invited to share and trust, also embraces this logic of resistance to revision. She, too, thinks that she knows someone "better than" he knows himself: her husband Brian.

> A feeling of uneasiness stole upon her at the inconceivable suspicion that she might have been wrong in her estimate of her husband's character....Impossible! She couldn't have been wrong....And all, she assured herself, because she understood him so well, because she had,

actually, a special talent for understanding him. It was, as she saw it, the one thing that had been the basis of the success she had made of a marriage that had threatened to fail. *She knew him as well as he knew himself, or better.* (187; emphasis added)

The irony Larsen has so carefully designed here is that Irene's marriage is decidedly *not* the "success" she dreams it to be. Her relationship with Brian is a colossal failure precisely because she won't allow him a margin of unknowability. Because she needs "to keep her life fixed, certain" and because for her "security was the most important and desired thing in life" (235), she is terrified of change and refuses to revise her understanding of her husband. Indeed, the more he seems to change, the more she hardens. Her old friend is indeed a mystery to her, but Irene turns the elusiveness of Clare's identity into a settled preconception of the exotic and the beautiful—or, as critic Cheryl Wall writes, "she is not responding to the person before her so much as to her own notions of Otherness."9 By fixing Brain in her unchanging conception of his identity— which she mistakes for a "special talent for understanding him"—she has exhibited a temperament characteristic of a racist like Bellew. Both are stubbornly unwilling to let another's identity be a "wraith" and to acknowledge, with humility, that one cannot, after all, finally and fixedly know another. If we are appalled by Bellew's statement, "I know people who've known them [blacks], better than they know their black selves," we should look with equal skepticism on Irene's belief that "She knew him [Brian] as well as he knew himself, or better." Larsen surely intends us to register the almost identical phrases in which these characters mistakenly assert their mastery of knowing who others are.

Passing explores not just the risks of assuming that we know what it means to know an "other" who is different from us, but also the dangers of choosing whether to project or conceal the differences that might enable others to recognize us for who we feel we are. By trading away her difference and passing as white in order to gain wealth and security, Clare has struck a painful bargain. Although the difference constituted by her blackness is virtually invisible and therefore more of a social possibility than a natural fact, its social and personal significance is indissoluble. It matters to her, and it matters to her friends who gaze appalled at her marriage to a racist. Not only has she cut herself off from the community she longs to return to, but she has cast aside a vital signifier through which she might be recognized as the person she likes to think she is. Of course, if her (invisible) blackness is taken to have a fixed and determinative meaning (which is how Bellew would read it), then it would work to obstruct her being recognized by him and others. But is there not some other way her blackness might be read?

Political theorist Iris Marion Young would say that there is, and that Clare's racial identity could be understood as what Young calls a "resource for democracy." "A democratic public," she writes, ideally "arrives at objective political judgment from discussion not by bracketing these differences [of race, age, gender, and the like] but by communicating the experiences and perspectives conditioned by them to one another."[10] Young's hope that differences might be seen as means of democratic communication rather than impediments to it raises a difficult question, however: how can a democratic polity respect the differences among its citizens and at the same time promote the shared values that they apparently require in order to govern themselves? Addressing this concern, political theorists at first tried to establish the universal "grounds" or "norms" by which citizens could decide which differences to allow and which to exclude. Predictably, these principles turned out to reflect western European preconceptions and values, so theorists began trying instead to articulate the "conditions" that make possible "dialogues" through and across difference. Such dialogues, suggests James Tully, "rooted in the everyday world of belonging and difference, informed with both caring attentiveness and degrees of critical reflexivity…could nurture the intersubjective bonds of solidarity of a genuinely 'democratic cosmopolis.' "[11]

But what exactly do "caring attentiveness" and "degrees of critical reflexivity" consist of in practice? What does "communicating the experiences and perspectives" of differently positioned people entail? After all, if the differences among democratic citizens run very deep, then their ability to know one another is dubious, and so is their ability to communicate effectively, caringly, and self-reflexively. Cognizant of the need to understand more richly what it means to "know" an "other," political theorists are starting to produce phenomenological accounts of democratic communication. Romand Coles, for example, has suggested that theories of democracy need to attend not just to the importance of how "politically marginalized people would gain voice," but to "practices of listening," or "practices of difficult receptivity."[12] In short, the question is not only whether "the subaltern can speak" but whether she can be heard.

In the novel, the threads of these questions are cut short by Clare's decision to conceal her racial difference from whites: because she hides her blackness from them, neither she nor they are forced by it to improve their practice of listening. Yet these issues come alive in the novel's tragic denouement. When at the end Irene kills Clare because Clare provokes the "inconceivable suspicion" that her understanding of Brian has all along been "wrong," Clare seems to embody "the menace of impermanence" that Irene had tried so desperately to evade. But while the novel points us toward this conclusion, it does not allow us to settle there. Critics have persuasively argued for other ways of understanding the ending—that the sexual desire Clare kindles in Irene is what provokes Irene to kill her, or that the narrative itself is forced to kill her because "the subplot of Irene's developing if unnamed and unacknowledged desire for Clare" is too dangerous to tell. These multiple readings can all be true because the larger point that *Passing* works to make is that *all* such identifications must be tentative and provisional. As Claudia Tate has put it, our "inability to arrive at a conclusion in and of itself attests to Larsen's consummate skill in dramatizing psychological ambiguity."[13] Clare Kendry represents a difference that cannot be placed or measured. She stands in a zone of radical indeterminacy that forces other characters within the novel, as well as the readers of the novel, to confront the limits and dangers of any settled and certain understanding of what it means to know and recognize an other. Her story thus qualifies our conclusion that democratic citizens should cultivate dignity-nurturing relationships. It may be true that they should not pass each other with "unseeing eyes," but nor should they presume that they are able to see and know *all* of who another person is.

Passing also warns that an indeterminacy like Clare's (is she black or white?) should not be understood simply as a radical emptiness or absence. There *is* something there—a wraith—even if it cannot be named. The novel underscores the difficult paradox that just as one must recognize a difference without presuming to know what it means, so should one be willing to project a difference without presuming to know how it will be taken. In a racist society, obviously, this second willingness is not an option. Nor, as the novel suggests through its tragic ending, is the alternative choice of passing.[14] Like Chesnutt, then, Larsen is deeply committed not just to asserting the importance of recognizing the personhood of another citizen but to exploring the *difficulty* of doing so when that other person exhibits a difference (whether of race or gender or sexuality or ethnicity) that is important to him or her.

"Trying to Be Like Friends": James Baldwin's In Another Country

Like *The House behind the Cedars* and *Passing*, James Baldwin's novel *Another Country* is concerned—if not obsessed—with what can happen or fail to happen when two human beings look one another in the eye. Scene after scene pivots on such exchanges, for they epitomize the larger question on which the novel as a whole rests: can we know each other across or through or despite our differences, and if so how? The novel is "preoccupied," critic Brandon Gordon writes, "with precisely this problem of how literature can make the knowledge of what it is like to be African American available to the [white] reader"; and its major insight, he suggests, is that a white person must feel "the physical pain…of what it means to be black." But Gordon's account doesn't quite do justice to the novel's nuances. *Another Country* isn't trying to convey "what it is like to be an African American," which implies both that Baldwin believed there was a single African American experience and that could it could be represented to and known by whites. Neither of these things is the case. Rather, as Kevin Ohi has argued, critics who read the novel as an uplifting account of its "characters…revealing themselves to themselves and to others" overlook that "self-revelation almost always appears in the novel as a poignantly yearned-for impossibility" and miss Baldwin's point that they "in fact reveal only the fact of having an incommunicable secret." Like Nella Larsen's *Passing*, then, *Another Country* provides a pedagogy of democratic interpersonal communication that urges its readers to understand that complete knowledge of another person is neither possible nor desirable. To know them, we have to accept and respect precisely what we *cannot* ever know about them. And as Ernesto Javier Martinez argues, the novel's interests are ethical, not just epistemological: "What Baldwin's characters can *know* about themselves and their social contexts is intimately related to what they are willing to *do* in the social domain."[15]

The ethics in question are specifically democratic. In order to recognize one another's dignity, we must work through and around the incommunicable individual suffering that has been caused by oppressions such as racism, homophobia, and patriarchy. We also have to recognize our own complicity with those forces. As Lawrie Balfour writes: "recognition of black Americans by whites does not alone suffice. Baldwin contends that white Americans will not have accepted the equal humanity of blacks until they are able to admit the racial construction of their own identities and ask how that construction affects their commitments." *Another Country* vividly dramatizes just how difficult—and necessary—such recognition and admission are. While condemning those oppressive forces and wishing to bring their histories to an end, Baldwin also believes that we have to do much more than condemn them. We also have to do the hard ethical work of *living through* them moment by moment without "innocence." This effort is bound to be messy, mistake-ridden, and painful, but the alternatives are all "too easy." Baldwin is well aware that this espousal of gradualist effort could easily be confused with the naive liberal belief that we can slowly bring about change by standing in one another's shoes, so he takes pains to distinguish his own democratic commitments from those of mainstream American liberalism by holding several plainly liberal characters up for scrutiny and criticism. At the same time, as we shall see, his novel and his essays warn against the radical Left's tendency to displace the scene of democratic politics away from the here and now and to project them exclusively into the before and the after—into the interminable critique of the causal origins of oppression and into the dream of its eventual and uncompromised defeat in some postrevolutionary future.

The novel's cast of characters is large, and the differences Baldwin sets in play are many. There are differences between black and white characters, between straight and bisexual characters, and between men and women. To list these differences as I have is to risk reducing the novel to a prime exhibit in the multicultural curriculum that guided so much work in the humanities and social sciences in the 1980s and 1990s. But Baldwin's novel, published in 1962, is neither a celebration of difference per se nor an analysis of the ways political and economic powers emphasize and exploit difference in order to divide and dominate people. Baldwin does take careful note of the fact that even an artsy bohemian couple living in Greenwich Village assumes that the wife should quite literally serve her husband—breakfast, lunch, cocktails, dinner—and then do the dishes and put the children to bed, all while he works on his novel. And Baldwin is very attuned to the power dynamics that can both enliven and corrupt sexuality, whether between men and women or between men. But Baldwin's sensibility is not interested in "power" in either the Foucauldian or the Marxist sense. While he understands that forces much larger than individuals are constantly shaping and constraining their choices, he focuses on the moments when they exercise, or fail to exercise, that margin of agency for which they are responsible.

And yet history does make frequent appearances in the novel, for Baldwin's interest in racial difference is also an interest in the present consequences of a long history of white racism. The racial question he dramatizes is whether a white person and a black person can love and know and communicate with each other across the abyss of the history that divides them. This question gets played out primarily through two relationships: first, a friendship between Vivaldo (a working-class Italian-American living in the Village and trying to be a novelist) and Rufus (a black musician from a poor family in Harlem); then, after Rufus's suicide, a love affair between Vivaldo and Rufus's younger sister, Ida. The main challenge this history poses in the novel is that it causes Rufus and Ida to feel "the rage of the disesteemed"—which is an emotion Vivaldo can never fully understand. Not being black himself, he simply cannot grasp why his black friends hate all whites, including even those whites whom they love and who love them.

As the novel opens, Rufus is full of self-loathing because he cannot help hating the white woman, Leona, with whom he has fallen in love. Hating her, he beats her, and that she endures his abuse only strengthen his suspicion that she loves him only because she is drawn to the myth of black sexual prowess. This destructive cycle has been caused by past histories of racism for which neither of them is responsible and which neither of them can now manage. Into this situation steps Vivaldo, Rufus's best friend. Vivaldo is a good man, but he cannot quite admit to himself how deeply racism has caused Rufus to suffer. (He is, as Susan Feldman suggests, "the novel's staunchest representative of white liberalism.")[16] After sending Leona away, he offers to stay with Rufus—and out pours Rufus's hatred of all whites:

> I don't need no company. I done had enough company to last me the rest of my life.... How I hate them—all those white sons of bitches out there. They're trying to kill me, you think I don't know? They got the world on a string, man, the miserable white cock suckers, and they're tying that string around my neck, they're killing me.... Sometimes I lie here and listen, listen for a bomb, man, to fall on this city and make all that noise stop. I listen to hear them crying, man, for somebody to come help them.[17]

Baldwin carefully sets forth Vivaldo's complex response:

> "Rufus. Rufus. What about—" He wanted to say, What about me, Rufus? I'm white. He said, "Rufus, not everybody's like that." (426)

Vivaldo's first impulse is to offer himself as an example of white virtue and innocence, however rare that might be. But he thinks better of it, probably because he is intelligent and good enough to realize that, under these circumstances, such a reply would be egotistical and even vain. Moments like these give us a clear sense of why Rufus considers Vivaldo to be a friend. A few minutes later, Vivaldo says, "I just want to be your friend.... That's all. But you don't want any friends, do you?"

> "Yes, I do," said Rufus, quietly. "Yes, I do." He paused; then slowly, with difficulty, "Don't mind me. I know you're the only friend I've got left in the world, Vivaldo."
> And that's why you hate me, Vivaldo thought, feeling still and helpless and sad. (428)

The power of racism's legacy to enter into and distort and even destroy relationships is shown repeatedly in the novel. After Rufus's suicide, when Vivaldo goes to a nightclub to hear Ida sing, he thinks about how the black musicians who accompany her must think of him:

> It was too clear that if he had been a powerful white man, their attitudes would have been modified by the assumption that she was using *him*; but it was obvious that, as things were, he could do her no good whatever and, therefore, he must be using *her*. (652)

Baldwin is doing two things here. On the one hand, he's suggesting that the history of race relations prevents these musicians from seeing Vivaldo's relationship with Ida for what it is: Vivaldo most certainly is *not* "using" her in the customary racialized sense, the sense Ida herself refers to later when she tells him, "But I'm black, too, and I know how white people treat black boys and girls. They think you're something for them to wipe their pricks on" (656). At the same time, though, Baldwin is imbedding an irony that Vivaldo will come to acknowledge only at the end of the novel, when Ida makes clear that he *does* use her in a different sense, one that has little to do with race: he uses her in that he needs to love her in order to feel self-esteem. This need prevents him from being honest with her, because he knows that by being honest he might lose her.

But before we get to this aspect of their relationship, we should first see in more detail how the long history of racism continually threatens it. After Ida's remark about how "white people treat black boys and girls," Baldwin writes:

> "After all this time we've been together," he [Vivaldo] said, at last, "you still think that?"
> "Our being together doesn't change the world, Vivaldo."
> "It does," he said, "for me."
> "That," she said, "is because you're white." (656)

Vivaldo is hurt; he takes her point personally. But Ida is naming something real that he will have to learn if he is ever going to have an honest relationship with her: as a white man, he *does* live in a different world from hers. Even when they are "together," she is also away from him in a world he has no access to. Their being together might change the world for *him*, and maybe *he* can think of their relationship itself as changing the world, but if so that is because he is *white*. If he were black, he would still have to experience moments when the hard fact that the world has not changed would thrust its racist leer in his face. If he were black and had a wider awareness of the systemic power of racism, he would be much less likely to imagine that one good relationship could change the world. Vivaldo is, in a word, "innocent," as Baldwin uses that word in his essays, where it means a cowardly and guilty unwillingness to face squarely the damages caused by the history of white racism. This innocence enrages her (as it does Baldwin himself). "How can I believe you love me?" she demands. "How can you love somebody you don't know anything about? You don't know where I've been. You don't know what life is like for me" (657).

In a conversation with Cass, a white female friend, Ida makes the same point. Again, Baldwin takes care to let us know that Cass is no villain; she is a sensitive, intelligent woman who is aware of racism and tries to think about it in her relationships with black persons, including Rufus and Ida. Yet she, too, is innocent—as when Ida tries to explain to her that their situations aren't commensurable because their past histories are so different.

> "But imagine," Ida was saying, "that he came, that man who's your man—because you always know, and he damn sure don't come every day—and there wasn't any place for you to walk out of or into, because he came too late. And no matter when he arrived would have been too late—because too much had happened by the time you were born, let alone by the time you met each other."
>
> I don't believe that, Cass thought. That's too easy. I don't believe it. She said, "If you're talking about yourself and Vivaldo—there are other countries—have you ever thought of that?"
>
> Ida threw back her head and laughed. (679)

And she laughs for good reason: what is Cass suggesting—that she and Vivaldo emigrate to another country (hence the book's title) where racism has never existed? Even if there were such a place, its existence wouldn't gainsay the radical difference between the terms in which Cass and Ida can think about meeting that rare man who is "your man." For Ida, such a man happens to be white, and because he is white he necessarily comes "too late"—after white racism has caused her and her people irreparable damage. That history cannot be undone. Now it comes between her and Vivaldo. And this is why Ida, like Rufus, hates all white people:

> Cass, ask yourself, look out and ask yourself—wouldn't you hate all white people if they kept you in prison here?...Kept you here, and

stunted you and starved you, and made you watch your mother and father and sister and lover and brother and son and daughter die or go mad or go under, before your very eyes?...Some days, honey, I wish I could turn myself into one big fist and grind this miserable country to powder. Now, you've never felt like that, and Vivaldo's never felt like that. (680)

Yet Ida doesn't get the last word on this subject. Baldwin reveals that she is not always as correct as she supposes when he embeds an irony that comes into view later: even though Ida is right, her response is, as Cass supposes, "too easy." It's too reflexive; it isn't self-oppositional. When Ida thinks and speaks these words, she isn't really thinking or working.

In one of the novel's final scenes, Ida confesses to Vivaldo that she's had an affair with a powerful white record producer who can advance her career. Their conversation gets underway as follows:

He said, very gently, "Well, then what *is* it, Ida?" She said, wearily, "Oh, it's too many things, it goes too far back, I can never make you understand, never."

"Try me. You say you love me. Why can't you trust me?"

She laughed. "Oh. You think life is so simple....I always think of you as being a very nice boy who doesn't know what the score is, who'll maybe never find out. And I don't want to be the one to teach you." (535)

She tries to explain herself by reminding Vivaldo that her life has been different, that she has grown up knowing the score, and that this knowledge requires her to adopt a ruthlessly Hobbesian view of the world in order to survive or succeed:

"Because I'm black," she said, after a moment, and sat at the table near him, "I know more about what happened to my brother than you can ever know. I watched it happen—from the beginning. I was there." (737)

Vivaldo both understands, partially, and objects:

"Nothing you've said so far...seems to have much to do with being black. Except for what you make of it. But nobody can help you there."

She sighed sharply, in a kind of rage. "That could be true. But it's too easy for you to say that."

"Ida, a lot of what you've had to say, ever since we met, has been— too easy." He watched her. "Hasn't it?" And then, "Sweetheart, suffering doesn't *have* a color. Does it? Can't we step out of this nightmare?" (740)

What Baldwin wants his readers to see is that Ida and Vivaldo are *both* right, and that the truth of who they are individually and collectively is more completely perceived if we combine both of their perspectives—however at odds they may be. Ida is surely correct when she points out Vivaldo's innocence to him and when she claims that there are aspects of her identity that he can never understand—the most significant one being the rage she and Rufus feel that Vivaldo and Cass cannot. At the same time, though, Vivaldo does name something important when he says that Ida too readily traces all her problems back to her blackness, which becomes therefore the overdetermining explanation of everything. To her credit, Ida implicitly agrees, but she also retorts, rightly, that "it's too easy for you to say that."

This conversation suggests, then, that the problem they have to overcome is the tendency they both have—and that we *all* have—to believe and say things that are "too easy." Baldwin plainly has a good deal of compassion for these two characters who are working very hard to know each other and be honest with each other. Yet even they slip into the "easy" way of seeing things rather than facing and living through the hard ways. When Ida looks at Vivaldo, she sees someone who "doesn't know the score," by which she means someone who hasn't suffered enough to arrive at her thoroughly wised-up view of the world. And up to a point, she is right: he can no more see the privilege his whiteness has conferred on him, and the suffering her blackness has imposed upon her, than he can see the back of his head or the dark side of the moon. In these ways, he surely doesn't know the score, and the challenge he faces is to continually bring an awareness of his ignorance (of what he does not know) into his relationship with Ida. But Vivaldo too is right when he says that "suffering doesn't have a color" and when he suggests that there's an innocence in *her* assumption that by being black she automatically knows the score—all of it. Vivaldo can see something about Ida that she cannot: that some of her suffering is *not* caused by her being black. The challenge for Ida will be to bring her awareness of what she can't know—what it's like *not* to be black, what it's like to be a man, what it's like to be a Catholic Italian-American—into her relationship with Vivaldo.[18]

All this is to say that recognizing and nurturing democratic dignity is more difficult and complex than we might at first suppose. In order for Vivaldo to continuously affirm Ida's dignity, he must be able to see her, which means he must also see a particular history; she is not just an abstract self or soul but an individual person formed in part by complex historical forces, including racism and slavery—which she understands much better than he. Yet, as he understands a bit better than she does, she also needs to be seen as *more* than a historical person; she needs to be seen and to know herself as a person with human motives and needs, who suffers and undergoes experience in the ways most other humans do, regardless of their race or history. He must see her historically *and* existentially, and she must see him in the same complex and delicate manner.[19]

Implications for Democracy

Baldwin's novel suggests, then, that what we have been calling "human dignity" is more complex and dynamic than that phrase implies. Dignity is not something ethereal and abstract that takes identical form within every person and lies there, waiting for recognition or fearing denial. Instead, as *Another Country* shows, a person's dignity is thoroughly woven into his or her idiosyncratic personhood, into who that person is that no one else is or ever can be. To see and nurture another person's human and democratic dignity, therefore, we must learn to see him or her both historically and existentially. For black persons and white persons, this means acknowledging the history of racism and its legacies in the present. As Lawrie Balfour argues with respect to Baldwin's essays, his work instructs us that "theories of politics that abstract from racial identity may move too quickly into the raceless future without struggling with the significance of a race-conscious present."[20] Yet as both Baldwin and Larsen warn, seeing this history and knowing what it means— especially for each individual person—is probably impossible. They suggest that we should enter into our relationships with other citizens knowing in advance that we never can see *all* of any person; aspects of him or her will always be out of reach and out of sight, including (perhaps especially) the aspects that are traceable to the history of race and racism. The key, therefore, is to know *that* we don't know *what* we don't know and then to be vigilantly alert for those occasions when, through the creative workings of vulnerability that has been risked and trust that has been built, we get a glimpse of these aspects. In some cases, these will be glimpses of categorical historical phenomena: a straight person might think he's getting a glimpse of what it's like to be gay or lesbian, a woman might infer that she is getting a glimpse of what it's like to be a man, a white woman might suppose she is getting a glimpse of what it's like to be a black woman, and so on. In all such cases, as Larsen's novel in particular advises, we should be aware that these categories must take their specific meaning from the particular person to whom they apply. All we can and should hope to get a glimpse of what is it's like for *that* person to be gay or lesbian, or black, or white, or old, or rich. What we should be listening for is *their particular experience and interpretation* of that category. If we take the category to have meaning in itself, we become despite our best intentions "innocent" racists or sexists or homophobes or the like.

We live in a society composed of persons with these and many other differences. If we seal ourselves off from each other, if we deny or foreclose on the possibility of relationship with each other, then we clearly are not putting ourselves in a position to recognize and affirm each other's democratic dignity. Democratic citizenship is relational citizenship. But as we have seen, that insight opens the door to very difficult questions and challenges: what does it mean to recognize and affirm dignity? what *is* dignity? if history and categorical forms of difference enter into and compose personhood, should we abstract these out in order to recognize and affirm dignity? if not, how do we take them into account without thereby losing sight of the idiosyncrasy of each person?

As I hope my discussion of these two novels has shown, the answer to this last question is complex. These works suggest that we can never finally determine the *meaning* of these forms of difference. At best, we can begin to know what they mean for a particular person. Relational democratic citizenship is therefore characterized by a profound modesty. We understand that our knowledge of one another is and always will be limited and incomplete. This is why respect is the attitude we should bring to democratic relationships: I affirm and nurture a person's dignity by respecting her; as the word itself implies, this means observing certain limits and boundaries to what I can know about her. This incompleteness also characterizes our knowledge of ourselves: try as we might, we can never get to the bottom of our entanglements in, and complicity with, history and all of its cruelties. As Robert Tomlinson has pointed out, Baldwin's conviction that our efforts to know must inevitably fail—and that we are morally obliged to keep trying nevertheless—is what makes his vision so profoundly tragic.[21]

To bring into sharper focus the contribution these two novels might make to our understanding of the practice of democratic citizenship, I'd like to conclude by comparing their interest in relationships with the views of two writers commonly taken to express this nation's democratic character and aspirations: Ralph Waldo Emerson and Walt Whitman. Emerson had what we might call a zero-sum-game understanding of democratic personhood: *either* we are self-reliant *or* we are oppressed by our society's relentless pressure to conform. Because relationships are one of the main ways society conditions and manipulates us, Emerson believed that we should spurn them whenever they threaten our autonomy and integrity—and, yes, our dignity. In a passage typical of his views, Emerson writes in "Self-Reliance": "The doctrine of hatred must be preached as the counteraction of the doctrine of love when that pules and whines. I shun mother and father and wife and brother, when my genius calls to me."²² Evidently, Emerson seldom if ever imagined that relationships could be plastic and malleable; he was even less disposed to imagine that relationships, when properly understood and practiced, could actually affirm and nurture individual personhood ("genius") and dignity.

Like Emerson, Walt Whitman believed that democratic personhood is something we must form and make, not something simply given to us. The right to vote, he saw, is just the beginning, not the fulfillment of "the grand experiment" of democratic citizenship: "to become an enfranchised man, and now, impediments removed, to stand and start without humiliation, and equal to the rest; to commence, or have the road clear'd to commence, the grand experiment of development, whose end (perhaps requiring several generations,) may be the forming of full-grown man or woman—that is something." But as many of Walt Whitman's readers have noted, unlike Emerson he regarded relationships as indispensable to democratic personhood. Hoping to counteract what Alexis de Tocqueville had diagnosed as American democracy's tendency to produce an individualism marked by loneliness, selfishness, and greed, Whitman argued: "Not that half only, individualism, which isolates. There is another half, which is adhesiveness or love, that fuses, ties, and aggregates, making the races comrades, and fraternizing all."²³

However, in his eagerness to love his fellow citizens and to identify with them despite their differences, Whitman seems unaware that democratic relationships require respect, not just empathy. Too often he speaks of democracy in terms of "merging," "fusion," even "lump" and "mass." Too often he claims to be able to identify with others in an unqualified way. We should certainly admire him for saying, "I am the hounded slave.... I wince at the bite of the dogs," especially since in doing so he broke with the racist working-class culture of mid-nineteenth-century New York City he affiliated with.²⁴ But at the same time, we should take note of all that is lost through this erasure or suppression of the differences between himself and a runaway slave. At the very

least, and as the work of Frederick Douglass and Harriet Jacobs makes abun-
dantly clear, Whitman failed to imagine that an enslaved person might bring
distinctive and valuable knowledge with him—knowledge that Whitman
himself could not have acquired, including knowledge about the meaning of
democracy and the practice of democratic citizenship.

Danielle S. Allen has pointed out that the strongest advice we give to our
children about the practice of democratic citizenship is "Don't talk to strangers." She has proposed that we adopt instead "a new mode of citizenship in
friendship understood not as an emotion but a practice."[25] She thinks of this
new mode as a form of "rhetoric" (in the Greek, not in the pejorative, sense
of the word):

> Political friendship consists finally of trying to be like friends. Its payoff
> is rarely intimate, or genuine, friendship, but it is often trustworthiness
> and, issuing from that, political trust. Its art, trust production, has long
> gone by the abused name of rhetoric. Properly understood, rhetoric is
> not a list of stylistic rules but an outline of the radical commitment to
> other citizens that is needed for a just democratic politics. (157)

Allen captures very well the sense of measure, or restraint, that these black
writers urge us to adopt in forming relationships that affirm and nurture democratic dignity. What I find especially helpful is her emphasis on the practice
(or form) of such relationships rather than on their content. This concern
with form is what prompts her to speak of the "art" of citizenship. Larsen and
Baldwin likewise aim not to prescribe *what* we should feel and know but to
guide us in *how* we should feel and know. Their understanding of the art of
citizenship protects the "inner ocean" of each person, that sense of idiosyncratic self so dear to Emerson; yet it also places us in a web of democratic relationships so important to Whitman, making clear that these should not be
imagined as a bear hug or a "merging" of selves into an undifferentiated mass.
"Unless we continually explore the network of complex relationships which
bind us together," Ralph Ellison wrote, we will "continue being the victims of
various inadequate conceptions of ourselves, both as individuals and as citizens of a nation of diverse people."[26] The fictions of Larsen and Baldwin contribute to our public philosophy of democracy by underscoring the complex,
perhaps inescapably tragic dynamics of such relationships, thereby pointing
us toward a more successful practice of the art of democratic citizenship.

4

"A Greater, Broader Sense of Humanity and World Fellowship"

BLACK WORLDLY CITIZENSHIP FROM DOUGLASS TO MALCOLM X

IN THE WINTER of 1845, Frederick Douglass had to flee from the United States to avoid recapture by his master (who had been alerted to Douglass's whereabouts by the recent publication and success of *Narrative of the Life of an American Slave*). Douglass escaped to Ireland, Scotland, and England, where for eighteen months he toured extensively, giving warmly received lectures to abolitionist and temperance audiences. In a letter to William Lloyd Garrison, which Douglass intended for publication in Garrison's newspaper the *Liberator*, he wrote: "I can truly say, I have spent some of the happiest moments of my life since landing in this country. I seem to have undergone a transformation. I live a new life. The warm and generous cooperation extended to me by friends of the despised race . . . the spirit of freedom that seems to animate all with whom I come in contact, and the entire absence of anything that looked like prejudice against me, on account of the color of my skin—contrasted so strongly with my long and bitter experience in the United States, that I look with wonder and amazement on the transition."[1] Douglass also declared that he underwent this transformation as a man without a country, as an exile or even as an "outlaw" from his native land: "I have no end to serve, no creed to uphold, no government to defend; and as to nation, I belong to none. I have no protection at home or resting-place abroad. The land of my birth welcomes me to her shores only as a slave, and spurns with contempt the idea of treating me differently; so that I am an outcast from the society of my childhood, and an outlaw in the land of my birth" (372).

Surprising as it may seem, Douglass's experience as a man who belonged to no nation should speak powerfully today to all Americans. For whatever their race or ethnicity, Americans today must come to terms with what globalization and an interconnected, interdependent world portend for their democracy and their citizenship. The challenge is hardly unique to citizens of the United States. All the nations of the world are being forced to adjust their traditional conceptions of their identity, or *ethnos*, to an omnipresent global culture produced and largely dominated by transnational financial and media institutions. Moreover, all the nations of the world are being pressured to adapt as conventional conceptions of national sovereignty clash with the emerging need for systems of global governance capable of dealing with these institutions, and with global problems like pandemics, terrorism, and degradation of the biosphere. Along with these issues, the world's democracies in particular are having to deal with a conceptual contradiction between the idea on which democracy is based—that of a singular self-governing demos—and the necessity of ceding some authority to international institutions of governance. As Judith Shklar puts it: "If 'we the people' are the sole source of public authority, who are the people? If democracy is government by and for the people, who does and does not constitute the people? No question has been more vexing for modern democratic thought, because it arises not only when self-government is defined, but also whenever democratic governments have to consider their relations to aliens and to other states and peoples."[2] Finally, and complicating its response to all of these challenges, the United States will have to transform its long-standing myth of American "exceptionalism" in order to make it more compatible with international interdependence and global partnership. Sooner or later, in short, Americans will have to fundamentally reimagine what it means to be "American" in the world of the twenty-first century. They will have to balance their national with a nationless identity.

Some political theorists have argued that this can be done only if citizens identify their national identity and democracy with universal truths and principles. Martha Nussbaum, most notably, has proposed that young Americans be taught "that they are, *above all*, citizens of a world of human beings, and that, while they happen to be situated in the United States, they have to share this world with the citizens of other countries."[3] She goes on to suggest that "We should recognize humanity wherever it occurs, and give its fundamental ingredients, reason and moral capacity, our first allegiance and respect" (7). Her position rests, Nussbaum says, on what "is justifiable in universalist terms," and she believes that US public philosophy should strive to emphasize the universalism already built into our civic national identity: "If we really do believe that all human beings are created equal and endowed with certain inalienable rights, we are morally required to think about what that conception requires us to do with and for the rest of the world" (13).

Nussbaum's call to subordinate national to international civic identity in accordance with universal principles of justice has drawn fire from a number of critics. Benjamin Barber points to two problems: "First, she underappreciates the success of the American experiment in grafting the sentiments of patriotism onto a constitutional frame defined precisely by the 'substantive values of justice and rights' she prizes. And second, she underestimates the thinness of cosmopolitanism and the crucial humanizing role played by identity politics in a deracinated world of contracts, markets, and legal personhood."[4] Lawrie Balfour expands on Barber's second criticism by arguing that Nussbaum's version of universalism slides over some historical thorns that pose a sharp challenge to it. Nussbaum "sidesteps questions about the lingering shadows" of a long history of European imperialism that sought to justify itself by creating and maintaining racial hierarchies, so her conception of the world today seems naively abstract.[5] Thus, when Nussbaum writes that young Americans should be taught that they have to "share this world with the citizens of other countries," she overlooks the hard fact that most of these Americans have benefited from that history of racial hierarchy, while many of the "citizens of other countries" have been its victims. Her choice of the verb "share," with its implications of equal responsibility for the world as it is, seems inadequate to what we know about the powers that have *made* the world what it is: Do Americans *share* with others resources that they have taken from them? Nussbaum's universalism, in short, ignores the historical particularity of racism. As we face the challenges of living in a more interconnected world, we cannot simply overlook the history of race and racism and imagine that all people are for moral purposes "the same."

Some political theorists have argued also that no conception of universalism can truly be universal, since as Judith Butler observes, "the meaning of 'the universal' proves to be culturally variable" and "standards of universality are historically articulated."[6] While Americans might "really believe" that their principles are universal, this does not make them so. Consequently, they must now reimagine the relation between their religious and ethical traditions and those of other peoples. As Seyla Benhabib (herself something of a Kantian) puts it, to negotiate the challenges of the demos's boundaries in a more interdependent world, we should "engage in reflexive acts of self-constitution, whereby the boundaries of the demos can be readjusted." And this will require us, writes Bonnie Honig, to reimagine our national identity in ways that "scramble" the "binaries of cosmopolitanism versus patriotism."[7]

In the pages that follow, I suggest that a number of black American artists and activists anticipated all of these political theorists and initiated precisely the kinds of reimagining of democratic national citizenship they call for. To see how this might be so, let us first return briefly to Frederick Douglass's writings from Ireland and England. As literary historian Fionnghuala Sweeney has suggested, the perspective his travels afforded prompted Douglass "to challenge and rework the racialized tenets of the US cultural imaginary, the internalized image of the national ideal that underpinned political reality and representative norms."[8] One especially effective form of that reworking, I suggest, was his recovery of the transnational implications of the founding document of US national identity: the Declaration of Independence. This retrieval was made possible, he lets us know, by his discovery of a space not delimited by any national borders, a space he would later call "the high ground of human brotherhood."

"I have ever found the Abolitionists of this country [Ireland] the warmest friends of America and American institutions," he wrote to newspaper editor Horace Greeley:

> I have frequently seen in their houses, and sometimes occupying the most conspicuous places in their parlors, the American Declaration of Independence. An aged Anti-Slavery gentleman in Dublin...has the Declaration of Independence and a number of the portraits of the distinguished founders of the American Republic. He bought them many years ago, in token of his admiration of the men and their principles. But, said he, after speaking of the sentiments of the Declaration— looking up as it hung in a costly frame—I am often tempted to turn its face to the wall, it is such a palpable contradiction of the spirit and practices of the American people at this time.[9]

The principles of the Declaration, Douglass suggests, belong to the Irish as much as to the United States, just as the document itself hangs on their walls not just on Americans'. In his lectures in Britain, therefore, he ridiculed the hypocrisy of the American appropriation of the Declaration for its narrowly nationalist purposes. In a speech of March 30, 1847, he sarcastically declared that Americans "made the loudest and clearest assertions of the rights of man; and yet at that very same time the identical men who drew up that Declaration of Independence...were trafficking in the blood and souls of their fellow men."[10] In another speech, he declared:

I confess, that although I am going back to that country, though I have many dear friends there, though I expect to end my days upon its soil, I am, nevertheless, not here to make any profession whatever of respect for that country, of attachment to its politicians, or love for its churches or national institutions. The fact is, the whole system, the entire network of American society, is one great falsehood, from beginning to end.[11]

Yet these words do not express the whole of Douglass's attitude toward the United States. With the self-opposing energy characteristic of so much black thought about democracy, he often voiced a quietly persisting patriotism, a deep affiliation with the homeland that had outlawed him: "America will not allow her children to love her," he complained in an April 1846 letter to Garrison. "She seems bent on compelling those who would be her warmest friends, to be her worst enemies.... I will continue to pray, labor, and wait, believing that she cannot always be insensible to the dictates of justice or deaf to the voice of humanity." In another letter he wrote: "I long to be at home—'home, sweet, sweet, sweet home! Be it ever so humble, there is no place like home."[12] And in a letter he wrote later that month to Greeley, he portrayed himself as a "friend" of the United States: "I am one of those who think the best friend of a nation is he who the most faithfully rebukes her for her sins—and he her worst enemy who, under the specious and popular garb of patriotism seeks to excuse, palliate, and defend them."[13]

In short, the experience of being nationless allowed Douglass to reconceive the meaning of his nation and of its founding document, the Declaration. Further, and more paradoxically, his critical distance as an outlaw enabled him to conceive of a version of patriotism that preserved—indeed promoted—these insights. He began voicing this newly acquired perspective as soon as he returned to the United States. In doing so, he took another step toward what we might call a *theory* of transnational democratic citizenship by articulating the vantage point that had made these insights possible. Thus, in the very first speech he gave back in the United States, he defended the speeches he had given abroad, and pointed to prenational space from which and toward which he spoke. "I do not hate America as against England, or against any other country or land. I love Humanity all over the globe.... I never appealed to Englishmen in a manner calculated to awaken feelings of hatred or disgust, or to inflame their prejudices toward America as a nation...I always appealed to their manhood, *that which preceded* their being Englishmen."[14] And in *My Bondage and My Freedom*, written four years later, he made the

same claim: "Again, let it also be remembered—for it is the simple truth—
that neither in this speech, nor in any other which I delivered in England, did
I ever allow myself to address Englishmen as against Americans. I took my
stand on the high ground of human brotherhood, and spoke to Englishmen
as men, in behalf of men" (379; emphasis added).

This "high ground of human brotherhood" served, then, as the ground
from which he could perceive that the Declaration and its principles might
speak for and to all men and women, not just Americans, by appealing to an
identity that "preceded" their national identities. Is it possible that his status
as a nationless outlaw disposed him to perceive what we too easily forget: that
the signers of the Declaration were *outlaws* before they became founders? For
they, too, were briefly nationless as they rebelled from one nation in order to
form a new one. Like Douglass, they stood *not* on the ground of the United
States, but on the "high ground of human brotherhood," where they made
their declaration with "a decent respect for the opinions of mankind."

While Douglass's sojourn abroad encouraged him to adopt this transnational perspective on the principles expressed in the Declaration of
Independence, his abiding affiliation with his country disposed him to
take this now-renewed document back to his countrymen, dusted off, so to
speak, and freed from all of its musty nationalist trappings. When in 1847
he stepped back within the horizon of his nation, he believed that he now
knew something about the founding principles of US democracy that most
white American citizens had forgotten, or knew only weakly and abstractly.
It is well known that his colleagues in the Massachusetts Anti-Slavery Society
were dismayed when he told them that he intended to start his own newspaper and thereby assert his independence from their oversight. Less remarked
upon, however, are the specific words Douglass later used to describe this fall-
ing out: "My American friends looked at me with astonishment.... A slave,
brought up in the very depths of ignorance, assuming to instruct the highly
civilized people of the north in the principles of liberty, justice, and humanity! The thing looked absurd" (390). Clearly, Douglass was claiming not just
independence from the Garrisonian wing of the abolitionism movement but
his right to speak as a philosopher of democracy and to instruct his fellow
citizens in its principles.

In response to the challenges of twenty-first-century democratic citizenship, Seyla Benhabib has called for us to notice and "conceptualize those
moments when a space emerges in the public sphere when principles and
norms that undergird democratic life will become permeable and fluid to new
semantic contexts, which enable the augmentation of the meaning of rights."[15]

Douglass, clearly, found and noticed such a "space." It was his literal and legal nationlessness that prompted him to place US democracy in a "context" that would "enable the augmentation of the meaning of rights." His genius was to suggest that that context was not "new": it was instead the *original* position, the nationless context within and from which the founders themselves had penned the Declaration of Independence. By claiming that he spoke to the British not in their role as Englishmen but as what they were *before* they constituted any nation, Douglass was reminding his American audience of what Benhabib calls its "*pre*commitment to certain formal and substantive interpretations of rights" (33). In this way Douglass was able to "scramble" the "binaries of cosmopolitanism versus patriotism."

In the pages that follow, I trace the ways James Weldon Johnson and Malcolm X undertook in the twentieth century the kind of reimagining of nation, demos, and citizenship that Douglass prefigured in the nineteenth. A shared condition predisposed all of them (along with many other black Americans) to take a broader, more worldly view of life than most of their white fellow citizens. This was the bare fact that their black ancestors had been kidnapped, sold into slavery, and forcibly brought to North America. Their knowledge of their African past and their experience of exclusion and injustice gave them what Du Bois called a "double consciousness," the faculty (or curse) of being able to see things from both an American and an outsider's perspectives. It also disposed many to seek a form of citizenship that melded African diasporic self-identification with national citizenship. In the early twentieth century, this inclination enabled Du Bois to see that white racism was a global problem, present wherever European and US colonizers had established their dominion, and that the black struggle to achieve democracy within the borders of the United States was thus inextricably linked to a worldwide struggle of people of color to liberate themselves from European colonization.

Historian Nikhil Pal Singh has shown how Du Bois's insight was taken up and interpreted in different ways by black artists and intellectuals active from the 1930s through the 1960s. Singh takes pains to make clear that there was no singular, unitary black position on the large question of the relation between black American political struggle and global anticolonialist movements; indeed, he calls attention to a matrix of vigorous debate within which several generations of black Americans pondered this issue. Yet he also demonstrates that, however varied their positions, all believed that the fate of black Americans and of US democracy would ultimately require thinking on a transnational, even global scale. Thus, well in advance of the rest of the US polity, they and many other black Americans were grappling with the perplexing and complex relation between national democracy and worldly citizenship.[16]

James Weldon Johnson: "The Myriad Threads of Influence"

In May 1920, James Weldon Johnson was returning by steamship to the United States from Haiti, where he had gone on a secretive NAACP mission to investigate abuses occurring under the US military occupation of the island. Seasick and exhausted after several nights on deck, he bribed one of the stewards to set up a makeshift bed for him in the all-white smoking room. It was crowded day and night with workers from the Panama Canal drinking, smoking, swearing, and gambling. "These men who crowded the smoking room were Canal employees of the artisan class—engineers, machinists, plumbers, electrical workers, and helpers," Johnson writes in his autobiography, *Along This Way*. "They were rough; their language was coarse and profane. But I gave the best attention I could to what they said, because it presented an interesting and important view of life, a view that I was unfamiliar with, a view that disclosed one of the most discouraging aspects of the racial situation."[17] What he noticed in particular was a phrase these men used over and over again while he sat watching them:

> One expression that they constantly used brought to me more vividly than anything else ever had a realization of the Negro's economic and industrial plight, of how lean a chance was his with his white brothers of the proletariat. The expression which I heard at least a hundred times was, "Never let a nigger pick up a tool." "Never let a nigger pick up a tool." "Never let a nigger pick up a tool." This expression echoed in my mind for a long time.... For no condition under which he struggles oppresses the Negro more than the refusal of a fair and equal chance to earn a living—to say nothing of earning it in ways in which he is able to prove himself well fitted. (529)

Johnson was forty-nine years old at the time and serving as field secretary of the NAACP. Best known today as the author of the novel *Autobiography of an Ex-Colored Man*, he was a man of many parts. He had worked as a backwoods teacher in Georgia and as a high-school principal in his home town of Jacksonville, Florida; he had traveled abroad as a member of the hugely successful trio of songwriters known as the Johnson Brothers and Bob Cole; he had worked as a political operative and fundraiser for the Republican Party in New York City; he had written and published numerous poems, reviews, and essays. He had served as US consul to Puerto Caballo in Venezuela and then to Corinto in Nicaragua, where he had been involved in defeating the revolutionary uprising of 1910; he had joined the NAACP in 1915 and spent the next two years traveling the length and breadth of the United States, helping to organize new chapters, raising funds, and investigating lynchings; he had met with President Wilson in 1918, he knew former president Theodore Roosevelt, and soon he would take facts he had obtained in Haiti about the harsh American occupation there to Warren Harding, who would turn them into powerful political ammunition in his successful presidential bid against Democrat James M. Cox in 1920.

In *Along This Way*, he writes that he had searched often for the "Key" that would explain how a black boy from Jacksonville could have become such a man of the world, equally at ease in the Oval Office, a Paris nightclub, or a sharecropper's shack in Georgia, and able to listen with cosmopolitan composure to coarse white laborers repeatedly saying, "Never let a nigger pick up a tool."

> Since I have reached the point in life where the glance is more and more frequently backward, I look searching to discover the Key. I try to isolate and trace to their origins the forces that determined the direction I have followed. This is a fascinating but inconclusive pursuit. The Key I do not find. I cannot separate the many forces that have been at work. I cannot unravel the myriad threads of influence that have drawn me here or there.... The number of forces, within and without, at work upon each of us is infinite. Many of these forces are so subtle, so tangential that they are not even perceived.... The forces at work on each individual are so manifold, so potent, so arbitrary, and often so veiled as to make fatalism a plausible philosophy. (237)

If any African American of his generation could be described as embodying the American success story, that person was James Weldon Johnson. Yet these reflections—along with others placed throughout his autobiography— seem deliberately to reject that story's tale of a solitary individual winning his way to success by dint of pluck and industry. Indeed, Johnson repeatedly insists that he has no wish to be understood this way, emphasizing instead the chance meetings and personal relationships that guided him now in one direction, now in another. He tells us, for example, that when he was a very young man trying to decide whether to stay in Jacksonville or move to New York, he felt that he "was at the fork, at the crossroads; no, I was standing lost in the woods. I did not know which direction to take, but I knew whichever I took would be fateful. I finally arrived at a fixed purpose." So far, we may think we are reading a Horatio Alger story or "Self-Reliance" by Ralph Waldo Emerson. But Johnson continues in a markedly different vein: "Just how I reached it I cannot tell. Was I governed by prescience or led by the wish? Was it blind luck or just a good guess? Someone has said that a large part of the whole business of life is good guessing. That someone was, I think, pretty close to the truth" (465). Years later, when Johnson was offered a position at the NAACP, the offer came as "a genuine surprise. I had not received the slightest intimation of its likelihood; nevertheless, under my surprise I was aware that what had come to me was in line with destiny. Out of such tenuous stuff had it come—the *unspoken reactions between me and two other men*, J. E. Spingarn and W. E. B. Du Bois—that it could not have been other than the resultant of those mysterious forces that are constantly at work for good or evil in the life of every man" (472–73; emphasis added).

What these and other passages express is a keen sensitivity to life's contingency and an appreciation—like that we find in Charles Chesnutt, Nella Larsen, and James Baldwin—of the "tenuous stuff" of relationships citizens form with one another. Johnson's autobiography offers, then, a self-conscious alternative to the American success story. His is a story that encourages us to feel the "myriad threads of influence" that make us who we are and to realize that "the number of forces, within and without, at work upon each of us is infinite." No single factor, Johnson believed, could be plucked from the whole and considered determinative of one's destiny. Many chance encounters, relationships, and influences played a role, and so, too, did his own will as he responded to those chances. Johnson succinctly condenses his worldly rejection of the success story's narrative of self-sufficient striving in the phrase *lucky breaks*: "I have no intention of depreciating my own intelligence and industry," he writes, "but the farther back I am able to look, the more clearly I discern that such results as I have gained may be, in a fair degree, traced to 'lucky breaks.' If I were giving an exhortation on the subject to young people, I should say, '*Do not trust to luck*, but be, in every way, as fully prepared as possible to measure up to the 'lucky breaks' when they come" (569–70).

Johnson's having this understanding of his life may explain why he so seldom felt threatened in his encounters with others, however different or even hostile they might have been. It may also have contributed to his skill in diplomacy, and to his use of what critic Brian Roberts has called "strategic indirection," or working to win black American democratic rights by demonstrating their mastery of the arts, not just through direct political struggle. Johnson always felt that something could be gained from an encounter, even one with a bullying white racist, so that closing down the opportunity to benefit from such an encounter should be the option of last resort. The urbane confidence and commitment to conviviality that allowed him to form relationships with rich white men as well poor black sharecroppers flowed from his understanding that his self was actually being formed by multiple chance encounters with others, even when they were men who kept repeating, "Never let a nigger pick up a tool." His writing thus exemplifies Alasdair MacIntyre's point that "political theories are, by and large, articulate, systematic, and explicit versions of the unarticulated, more or less systematic and implicit interpretations, through which plain men and women understand [their] experience of the actions of others in a way that enables them to respond to it with their own actions."[18] We can witness Johnson continuously working to reflect upon "the actions of others" so as to bring his own "implicit interpretations" into more explicit, self-conscious form: "I gave the best attention I could to what they said, because it presented an interesting and important view of life, a view that I was unfamiliar with, a view that disclosed one of the most discouraging aspects of the racial situation."

Another way to perceive the philosophical implications of Johnson's narration of his life story is to read it as repeatedly and deliberately dramatizing what Gilles Deleuze has called "the contingency of an encounter with that which forces us" to think. Deleuze argues that we need a more flexible way of thinking about thought itself, one that is more attentive both to its affective side (thinking is also *feeling*) and to its complexity (thinking is actually many processes occurring so quickly as to feel simultaneous). If we really pay attention to what happens when we think, and especially to what provokes us to think, we will quickly see the importance of what he calls a "fundamental *encounter*."[19] *Along This Way* narrates many such surprising and contingent encounters, moments when Johnson collides with experience—usually but not always in the form of a person—and instead of shrinking from the shock makes all he can of it. "I regard it as curious, almost as a matter of destiny," he writes toward the end of his autobiography, "when I think of the number of times my life has touched the life of some other individual in an apparently cursory and transient way, and then consider how that contact marked the beginning of an important phase in my own life" (569–70).

Among the many such relationships Johnson describes in *Along This Way*, two were especially important. The first was with Dr. Summers, a white man who hired Johnson to be his personal assistant when Johnson was seventeen years old. Languid, brilliant, cynical, depressed, Summers exercised a powerful influence on Johnson. He put his library at Johnson's disposal, and soon Johnson was reading books that would have scandalized his professors at Atlanta University. One of these, Paine's *The Age of Reason*, became such a favorite that he took it home and read it so often that his father eventually ordered him to remove it from the house. "Of course, he [Summers] was educated," Johnson recalls; "but I had by now known a number of educated people. What was unprecedented for me was that in him I came into close touch with a man of great culture. He was, moreover, a cosmopolite. He had traveled a good part of the world over, through Europe, to North Africa, to Greece and Turkey. He spoke French and German, the latter, because of his student days in Germany, as fluently as he did English. He had a wide knowledge of literature, and was himself a poet" (238).

The relationship that grew up between these two men became strong and intimate. Johnson eventually realized that Summers was addicted to ether; he did some research about the drug, discovered how dangerous it was, and tried hard to persuade Summers to quit. "I dared to speak to him about so personal a matter because from the beginning the relationship between us was on a high level. It was not that of employer to employee. Less still was it that of white employer to Negro employee. Between the two of us, as individuals, 'race' never showed its head. He neither condescended nor patronized; in fact, he treated me as an intellectual equal" (238).

Johnson's remarkably worldly disposition was strengthened as well by a second important relationship. This one was with an entire community in "backwoods Georgia" that he came to know while teaching there in the summer of his junior year in college:

> In all of my experience there has been no period so brief that has meant so much in my education for life as the three months I spent in the backwoods of Georgia. I was thrown for the first time on my own resources and abilities. I had my first lesson in dealing with men and conditions in the outside world. I underwent my first tryout with social forces. Certainly, the field was limited, the men and conditions simple, and the results not particularly vital; nevertheless, taken together they constituted the complex world in microcosm. It was this period that marked the beginning of my psychological change from boyhood to manhood. It was this period which marked also the beginning of my knowledge of my own people as a "race." (265)

Johnson lived with a family in an old, unpainted wooden house with just two rooms separated by a thin partition that didn't reach to the ceiling and windows without glass. But the only things that dismayed Johnson were "the lack of conveniences for taking a bath, and the lack of a suitable light by which to read or study at night" (255). Johnson passed the hours after dinner sitting on the front porch with his hosts and their neighbors, talking and listening, learning about the lives they led and pondering the nature of his relations with them. So, too, in his work as a teacher: "As I worked with my children in school and met with their parents in the homes, on the farms, and in church, I found myself studying them all with a sympathetic objectivity, as though they were something apart; but in an instant's reflection I could realize that they were me, and I was they; that a force stronger than blood made us one" (266–67).

Perhaps because he was the child of parents who, though poor, had never had to worry about getting enough food on the table, or perhaps because he had gone to college and been inducted into the black "elite" that was supposed to guide the black "masses" toward civilization and citizenship, Johnson was at first inclined to look down on these people of the Georgia backwoods. But the longer he lived with them and the more he learned about their habitual bravery, the more he came to respect them: "I was anxious to learn to know the masses of my people, to know what they thought, what they felt, and the things of which they dreamed; and in trying to find out, I laid the first stones in the foundation of faith in them on which I have stood ever since. I gained a realization of their best qualities that has made any temptation for me to stand on a little, individual peak of snobbish pride seem absurd. I saw them hedged for centuries by prejudice, intolerance, and brutality; hobbled by their own ignorance, poverty, and helplessness; yet, notwithstanding, still brave and unvanquished" (266).

After his first year of college, Johnson writes, he "began to get my bearings with regard to the world and particularly with regard to my own country. I began to get the full understanding of my relationship to America, and to take on my share of the peculiar responsibilities and burdens additional to those of the common lot, which every Negro in the United States is compelled to carry" (220). Arguably, one purpose of Johnson's autobiography was to discharge precisely this "peculiar responsibility" by encouraging his fellow citizens to get some distance from conventional narratives of the successful, self-reliant, self-made man. Again and again, he calls our attention to his discovery that, as Chesnutt put it, "connected with our kind we must be." He keeps emphasizing the importance of his encounters with others because he wants his readers to see that success has everything to do with a web of inter-dependent relationships—with what Martin Luther King Jr. would later call a "garment of destiny"—in which all men are caught.

Although I have avoided using the word "cosmopolitan" to describe Johnson's disposition, preferring Singh's "black worldliness" instead, we might pause here to consider Johnson's thinking in relation to what Walter Mignolo has called "critical cosmopolitanism."[20] Mignolo distinguishes between forms of cosmopolitanism that emanate from colonizing nations and forms that take the "perspective of coloniality," or the colonized. Only the latter will be truly useful to "an increasingly transnational (and postnational) world" (724), Mignolo argues, because the former are able to conceive of world conviviality only condescendingly, that is, in terms of "underdeveloped" or "exotic" peoples being "included" in a global culture built atop a European democratic legacy originating in ancient Greece. Indeed, all "universals" as conceptualized by the colonizing nations tend to express a Eurocentric particularity claiming to be universal. What Mignolo proposes as a substitute is what he calls "connectors" (742). A "connector" is a term or concept that the colonized have taken from the lexicon of colonizing powers and interpreted in their own way. Mignolo offers as an example the Zapatistas' use of the word "democracy." They "have no choice but to use the term that political hege-mony imposed," but "it is conceptualized not in terms of European political philosophy but in terms of Maya social organization" (742). The term or con-cept then becomes "a connector through which liberal concepts of democracy and indigenous concepts of reciprocity and community social organization for the common good must come to terms." Such examples give Mignolo hope that "The entire planet could, in fact, endorse a democratic, just, and cosmopolitan project as far as democracy and justice are detached from their 'fundamental European heritage,' from Greece onward, and are taken as con-nectors around which critical cosmopolitanism would be articulated" (743).

Johnson's *Along This Way*, with its repeated emphasis on "myriad threads of influence" and contingent encounters with others, can be read as express-ing something very close to the critical cosmopolitanism Mignolo calls for. Johnson's perspective is in a very real sense that of "coloniality," and he him-self—perhaps as an actual person, and certainly as the imagined protagonist of his own life story—is a "connector." The African American who has just investigated the US military occupation of Haiti and who can listen calmly to white Panama Canal workers repeatedly insisting, "Never give a nigger a tool," is very self-consciously exhibiting and modeling a critical cosmopolitan disposition. Having brought his readers along the way with him, he induces them to take this perspective themselves and to witness as he, a black man, comes to terms with the wages of whiteness in a transnational labor market. This form of cosmopolitanism is not very different from black worldliness. "In a world defined by complex webs of interdependency," Singh writes of black intellectuals of the 1930s and 1940s, "they recognize[d] that patterns of injustice are not confined within national borders and that antidotes cannot be sought through exclusively domestic measures" (119). Johnson's work provides exactly such pattern-recognition—not by way of a theoretical analysis, to be sure, but by way of first-person storytelling about personal encounters and relationships. Again and again Johnson positions himself as a "connector" in a double sense: among the persons he meets in his life story and between himself and his white and black readers. This is one way he fulfilled what he called his "relationship to America."

"The True Believer Recognizes the Oneness of All Humanity"

In the winter and spring of 1964, Malcolm X was in a state of spiritual and intellectual crisis. In December, he had been removed from his position as minister of the Nation of Islam's Mosque No. 7 in Harlem and ordered to refrain from making any public statements on any issue. Ostensibly a punishment for his controversial remarks about "chickens coming home to roost" in the assassination of John F. Kennedy, this suspension was to last just ninety days. But in fact the leadership of the Nation of Islam (NOI) had become deeply suspicious of Malcolm and aggravated by what looked to its leaders like an escalating pattern of disobedience to their orders. In particular, they viewed his recent speeches as direct challenges to their relatively apolitical version of black nationalism. At first Malcolm assumed that his suspension would be, indeed, a temporary one; but as the dreary winter months passed and the rift widened, he slowly realized that the NOI would never allow him to resume his position as its principal spokesman.

Facing the likelihood of losing his spiritual mentor, Elijah Muhammed, his political base, and his means of financial support, Malcolm began to rethink both his future and his political philosophy. On March 8, he announced his decision to quit the NOI, and soon thereafter he began building his own black nationalist organization, which he would later call the Organization for African American Unity (OAAU). On March 29 he gave a speech in which he signaled some of the changes in his thinking.

"The Ballot or the Bullet," as its title suggests, was every bit as provocative as most of Malcolm's earlier speeches and addresses. Yet as Manning Marable points out in his recent biography of Malcolm, "at its core the speech actually contained a far more conventional message, one that had defined the civil rights movement as far back as 1962: the importance of voting rights. . . . What was most significant was his shift from the use of violence to achieve blacks' objectives to the exercising of the electoral franchise. By embracing the ballot, he was implicitly rejecting violence, even if this was at times difficult to discern in the heat of his rhetoric."[21] Marable may be overstating his case, but without any doubt Malcolm was rethinking his basic position on the possibilities and potential of US democracy. Hitherto, he had been guided by the NOI creed that whites were "devils" and their works—including constitutional democracy and the Constitution of the United States—merely the work of devils. Now he began to see a glimmer of hope in those institutions. When he gave a slightly revised version of the speech in Detroit, for example, he embraced a strategy that had been advanced decades earlier by W. E. B. Du Bois, declaring that if "Negroes voted together, they could turn every election, as the white vote is usually divided" (306).

During this period of personal and professional turmoil, when his thinking about US democracy was just beginning to change, Malcolm left the United States on April 13 to undertake a pilgrimage (hajj) to Mecca. The experience was transformative in two closely related ways. First, it prompted him to reject the fundamentally racist foundation of the Nation of Islam, the belief that all whites are devils; second, it encouraged him to adopt a broader humanism that emphasized both equality in submission to God and relationships among men and women who recognize themselves as part of the "human family." In a letter to Alex Haley on April 25, Malcolm wrote: "I began to perceive that 'white man,' as commonly used, means complexion only secondarily; primarily it describes attitudes and actions." In the Muslim world he had witnessed individuals who in the United States would be classified as white but who "were more genuinely brotherly than anyone else had ever been" (310). On April 26, Malcolm wrote in his diary, "The very essences of the Islam religion in teaching the Oneness of God, gives the Believer genuine, voluntary obligations towards his fellow man (all of whom are One Human Family, brothers and sisters to each other) . . . the True Believer recognizes the Oneness of all Humanity" (311). In a letter to his wife Betty, he more fully explained this change in his thinking:

> Throughout my travels in the Muslim world, I have met, talked to, and even eaten with people who in America would have been considered 'white'—but the 'white' attitude was removed from their minds by the

religion of Islam. I have never before seen *sincere* and *true* brotherhood
practiced by all colors together, irrespective of their color.... You may
be shocked by these words coming from me. But on this pilgrimage,
what I have seen, and experienced, has forced me to *re-arrange* much of
my thought-patterns previously held, and to *toss aside* some of my pre-
vious conclusions. This was not too difficult for me. Despite my firm
convictions, I have always been a man who tries to face facts, and to
accept the reality of life as new experience and new knowledge unfolds
it. I have always kept an open mind, which is necessary to the flexibility
that must go hand in hand with every form of intelligent search for
truth.[22]

Thus, like Douglass and Johnson, Malcolm gave authority to situated over
abstract knowledge; because he felt himself to be looking out from a contingent standpoint, he tried to be broad and flexible rather than narrow and rigid
in his thinking. He conceived of "truth" as something that must be "searched"
for because it is beyond what any individual can completely comprehend. As
Anna Hartnell observes: "The absolute certainty which grounded Malcolm's
earlier vision was supplanted by an understanding of God that could no
longer provide sanction to his political beliefs and actions. Possibly to an
even greater extent than King,... Malcolm's latter politics was cast as provisional and constantly open to what is other."[23] I do not mean to suggest that
overnight Malcolm came to believe that black Americans could win justice
through the democratic processes already in place. He did not suddenly—or
ever—become an integrationist. He remained deeply pessimistic about US
politics, claiming even after his return to the United States that there was no
important difference between Lyndon Johnson and George Wallace.[24] As
he remarked when challenged to explain his new attitude toward whites: "I
haven't changed. I just see things on a broader scale."[25]

But while Malcolm did not return from his travels suddenly optimistic
about US democracy as already understood and practiced, he did become
more interested in the possibility of reimagining, or *transforming*, that
democracy. In particular, he hoped to find a way to reconcile—or hold in
tension—his political orientation toward the distinctive struggles of black
Americans with his newer embrace of democratic humanism.[26] Clear signs
of this new interest appeared in a speech that must have stunned some of his
followers: "Separation is not the goal of the Afro-American," he declared on
May 22 in Chicago; "nor is integration [his] goal. They are merely methods
toward his real end—respect as a human being."[27]

Malcolm sought to achieve this end through the Organization of African American Unity, to which he now turned with renewed zeal. Although he did not himself write its "Statement of Basic Aims and Objectives," he certainly approved it—and read it aloud at a ceremony on June 28. This document can be understood, I would suggest, as an effort to rearticulate the basic values of US democracy—freedom, equality, dignity—by taking them out of their American exceptionalist framework and re-placing them in a transnational or global context. One paragraph of the document states: "DETERMINED to unify the Americans of African descent in their fight for human rights and dignity, and being fully aware that this is not possible in the present atmosphere and condition of oppression, we dedicate ourselves to the building of a political, economic, and social system of justice and peace." Another paragraph declares that the OAAU is "PERSUADED that the charter of the United Nations, the Universal Declaration of Human Rights, the Constitution of the United States of America and the Bill of Rights are the principles in which we believe and these documents if put into practice represent the essence of mankind's hopes and good intentions." By thus specifying that black Americans citizens were at the same time also human beings protected by international standards of human rights, the document and the organization did two things: it cut the ground from under American assumptions that the United States had a proprietary claim to be the custodian of those rights, and it suggested that, as an African diasporic community, black Americans were entitled to appeal not solely as Americans, but as human beings, to an international court of opinion. In this way, the OAAU placed the US Constitution and Bill of Rights firmly within an international network of norms and principles, while at the same time asserting that the "people of African descent here in the Western hemisphere" could claim not just their American rights as US citizens, but their "*human* rights and dignity" as citizens of the world.[28]

Malcolm lost no time turning this theory into practice. He decided that the OAAU should go before the assembled United Nations and lodge a formal complaint against the racist violations of human rights practiced routinely in the United States. (Malcolm was assassinated before this could be accomplished.) For both tactical and strategic reasons, this was a shrewd maneuver. In the short run, it would embarrass the United States and place the movement for "civil rights" in the United States within a broader, worldwide struggle for "human rights"; this shift would in turn encourage black Americans to experience their struggle as being simultaneously pan-African and domestic, helping them to reconcile their black nationalist aspirations with their demand for justice achieved through a transformed US democracy.[29] In the longer run, the OAAU's thinking laid the groundwork for a more porous and cosmopolitan understanding of US democracy itself. It could be seen, that is, as a classic example of Benhabib's "jurisgenerative process" through which a democracy reiterates and reimagines itself. "Although the demos, as the popular sovereign, must assert control over a specific territorial domain," she writes, "it can also engage in reflexive acts of self-constitution, whereby the boundaries of the demos can be readjusted" (36). The OAAU's plan was an effort at precisely such readjustment.

"To Place Oneself in That Larger Point of View"

I have not brought the stories of Douglass's, Johnson's, and Malcolm's travels together because they are representative of the totality of black experience or because they collectively constitute a theory of a more worldly form of US citizenship. My more modest aim is to explore what their perspectives might portend for political theory and US public philosophy as these struggle to reconcile the conflicting obligations of national and world citizenship.

Let us consider, then, how Douglass, Johnson, and Malcolm would enter the conversation between Nussbaum and her critics. On the one hand, I believe, they would certainly share Balfour's and Barber's view that the particularities of history should not be erased by principles claiming to be universal, and that political theory itself must take care to recall its own historical situatedness. On the other hand, I think that Douglass and Malcolm would agree with Nussbaum that *some* conception of universal moral truth is necessary to US democracy, and indeed to moral life of any kind. Malcolm's belief in the "the Oneness of all Humanity" is a belief in a universal truth. It is, moreover, a truth he will act upon and a truth that provides him a way to act simultaneously in both international and national arenas, bridging these and negotiating some differences between them. Likewise, when Douglass took his "stand on the high ground of human brotherhood," he was affirming a truth he considered to be universal.

But while these thinkers would favor a version of Nussbaum's universalism, theirs would look rather different from hers. Recall that the question that drives her argument is, to whom should I owe my primary allegiance, US democracy or humanity?

We might now observe that the question itself presumes the possibility of a certain detachment from circumstances, a theoretical perspective that is not situated anywhere. (This buried presupposition surfaces in her phrase "happen to be": Americans, she says, just *"happen to be* situated in the United

States.") The writers I have been discussing reject this way of addressing a problem. Because they understand their thinking to be rooted in its material and historical conditions, and to be the expression of a contingent standpoint, they have little interest in imagining such detachment, not even as a theoretical move or hypothesis. Douglass's nationlessness, we should recall, was *real*: it had been *forced* upon him, and as a fugitive slave he was quite literally an outlaw. Malcolm, too, discovered a new and richer meaning of humanity, but he did so because he was undertaking the hajj and traveling in Egypt and Saudi Arabia. Humanity was not something he hypothesized but an encounter, or experience, he underwent. Yet at the same time, Malcolm and Douglass never ceased to think of themselves as both American and black. Indeed, they immediately interpreted their discovery of humanity in the light of their political struggles back in their nation and demos. Each returned to his specific political struggle equipped with insights about the transnational implications of US democracy gained by traveling beyond its borders.

In short, Nussbaum's choice of worldly *or* national loyalty simply does not hold them. But the binary Balfour and Barber use—universal *or* historical— does not hold them either. Both men thought their way *through* the histories Balfour, Singh, and many other historians rightly underscore, but they did not stop there: they moved on *toward* a more worldly and flexible conception of the universal. They acknowledged history, but they did not allow it to fix the horizon of their thinking. (As Douglass declared: "We have to do with the past only as it is of use to the present.") Remarkably, the tensions between the world and the demos, and between the universal and the historical, did not tear them apart as much as it motivated and renewed them: the more international their outlook became, the more they were inclined to engage in a transformative rethinking of US democracy. Although their singular experiences do not add up to a theory, they do point toward a worldly outlook characterized by open-endedness, flexibility, and commitment. To use Judith Butler's words, we might say that they engage in "a difficult labor of translation" as they find their views continually enlarged through encounters with others. "That labor," Butler writes, "seeks to transform the very terms that are made to stand for one another, and the movement of that unanticipated transformation establishes the universal as that which is yet to be achieved and which, in order to resist domestication, may never be finally or fully achieved."[30]

Given Du Bois's importance as an early practitioner and advocate of black worldliness, it seems fitting to conclude with a brief look at two moments in his own thinking.[31] Like Johnson, Douglass, and Malcolm, Du Bois acquired a worldly perspective abroad that had a lifelong impact on his work, encouraging him to place the struggle of blacks in the United States within a broad international context of widening democracy. When he traveled to Germany in 1892 to complete his doctoral studies, he too experienced the "miracle" of affirmation, by whites, of his human and personal dignity. And just as Malcolm X would seven decades later, Du Bois felt that the recognition of democratic dignity he experienced was reciprocal; now, for the first time, he could look *back* at white folks and see the shared humanity that lay beneath *their* skin: "On mountain and valley, in home and school, I met men and women as I had never met them before. Slowly, they became, not white folks, but folks. The unity beneath all life clutched me. I was not less fanatically a Negro, but 'Negro' meant a greater broader sense of humanity and world fellowship."[32]

In "The Present Outlook for the Dark Races of Mankind" (1900), Du Bois shared this worldliness with his black American readers, urging them to view their struggle from what he called a "larger point of view":

[I]t is my purpose to consider with you the problem of the color line not simply as a national or personal question but rather in its larger world aspect in time and space. I freely acknowledge that in the heat of a burning social problem like this, when each of us feels the bitter sting of proscription, it is a difficult thing to place oneself in that larger point of view.... It is but natural for us to consider that our race question is a purely national and local affair, confined to nine million Americans and settled when their rights and opportunities are assured, and yet a glance over the world at the dawn of the new century will convince us that this is just the beginning of the problem—that the color line belts the world and that the social problem of the twentieth century is to be the relation of the civilized world to the dark races of mankind.[33]

Thus, like the other figures we've been reading, Du Bois *scrambles* the debate between Nussbaum and her critics. We find here Nussbaum's belief that Americans have an obligation to think beyond the securing of their own "rights and opportunities" and to shoulder some responsibility for helping others secure those same rights and opportunities in other parts of the world. But when he repeatedly contrasts the narrow, local, personal, and national with a "larger" framework that is "the world" as a whole, he expresses his deep awareness that perspectivalism and contingency shape our views and inevitably limit them. And Du Bois is careful not to advance his argument on the basis of a presumed American mission to bring its possession of certain universal truths to others. Quite the contrary, he perceives the struggle of blacks in the United States to be part of a worldwide anticolonial and antiracist struggle for democracy. Like James Weldon Johnson, Du Bois sometimes believed that the indispensable condition for human historical progress was human contact through contingent encounters: "Civilization is contact between human beings. No lasting culture arises from isolated groups or races. It is the fire of mind striking mind, the imitation of happy trials and guesses that spreads ideas and promotes invention and builds up civilized, progressive life."[34]

Political theorist William Connolly comes close to the spirit of Du Bois and the other black American thinkers I've discussed when he writes, "The task today is not to articulate one regulative idea that encompasses all others—the goal of Kantianism, religious ecumenism, and a single-entry universalism. Nor is it to rise above metaphysical differences, as if that were an easy or possible thing to do. The task today is to inspire more participants in each religious and metaphysical tradition to come to terms with its comparative contestability and to explore creative lines of connection to other orientations."[35] Connolly reminds us that although the very word "cosmopolitan" has an aura of grandeur or sublimity that sends our imagination on an expanding quest to *encompass*, we should instead feel it pushing us back inward, toward a sharper sense of our own *limitedness*. True worldliness is modesty, not magnanimity. Let us think of it as a radical openness to encounters—to the unpredictable things that happen when peoples meet along this way. By urging his listeners to place themselves "in that larger point of view" and to see beyond their own "burning social problem" to its global ramifications, Du Bois anticipates Connolly's cosmopolitan program of inspiring "more participants in [his] religious and metaphysical tradition to come to terms with its comparative contestability and to explore creative lines of connection to other orientations."

The pains these thinkers take to include both the universal and the particular, the global and the local, in their address to certain problems might encourage political theorists to rethink the very nature of theory, and of public philosophy as well. Perhaps the field should allow itself to express its ideas not just as arguments but as stories. For what Douglass, Johnson, Malcolm, and Du Bois offer is not arguments for a particular kind of worldly citizenship but narratives of their lived experience of it. If *they* could fuse worldly perspectives with democratic citizenship, then the possibility of others doing so becomes imaginable—becomes theoretically conceivable.[36] The word "theory" derives, of course, from the Greek *thea* (view, spectacle), and the value of theory has been that it does try to take a broad view of things by abstracting from a number of particulars. For theory to exist as a mode of thinking and inquiry distinct from the discipline of history, it must allow itself this latitude. Yet there are obvious dangers in a stance that tends to overlook the particular and to erase one's own situatedness as a thinker. Perhaps incorporating storytelling into theory might mitigate some of this danger, for the storyteller can easily display what the theorist so often forgets: a voice that knows it is speaking from a specific time and place. A story may aim to articulate a universal truth, but it doesn't have to shed its particularity to do so. Imagine what political theory would look like if Locke or Rousseau had narrated his theory of the social contract as a story: *Once upon a time the wanderers came out of the woods and decided to form a village.* Imagine if we were disposed to recognize a theory of democratic worldliness in a story that began, *From all available evidence, no black person had ever set foot in this tiny Swiss village before I came.*

5

"Religion in the Sense of Striving for the Infinite"

FAITH, PLURALISM, AND DEMOCRATIC ACTION

> ...while I do not deny that absolute and eternal truth *is*,
> still truth must be infinite, and as incapable as infinite
> space, of being encompassed and confined by one age
> or nation, sect or country—much less by one little crea-
> ture's finite brain.[1]
>
> —ANNA JULIA COOPER

AT THE START of the twenty-first century, Americans are deeply divided over the place of religious faith in public life and democratic politics; the splitting of the country into red states and blue states runs right along the fault line of this disagreement. Clearly, any progressive public philosophy for the twenty-first century will have to span this gap. But how?

Not so long ago, liberal public philosophy assigned a place for religious faith that most Americans accepted, if somewhat grudgingly. Faith belonged on the far side of the "wall of separation" between state and church, relegated to the realm of the private sphere where it was free to thrive but not to inter-fere with politics. For decades, this arrangement elicited little complaint from conservative Christians, whose main concern was to protect their religion from the corruptions of democratic politics and the grasping claw of "gov-ernment." Now all is changed. Conservative Christians insist that democratic politics be suffused with their religious faith and even guided by their inter-pretations of Christian scripture. Liberals and progressives are in retreat, real-izing slowly and reluctantly that that if they aspire to regain the commanding heights of politics, they will have to tear down their "wall" separating religion and politics and replace it with a more flexible and porous idea. Or metaphor. But what would that be?

This public perplexity has its counterpart in the world of philosophy and political theory. As we saw in the last chapter, a root question debated in these fields is whether universal truths of some kind—be they the religious truths of sacred scripture or the "self-evident" truths of the Declaration of Independence—are necessary to the project of collective self-governance. On the left today, most intellectuals are so keenly aware that convictions about what is true have changed over time, that they dismiss the very possibility of a truth being "eternal"; likewise, they are so conscious that different cultures have radically different notions of what truth is, that they cannot assent to the claim that a particular truth is "universal."

However, this most reasonable way of thinking brings a problem in its train: without a belief that certain truths are eternal and universal—self-evidently so, as the signers of the Declaration believed—how can a democracy resolve questions about what is right and what is wrong? That is, if all claims to truth are contingent on history and perspective, how does a democratic polity sort them out without recourse to certain truths and principles understood to be beyond political contestation—as standing outside history? How do we achieve the nonviolent conflict resolution on which democracy depends without having a shared set of principled agreements? Moreover, shared principles and truths also hold a political community together. Without a shared agreement that their democracy is based on a shared set of beliefs and values, how can citizens imagine and feel themselves to be a political community?

Over the past twenty years or so, radical conservatives have argued passionately and effectively that they cannot—that US democracy requires truths that are held by all citizens to be universal and eternal. Many have insisted as well, though with less success, that the only place where such transcendent truths can be found is in divine revelation—in the words and the will of God as expressed by the Bible. Intellectuals on the left have lagged behind. Like their liberal predecessors of the mid-twentieth century, they look with considerable suspicion on religious faith, regarding it as "irrational" and dangerous. Those few who take faith needs seriously have developed some complex and nuanced answers to the question of how belief in eternal and universal truths can be reconciled with a historical worldview and democratic pluralism, but they have been much less successful in making their ideas accessible and persuasive to citizens—that is, in crafting them into a viable public philosophy. Indeed, for progressives the asymmetry built into this contest is daunting: when, in rhetorical combat, has complexity ever triumphed over simplicity? I suspect that a great many Americans are ready to accept that truth must indeed be seen as a matter of history, culture, and perspective—that "it is turtles all the way down." But they are still waiting for an elegant explanation of how this conception of truth can be squared with a moral life, effective democratic practice, and a cohesive democratic community. Left-of-center intellectuals have failed so far to provide such an explanation.

A number of the black American writers and thinkers I have been discussing saw this whole picture differently. They knew from firsthand experience that those who hold power tend to represent the world in ways favorable to their own interests. After all, they knew that US democracy had represented them as only three-fifths of a person, and they knew that white racial thinking has represented "man" or "the human" as being essentially white and European. Their experience of these claims and their knowledge of their falsity predisposed them to be skeptical toward all claims of universalism and all claims to know the totality of truth. As a consequence, when they imagined God or the infinite or a transcendent order, they were inclined to figure these as being far vaster than anything a mere finite being could ever hope to represent or know. They did not, for example, simply replace a white God with a black God, or white Christianity with black Christianity, for they understood that in doing so they would reproduce the very error that their experience of racism had made obvious to them.[2]

Yet their belief that the infinite surpasses human understanding and human representation did not prevent them believing that some force has created and now sustains an "arc of the moral universe"; nor did their skepticism discourage them from using their belief in the divine as a pole star by which to orient themselves for encouragement and guidance as citizens in a social world. Their writings often express a deep belief in God and in the eternal truths of higher, or natural law; yet at the same time, these writings frequently remind us of the human inability to grasp fully the infinitude of a God, or of any version of a transcendent order, and they caution that we should remain humbly aware of our fallibility, mindful that we may be mistaken or misled even by our deepest beliefs. For how can the finite know the infinite?

The most eloquent expression of this conception of faith that I know of is Anna Julia Cooper's in her essay "The Gain from a Belief" (1892). Addressing skeptics who would urge an essentially secular understanding of life and of democratic citizenship, Cooper argues that what people who wish to *change* the order of things need most is "heroism, devotion, sacrifice; and there cannot be heroism, devotion, or sacrifice in a primarily skeptical spirit." Using a metaphor that recalls Douglass's, she writes, "At such times most of all, do men need to be anchored to what they *feel* to be eternal verities." But Cooper goes on to describe what such "belief" consists of: "I do not mean by faith the holding of correct views and unimpeachable opinions on mooted questions, merely; nor do I understand it to be the ability to forge cast-iron formulas and dub them TRUTH. For while I do not deny that absolute and eternal truth *is*,—still truth must be infinite, and as incapable as infinite space, of being encompassed and confined by one age or nation, sect or country—much less by one little creature's finite brain."

Along with this skepticism toward representation, the experience of unjust suffering also profoundly shaped the spiritual imaginations of the particular figures I will be discussing in this chapter. Such suffering both intensified their need to believe in a beneficent divinity and made such belief more difficult. A person who suffers injustice needs to believe that, however much power one's oppressors wield, an even greater power will eventually overturn them and restore the moral order of the universe. At the same time, the fact that the all-powerful divine being has deferred this day of glory year after year, generation after generation, casts doubt upon both its motives and its very existence. This deep ambivalence toward a transcendent order was accompanied by an equally painful ambivalence toward the meaning of one's suffering. Either it made sense of some kind within a cosmic order, or it was an intolerable condition that only human agency could change. For black Christians, these ambivalences were intensified by the role that the white churches played in supporting the slavery system and later Jim Crow by encouraging black Americans to be submissive and long-suffering, to accept their lot rather than resist it. Yet how could one survive enslavement and Jim Crow without faith in a God who would bring about a better day?

For these black Americans, then, faith was not a state in which to rest but a kind of work to do. Faith meant committing oneself to the arduous task of believing that the eternal and the historical, the infinite and the human, the sacred and the secular can be spanned. It meant believing, in other words, that these seeming opposites can and must be held in a dynamic tension that respects their difference yet imagines them intersecting in crisis moments of the present—what Douglass called "the ever-present now" and what King so famously invoked as "the fierce urgency of now." For this reason, their faith is sacred *and* secular, contemplative *and* active.[3]

The "Ring-Bolt" of Faith: Holding together History and Eternity

In *House of Bondage* (1890), Octavia V. Rogers Albert brought together a collection of her interviews with former slaves, including especially the

memories of a deeply religious woman named Charlotte Brooks. Speaking
to Albert, Brooks repeatedly emphasized that she never could have survived
enslavement without the support of her Christian faith and the comfort
provided by her religious mentor, a fellow slave named Aunt Jane Lee. "I tell
you, child," Brooks says, "religion is good everywhere—at the plow-handle,
at the hoe-handle, anywhere. If you are filled with the love of my Jesus you
are happy.... I can never forget Aunt Jane, for when old marster used to be
so hard on me it seemed I'd have to give up sometimes and die. But then the
spirit of God would come to me and fill my heart with joy. It seemed the more
trials I had the more I could pray."[4]

Yet Albert herself had a more ambivalent understanding of the relation
between religious belief and the slavery system, for she *began* her book by
asking her readers to "Consider that here in this Bible land, where we have
the light, where the Gospel was preached Sunday after Sunday in all portions
of the South, and where ministers read from the pulpit that God has made
of one blood all nations of men, etc., that nevertheless, with the knowledge
and teachings of the word of God, the slaves were reduced to a level with the
brute" (1–2). Albert was bitterly aware that the slave masters prayed to the
same Christ and the same God as she and Charlotte Brooks. Her understanding of her faith was thus shot through a wary consciousness that humans can
misunderstand and misappropriate the divine, turning it to their purposes
rather than submitting to its will. Faith that carries such consciousness with it
is both committed and open-ended, determined yet doubtful.

Here is civil right activist (and later congressman) John Lewis's description of his own experience of such doubt, some sixty years later. As a teenager,
he began to ponder some troubling paradoxes: "there was a contradiction
between what was and what ought to be.... For the most part, white Southern
Baptist churches didn't even want black people to step inside their buildings.
Yet within these very institutions, people were taught that Jesus Christ says to
love thy neighbor as thyself. How could that be? How could people reconcile
that belief with the way they lived? It was contradictory. It was illogical." Yet
Lewis's discovery of this contradiction did not lead him to despair. On the
contrary, it somehow carried him to what he calls "the Spirit of History" or
"faith":

> It was about this time that I began believing in what I call the Spirit of
> History. Others might call it Fate. Or Destiny. Or a Guiding Hand.
> Whatever it is called, I came to believe that this force is on the side of
> what is good, of what is right and just. It is the essence of the moral

force of the universe, and at certain points in life... this spirit finds you or selects you, it chases you down, and you have no choice; you must allow yourself to be used, to be guided by this force and to carry out what must be done. To me, that concept of surrender, of giving yourself over to something inexorable, something so much larger than yourself, is the basis of what we call faith.[5]

One last example of such faith: in the summer of 1830, Frederick Douglass ran into the woods trying to escape punishment at the hands of the brutal slave-breaker Edward Covey. "Well," he tells us, "now I am clear of Covey, and of his wrathful lash.... I am in the wood, buried in its somber gloom, shut in with nature and nature's God, and absent from all human contrivances. Here was a good place to pray; to pray for help for deliverance—a prayer I had often made before. But how could I pray?" Douglass goes on to explain his difficulty: "Covey could pray—Capt. Auld could pray—I would fain pray; but doubts (arising partly from my own neglect of the means of grace, and partly from the sham religion which everywhere prevailed, cast in my mind a doubt upon all religion, and led me to the conviction that prayers were unavailing and delusive) prevented my embracing the opportunity, as a religious one."[6]

As is so often the case with Douglass, this story carries deep reflection within it. On the one hand, he plainly blames his slave masters and the slave system for his loss of faith: their praying keeps him from praying, for how could their God be his God? But in his careful wording of this moment years after the fact, he also conveys that his *impulse* to pray, which had been crushed by repeated disappointments, still lived within him. We are meant to understand that when he asked himself, "How can I pray?" the question was itself a kind of prayer, reverberating in the hush that surrounded him. It reminds us that *all* prayers are offered in such a questioning spirit since we can never know if they are being heard, much less whether they will be answered.[7] Indeed, Douglass's ambivalence toward his faith is further underscored by his quiet self-criticism in this passage: he does not spare Covey and Auld, but he also blames his own "neglect of the means of grace" and implicitly criticizes himself for having allowed a single "sham religion" promoted by the slavery system to "cast...a doubt upon *all* religion"—that is, to *be* the infinitely larger structure of transcendent meaning that it claimed to represent.

What does the doubtful faith expressed by Brooks, Lewis, and Douglass have to do with democracy and with the relation between faith and democratic practice today? One answer is vividly dramatized by a moment in Douglass's long life as a political actor when he was forced to work out his uncertainty about the relation between man and God on the stage of national politics. He was a leading abolitionist at a time when the cause of abolition seemed to be failing. A new fugitive slave law had become the law of the land, and the slavery system was being allowed to expand rapidly into the new territories and states west of the Mississippi. Partly as a result of these defeats, the abolitionist movement was increasingly split by an argument over both principles and strategy. One the one side stood those who were working under the leadership of William Lloyd Garrison; they believed that a principled and effective war against slavery could not be waged through political means since the Constitution of the United States legitimated slavery in certain of its articles. The nation's founding document did not express the eternal truths known to mankind through Christian revelation but instead registered a deeply sinful historical compromise worked out by self-interested politicians trying to cobble together a nation. The Constitution in its present form was thus "a covenant with hell." It should be torn to shreds in a new revolution led by individual states like Massachusetts. By persuading citizens that slavery was a moral evil inconsistent with Christianity, abolitionists would spark movements to secede from the Union; eventually, they would force a new founding and write for the states of this new nation a new constitution—one that consistently and purely embodied the expressed will of God.

Opposed to the Garrisonians stood those we have come to call the "political abolitionists." They were convinced that the antislavery movement could not succeed if it continued to rely only on Garrison's highly principled strategy of abjuring politics and practicing moral suasion. The unabated spread of the slavery system convinced them that abolitionists would have to get involved with democratic politics, messy and compromised as these might be. They argued that the Garrisonians were in fact defeating themselves by ceding the whole question of the constitutionality of slavery to the system's defenders. Many came to see Garrison's uncompromising commitment to principle as a kind of fanaticism, or as an expression of selfish desire to remain morally pure while millions of enslaved persons continued to suffer. They proposed therefore a very different way of reading the Constitution. They argued in the first place that the people in "We the people" had ratified only the Constitution itself—not the debates and compromises surrounding it. They argued as well that the Constitution should *not* be read as a text that took its meaning from the historical context in which it was produced but as a set of laws and ideas cast into enduring form. It should be read literally, and when read this way it most certainly did *not* legitimate slavery: after all, the very words "slavery" and "slave" are nowhere to be found in it.[8]

As the power of the slavery system grew in the late 1840s and early 1850s, Douglass found the arguments of the political abolitionists more and more persuasive. Yet for a long time he remained troubled by a question that he put frankly to Gerrit Smith, one of political abolitionism's most powerful advocates:

> [T]here is a consideration which is of much importance between us. It is this: may we avail ourselves of legal rules which enable us to defeat even the wicked intentions of our Constitution makers? *It is this question which puzzles me more than all others involved in the subject.* Is it good morality to take advantage of a legal flaw and put a meaning on a legal instrument the very opposite of what we have good reason to believe was the intention of the men who framed it?[9]

The framers' *"intentions,"* Douglass continued, "you fling to the winds." But *why* did their intentions matter so much to him? Why—while waging a war against slavery—would he hesitate over the "morality" of using a "legal rule" to "defeat even the wicked intentions" of the founders?

The answer, I believe, is that he knew that such an interpretative strategy risked dishonoring the framers' own perspective on their actions and with it their historical agency. After all, if one ignores the intentions of others, one effectually discounts the possibility of their agency—and indeed, of their very personhood. The moral risk that concerned Douglass was not just that a pragmatic interpretative strategy could degenerate into amoral expediency but that it could deny the full personhood of one's predecessors in history and thus, implicitly, one's own. Douglass knew—as perhaps a former slave was disposed to know—that the historically committed actor risks denying the worth of his own intentions and personhood if he too easily dismisses the intentions and personhood of others.

Douglass did eventually break with the Garrisonians and side with the political abolitionists. He was convinced, he declared, that "I am only in reason and in conscience bound to learn the intentions of those who framed the Constitution in the Constitution itself."[10] So now we face a second puzzle: what brought about this change of mind? Some historians have emphasized Douglass's pragmatism or what Waldo Martin calls his sense of "expediency." Depressed by the growing power of the slave system, he embraced radical political abolitionism because he thought that it would be more effective than Garrison's moral suasion alone. Others emphasize the degree to which Douglass's many inconsistencies about strategy were consistently self-serving: "Douglass' ideology was thoroughly inconsistent, usually opportunistic, and always self-serving."[11]

I would add to these explanations that Douglass believed that political abolitionism accorded better with the intellectual and spiritual disposition he had acquired within slavery—including the ambivalence toward religious faith that he had felt in that moment in the woods, when he wanted to pray but could not. Douglass had begun his life within conditions of radical unfreedom. Unlike Garrison and Smith, both of whom could take for granted their freedom to think in a vacuum detached from the distorting exigencies of the material world, Douglass understood from the outset that his very ability to think at all was contingent on social forces and material circumstances. At the same time, he shared with both fellow abolitionists a deep commitment to God's eternal principles and higher laws that stand outside history as a guide and beacon to those who labor within it. Knowing himself to be located in this way at the crossroads of the historical and the eternal, he conceived of intellectual consistency quite differently than they did. Knowing that his thinking occurred in a realm where the winds of history constantly bend ideas to their always-changing meanings, not in a vacuum where ideas can have the purity of our highest ideals, he took consistency to mean setting a course and sticking to it even as history's winds blow now this way and now that.[12] Consistency for him did not mean subsuming history to eternity, or eternity to history, when they are clearly irreconcilable; it did not mean choosing between higher law and "the muck and mire" of existence; it did not mean choosing between faith in the eternal laws of God and faith in the political agency of men and women. Consistency meant, rather, the creation of a framework (or the embrace of a disposition) that allows these seeming contraries to coexist in a tense, dynamic relation with each other.

Douglass's most famous speech, "What to the Slave Is the Fourth of July?" is a brilliant demonstration of such an equilibrium. Most scholarly readers of this speech have emphasized just one side of its rhetorical strategy: by calling Independence Day "your" day, Douglass refused to identify with his free white audience. Instead, he took up a position on the "outside" of the American polity, a stance that gave him a valuable perspective on its shortcomings. "I shall see this day and its popular characteristics *from the slave's point of view*," he declared. "Standing, there, identified with the American bondsman, making his wrongs mine, I do not hesitate to declare, with all my soul, that the character and conduct of this nation never looked blacker to me than on this fourth of July."[13] Douglass insisted that he could not participate in a day of national celebration because his slave's perspective saw only the bitter ironies his countrymen hid from themselves: "Your high independence only reveals the immeasurable distance between us," he said. "This Fourth [of] July is *yours*, not *mine*" (368).

But Douglass's speech is even subtler than has heretofore been recognized. He embraces the slave's "point of view" not just as a rhetorical device to create a critical distance but because he sees *value* in that point of view: from within the conditions of enslavement, the slave sees and knows some things that the free white members of Douglass's audience did not. At the same time, though, Douglass links his singular perspective, with all its personal and cultural limitations, to his belief in truths that are "eternal"—true for all people in all times. His speech spans the space between the particular and the general, the individual and the national, the historical and the eternal, and holds them together in a tense and dynamic equilibrium.[14]

What most readers who stress Douglass's distancing himself from his audience overlook is a small detail: Douglass addresses his audience as "Fellow citizens" not fewer than eight times! If he had wished only to suggest that he was in no sense of the word an American, and in no way a communicant with his audience in this celebration of the nation's birth, he would never have employed this phrase. But he does, and its purpose is to bind his audience to him even as his rhetoric insists on "the immeasurable distance" between them. The "slave's point of view," we are poignantly reminded, is one that holds and takes into account other and even opposite points of view. As George Shulman has written: "Not speaking as a rebel rejecting the core ideals of the Republic but using their authority to justify his own, he [Douglass] casts himself as truly faithful to the legacy they [his audience] desecrate, and at once affirms the principles they profess and models a democratic way to practice them."[15]

This energy that holds opposites together in tension finds its most intense expression in a metaphor Douglass uses several times—that of a ringbolt: "The 4th of July is the first great fact in your nation's history—the very ring-bolt in the chain of your yet undeveloped destiny....I have said that the Declaration of Independence is the very RING-BOLT to the chain of your nation's destiny; so, indeed, I regard it. The principles contained in that instrument are saving principles. Stand by those principles, be true to them on all occasions, in all places, against all foes, and at whatever cost" (363–64). Packed into this metaphor is an extraordinary fusion of contingency and certainty, of the socially constructed and the morally absolute. Douglass and other abolitionists frequently used the metaphor of "chains" to call to mind the chains binding the three million slaves in bondage, and the "ring-bolt to the chain" resonated powerfully as a trope for unfreedom. This unlikely and jarring metaphor for "the saving principles" of the Declaration of Independence conveyed, then, an insight that was available to "the slave's point of view" but not necessarily to that of a free person: our principles actually fetter us because freedom is never absolute—it is always conditioned both by our circumstances and by the binding nature of our principles. In *My Bondage and My Freedom*, he had observed of his master, Captain Auld, that if he "had been brought up in a free state, surrounded by the just restraints of free society—*restraints which are necessary to the freedom of all its members*," Auld "might have been as humane a man ... as are members of society generally" (171; emphasis added). Perhaps this seeming paradox—that freedom requires all citizens to submit to "just restraints"—was much more obvious to a man who had lived at the mercy of unrestrained slave masters than it was to the free white men in his audience. Douglass's perspective suggests that democratic citizens must accommodate themselves to the paradox that the chains that bind them to their principles also secure their freedom and security. Without those principles, "the ship of state" will founder in the "heavy billows" of a national crisis. "Cling to this day—cling to it, and to its principles, with the grasp of a storm-tossed mariner to a spar at midnight" (364).[16]

Douglass had arrived at this understanding of democracy because many years of experience—both inside and outside the bonds of slavery—had taught him this self-contradictory lesson: on the one hand, as he put it in *My Bondage and My Freedom*, "the point from which a thing is viewed is of some importance" (148). At the same time, however, there are certain truths that remain true regardless of the point from which they are seen. Somehow a democratic mind has to contain this seeming contradiction; neither aspect of the lesson can be sacrificed to the other.[17] Douglass's own mind and the understanding of "thought" he acquired from his experience made it possible for him to do this work of holding opposites in tension with each other. Indeed, this disposition was exactly what he believed to be his contribution not just to the antislavery cause, but to the democracy that had yet to make a place for free black men and women. It was his answer to the question posed years earlier by his abolitionist friends: how could "a slave, brought up in the very depths of ignorance," assume "to instruct the highly civilized people of the north in the principles of liberty, justice, and humanity"?[18]

"To No One Type of Mind Is It Given to See the Totality of Truth":

While Frederick Douglass sought to fuse his commitments to the historical and the eternal through a particular understanding of "consistency" and in metaphors like the ringbolt, W. E. B. Du Bois took a different approach. Influenced perhaps by his exposure to Hegelian dialectics and certainly by his need to honor and yet check his indignation at white racism, he developed a distinctive intellectual and rhetorical style. In his writings and speeches, Du Bois often takes a partiality claiming to be a totality and shows it to be what it is—limited, not complete, local, not universal. He then creates or gestures toward a larger framework in which to place that particularity and thereby points toward the possibility of an unbounded "whole" in which parts retain their singularity and yet derive their meaning from their tense relation with each other. This vision of truth as something approachable only through endless enlargement of our outlook leads Du Bois to a particular understanding of religious faith as well: it springs from the utterly private suffering of individuals, suffering that can never be experienced or known by others, and which must turn to something equally unknowable for guidance and solace. Faith for Du Bois is not a settled state of certainty; it is a commitment by a finite being to *strive toward* the infinite, knowing all the while that arrival there, or full comprehension of it, is by definition impossible. "We must have religion in the sense of striving for the infinite, the ultimate, and the best," he writes. "But just as truly we must straitly curb the effort of any exclusive guild to be the single and final arbiter of individual interpretation of desired and desirable truth."[19]

Du Bois begins, then, by acknowledging some truth in the position he is contesting; he then moves on to expose that position's incompleteness, and he concludes by placing both his own and the other view within an enlarged and more inclusive framework. In his 1890 Harvard commencement address on Jefferson Davis, for example, Du Bois begins by acknowledging Davis as "a typical Teutonic Hero" and seems to applaud "the history of civilization during the last millennium," a history that has "been the development of the idea of the Strong Man of which he [Davis] was the embodiment." Davis was a "soldier and a lover," Du Bois declares, "a statesman and a ruler; passionate, ambitious and indomitable; bold reckless guardian of a people's All—judged by the whole standard of Teutonic civilization, there is something noble in the figure of Jefferson Davis."[20]

We can easily imagine the thrill that would have passed through many in Du Bois's mainly white audience as this young black man invoked—seemingly with approval—the increasingly popular theory of Anglo-Saxon racial superiority. But at precisely this moment, Du Bois's argument takes a sudden turn. Rhetorically assuming a dispassionate objectivity, he recoils from the limitedness of the Teutonic standard of civilization. "[J]udged by every canon of human justice," he observes, "there is something fundamentally incomplete about that standard" (243). Considered as a type, Davis is not so much wrong as partial, and so is "the type of civilization which his life represented." For such a civilization is narrowly based on "individualism coupled with the rule of might...; its ideals are power and conquest. Under whatever guise...a Jefferson Davis may appear as man, as race, or as nation, his life can only logically mean this: the advance of a part of the world at the expense of whole; the overweening sense of the I, and the consequent forgetting of the Thou" (243). Davis's "striking contradictions of character," Du Bois points out, "always arise when a people seemingly become convinced that the object of the world is not civilization, but Teutonic civilization." Only when one steps back and takes a broader view—as Du Bois now invites his audience to do with him—can one see that Teutonic civilization is "incomplete." The "world has needed and will need its Jefferson Davises," he graciously admits; "but such a type is incomplete and never can serve its best purpose until checked by its complementary ideas. Whence shall these come?" (244)

Du Bois is now ready to make his third move and resituate Teutonic civilization within a framework that is more whole and more inclusive because it contains different, complementary ideas. These would come, he asserted, from "the South" and in particular from "the Negro," who can offer the world a different ideal, "an idea of submission apart from cowardice, laziness, or stupidity, such as the world never saw before." The "change made in the conception of civilization" by this idea is profound: "the submission of the strength of the Strong to the advance of all—not in mere aimless sacrifice, but recognizing the fact that, 'To no one type of mind is it given to discern the totality of Truth,' that civilization cannot afford to lose the contribution of the very least of nations for its full development: that not only the assertion of the I, but also the submission to the Thou is the highest individualism" (244).

It is as much through the shape of his argument as through its content that we experience Du Bois's core claim: "To no one type of mind is it given to discern the totality of Truth." Even as his recoil has allowed him to see *more* of the truth than many in his audience, it has impressed upon him the impossibility of seeing *all* of the truth. His speech is not just about the virtues of Davis, or about his incompleteness, or about how that incompleteness can be remedied in a larger whole that includes the Negro's "complementary ideas." Most deeply, it warns that representation (cultural, aesthetic, political) tends to slide into synecdoche, and it demonstrates that the best way to resist this tendency is to develop a disposition, or a habit of mind, that moves as Du Bois's does: one must always seek for the "but also" that supplements and complements a partial representation and an incomplete understanding.

Du Bois delivered this essay as a speech when he was just twenty-two years old. Already he had forged the tone he would employ to great effect in much of his work, and already he had begun to exhibit a temper of mind remarkably suited to meeting the challenges of gaining democratic inclusion for African Americans and women in his lifetime. This temper presents a critical argument on behalf of inclusion as an act of generous fairness that includes whites in a larger and more complete whole. As one person in the audience wrote later, "His paper was on 'Jefferson Davis,' and you would have been surprised to hear a colored man deal with him so generously. Such phrases as a 'great man,' a 'keen thinker,' a 'strong leader' and others occurred in the address." A contributor to the *New York Nation* wrote, "Du Bois handled his difficult and hazardous subject with absolute good taste, great moderation, and almost contemptuous fairness."[21] *Almost contemptuous fairness*: the phrase nicely captures the dynamic of respect, recoil, enlargement, and recuperation that animates Du Bois's address.

During the next decade, Du Bois came increasingly to believe that this particular mode of thought and argument was an indispensable quality of what we would now call "democratic deliberation." In *The Souls of Black Folk*, after reprising an earlier critique of Washington's narrowness, Du Bois asserts that Washington was usually disposed to try to silence criticism. This, says Du Bois, "is a dangerous thing."

> Honest and earnest criticism from those whose interests are most nearly touched,—criticism of writers by readers, of government by those governed, of leaders by those led,—this is the soul of democracy and the safeguard of modern democracy.[22]

To understand fully what Du Bois takes such criticism to be, we might begin by noticing how much is packed into his phrase "nearly touched." *Touch* is a key word in his vocabulary of democracy—as when he writes in *Darkwater* that "Politics have not *touched* the matters of daily life which are nearest the interests of the people," or that "When voting *touches* the vital, everyday interests of all, nominations and elections will call for more intelligent activity."[23] In his *Autobiography*, Du Bois writes that teaching summer school in Tennessee (between semesters at Fisk) was an "invaluable" experience because he "*touched* the very shadow of slavery. I lived and taught school in log cabins built before the Civil War....I *touched* intimately the lives of the commonest of mankind—people who ranged from barefooted dwellers on dirt floors, with patched rags for clothes, to rough, hard-working farmers, with plain, clean plenty." And in another passage from his *Autobiography*, Du Bois writes: "This my training *touched* but obliquely," and "I could bring criticism from what I knew and saw *touching* the Negro"[24] (emphases added throughout).

Touch, I would suggest, registers Du Bois's commitment to a way of thinking that is not disembodied and distant but actually touches and is touched by its objects. Du Bois's implicit theory of democracy conceives of it as an endless process of "honest and earnest criticism" through which the multiple perspectives of those whose interests are "touched" become aggregated in a tense but (to use Cooper's words again) "stable equilibrium of opposition." "Democracy alone," he writes, "is the method of showing the whole experience of the race for the benefit of the future." Democracy rests, finally, on recognition of "the worth of" each person's "feelings and experiences to all" (555). "To disenfranchise" any group "is deliberately to turn from knowledge and grope in ignorance" (556). Therefore, "no state can be strong which excludes from its expressed wisdom the knowledge possessed by mothers, wives, daughters" and by other "excluded groups." And difference is crucial: "Human equality is not lack of difference, nor do infinite human differences argue relative superiority and inferiority." Indeed, genuine democratic inclusion cannot mean a universal sameness, the conformity of all difference to a single standard: "of all worlds, may the good Lord deliver us from a world where everybody looks like his neighbor and thinks like his neighbor and is like his neighbor" (561). There is a place in Du Bois's demos even for a Jefferson Davis—if he is willing complement his assertive self with a self that is willing to submit to the Thou of the community.[25]

Du Bois's emphasis on touch has further implications. As political theorist Thomas Dumm has observed in relation to Emerson's use of the word, its etymology—the Italian *toccare* means to strike or hit—should remind us that touching can be violent or conflictual.[26] Touching is direct, not mediated contact between persons. Unlike systems of representation, in which citizens communicate with each other by way of signifiers standing for things signified, or vest their political power in representatives who stand for them, a democracy that conceives of communication as touching risks the violence that unmediated contact carries in order to avail itself of the wisdom locked within individual suffering. Finally, Du Bois's commitment to touching expresses another reason why the "whole" or "all" he so frequently invokes is itself so resistant to representation. Composed of tangible and equal splinters of unknowable difference, it can never be summed up or enclosed in conceptual limits. Its circumference is always open to the possibility of further expansion.

Thus, a particular democratic epistemology informs Du Bois's suggestion that the contributions citizens make to the wisdom of the polity are best described as *touching* the matters being deliberated and as *touching* each other. Du Bois's verb carefully evades the tradition of Cartesian, spectatorial "knowing" because he wishes to convey that the source of democratic knowing is suffering. It is pain. The authority of each person's perspective rests, somewhat paradoxically, on the utter privacy of his or her suffering. "[I]n the last analysis," Du Bois writes, "only the man himself, however humble, knows his own condition." That is, "in the last analysis only the sufferer knows his sufferings," and "human beings are, and must be, woefully ignorant of each other" (*Darkwater*, 554). Democracy can transform this private pain into a political good, however, when citizens understand that it is the source of each individual's distinctive knowledge, of what he or she can distinctively contribute to the group's inevitably combative deliberations.[27]

By figuring suffering as the source of the most important knowledge citizens can bring to their democracy, Du Bois was thinking within a long Christian tradition and more specifically within a long African American tradition that accords value to suffering. As black theologian Gayraud S. Wilmore has written, many black Americans have felt themselves to be formed in part by what he calls a "matrix" of suffering:

> Black humanity in America is formed in the matrix of psychological and physical suffering, segregation, discrimination and the ever-present remembrance of a previous condition of involuntary servitude. Out of this condition has come a type of person, a type of human being whose sensibilities and perceptions, religious and secular, are rarely identical with those who are "born White" in America. This does not, however, make such sensibilities invalid. Indeed it may give them a certain depth and richness, a certain passion for justice that can discern in the truth about Jesus Christ that which modern White Christians have both forgotten and ignored.[28]

Yet while unjust suffering may have these redemptive qualities, neither Du Bois nor Wilmore suggests that these qualities justify such suffering or adequately explain it. On the contrary, they insist that the forces that cause injustice must be resisted and vanquished. The challenge, therefore, is to make unjust suffering meaningful without at the same time allowing it to become either acceptable or determinative of one's identity. Theologian and activist Pauli Murray described this challenge in these words:

> For those of us who have been born into a group which has been the object of contempt, injustice, and oppression, the figure of the Suffering Servant, the example of Jesus Christ, presents us with a most difficult dilemma. On the one hand we strive for self-respect and pride in ourselves and our achievements against those who would deny our humanity and our personhood. On the other hand we are told that self-pride is a stumbling block to salvation. Are we expected to endure injustice submissively? To give our backs to the smiters? Not to be rebellious when all around us we see evil and injustice?[29]

Murray confesses—to her congregation and to us—that she has never been able to resolve this dilemma definitively: "I would be dishonest if I told you that I have answers to these questions. I wrestle with them daily. For in them lies the ultimate test of our faith in God—a faith that God is in control of the universe and of our own destiny; that God moves in history;…that what we suffer is a part of God's ultimate plan; that we are in fact God's Suffering Servants in the salvation history of the world" (261). Like Douglass, Brooks, and Lewis, Murray experiences her faith not as a state to which she can leap and stay, but as a constant testing of herself as she tries to span the poles of irreconcilable obligations to the eternal and the historical.

Du Bois's suggestion that suffering is, in the last analysis, a private experience also suggests that suffering cannot on its own serve as the determinative basis of group solidarity. Two persons may have suffered from the same cause, but their experience of such suffering is bound to be different. If "in the last analysis only the sufferer knows his sufferings" and if for that reason "human beings are, and must be, woefully ignorant of each other," suffering is less the basis of solidarity than a prompt for it. Human beings must reach out to each other across the gulf into which their suffering has cast each of them. Rightly understood and practiced, democracy can provide the means for such a reaching out and a reason to do so.

Following this trail of key words in Du Bois's vocabulary of democratic theory—*criticism, whole, touch, difference, suffering*—we should not be surprised to find ourselves coming to *imagination, dream, infinity*. For if the democratic *whole* is always open to further revision and wider inclusion, and if it embraces "infinite human differences" rooted in distinctive experiences of suffering, then it is by definition infinite. And this infinite can only be envisioned by imagination, not grasped by reason, much less by empirical sociology.

Hence Du Bois's unyielding commitment to the belief that the imagination plays an indispensable role in the creation of a democratic political culture. As he wrote in a letter to Ben F. Rogers: "I was extremely emotional on the race problem while I was a student at Harvard and my emotion was curbed by the philosophy of William James and the historical research under Hart. They did not quench; they directed it. I was never 'primarily a historian.' If anything, I had the urge to be a creative artist but the literature which I wanted to write was not the kind which the public was willing to read."[30] Even as his appreciation of Karl Marx's dialectical materialism deepened, he continued to celebrate and affirm the politically transformative powers of the imagination. In his 1941 essay on Phillis Wheatley, for example, he presents her as a visionary whose prophetic dreams were later realized in the work of seven major African American writers, including David Walker, William Wells Brown, Charles Chesnutt, and Paul Laurence Dunbar: "It is these imagined visions of Phillis... that made her Phillis the Blessed." Almost certainly implying a reference to himself in particular and to African American experience in general, Du Bois writes: "Always a certain sense of mystery lurked in the furtherest [*sic*] reaches of Phillis' consciousness—the miracle of her sudden transport to this far land; the hoarse voice of the Visions, the deep dire Visions, thus floated and drifted, loomed and died in her thoughts and dreams. In the only home she knew—and the only friends she had, she was always partly a stranger. Only her phantasy was real, only her dreams were true. She could not help but have visions—prophetic visions—she who in a single childhood had encompassed the ends of the earth."[31]

When Du Bois writes, "The real argument for democracy is... that in the wisdom of the people we have that source of endless life and unbounded wisdom which the rulers of men must have" (555), his tropes of the "endless" and "unbounded" are of crucial importance: he is striving to express his understanding of democracy as a horizonless whole that cannot be precisely delimited because it is by nature infinite. This conception of the whole helps explain why Du Bois himself was and remained an imaginative writer throughout the entire span of his career. A secularist to the core and a rationalist master of empirical argument and icy logic, he nonetheless crowded his oeuvre with what a commitment to reasoned discourse would seem to exclude—specters of the unknown and the unknowable. Du Bois's poems, novels, and books of creative essays demand that his readers continually lift their eyes from the here and now to contemplate a world that can be approached only through the imagination. His political theory may thus be said to return us to the original meaning of *theoria* as contemplation of the divine, when that is understood to be something beyond our knowing or naming.[32] As he wrote in a 1933 editorial in the *Crisis*:

> He [the young Negro] should see in the church an expression of the desire for full and ultimate truth; that desire for goodness and beauty, which is ingrained in every human being; and on the other hand, and just as clearly, he should frankly denounce all attempts on the part of any organized body of human beings when they declare that they know it all and that God has personally told them about it. That is a plain lie and they know it and everybody else ought to know it. We must have religion in the sense of striving for the infinite, the ultimate, and the best. But just as truly we must straitly curb the effort of any exclusive guild to be the single and final arbiter of individual interpretation of desired and desirable truth.[33]

Du Bois's "criticism" as the "soul of democracy" is thus a mode of thought that continually tries to make room for the differences it encounters by habitually seeking an enlargement of the whole. Within that whole, differences persist and touch each other in Ellison's "cooperative antagonism." Democratic practice understood as such criticism would consist not of exchanging reasons, nor of reasoning per se, but of bringing to bear knowledge gained by suffering that can never be abstracted and then represented because it is essentially private and incommensurable. Such democratic practice is always aware of what Elaine Scarry calls "the difficulty of imagining others."[34] It touches rather than perceives things because it is informed by individual knowledge derived from the authority of personal suffering. That touching is at once near and intimate (not distanced) and yet also cognizant that it must be, in the best sense of the word, superficial. For when we *touch* upon something or someone, we do not presume to penetrate to an essence. Nor do we proceed by abstracting out what is purportedly held "in common" by all the differences that surround us. Suspicious of representation and alarmed by synecdoche, our touching locates knowledge precisely in what is separate and unique rather than in what is universal and shared (and shareable).

Some forty years earlier, Anna Julia Cooper was thinking analogously when she chastised black male leaders for presuming to represent the entire race and failing to take account of the different and equally important role played by black women: "our present record of eminent men, when placed beside the actual status of race in America to-day, proves that no man can represent the race. Whatever the attainments of the individual may be, ... he can never be regarded as identical with or representative of the whole." (Yet she might have slipped into the very error she deplored when she went on to claim, more famously: "Only the BLACK WOMAN can say, 'when and where I enter, in the quiet, undisputed dignity of my womanhood, without violence and without suing or special patronage, then and there the whole *Negro race enters with me.*'"[35]) Josephine St. Pierre Ruffin voiced the practical implications of such a view in 1895, when she defended the nascent National Association of Colored Women: "Our woman's movement is a woman's movement in that it is led and directed by women for the good of women and men, for *the benefit of all humanity, which is more than any one branch or section of it.*"[36]

"I Am Not Afraid of the Word Tension"

I want to conclude with two more stories about individuals whose faith informed their democratic politics in ways that figure faith as being both adamantine and flexible, committed yet contingent. Different as their characters and careers are often taken to be, both Martin Luther King Jr. and Malcolm X believed that politics should be infused with faith, and for both men that faith was one that could hold in tension their irreconcilable commitments to honoring black suffering and seeking to end it. To use Murray's words, both had faith that "God moves in history," and that their suffering therefore had meaning; yet both also believed that they should not be "expected to endure injustice submissively," and both resolved, therefore, to alter history. The key always was to hold these contradictory commitments in tense equipoise.

We can hear King striving to sustain such tension between acceptance and defiance, submission and action, suffering and soldiering, when he declares, "I mean to say that a strong man must be militant as well as moderate. He must be a realist as well as an idealist."[37] One phrase he used to describe the attitude, or posture, he aimed for was "militantly nonviolent" (348). Another was "nonviolent tension," as when he wrote: "This may sound rather shocking. But I confess that I am not afraid of the word tension. I have earnestly worked and preached against violent tension, but there is a type of constructive nonviolent tension that is necessary for growth" (291). *Militant nonviolence* and *nonviolent tension*, like Douglass's *ringbolt to the chain of destiny*, are phrases that seek to juxtapose and hold together seeming opposites. Like Douglass, then, King strove to reconcile his belief in eternal truths with his knowledge of human fallibility. As historical actors in "the muck and mire" of human existence, both men knew that perfect logical consistency is achievable only in theory, in an intellectual space removed from the world. They knew as well that a believing democratic *activist* would have to understand and practice consistency differently.

In the eyes of many black Americans, including Malcolm X, King gave too much emphasis to the side of faith that affirmed that "we are in fact God's Suffering Servants in the salvation history of the world." Malcolm intended to emphasize the other side—the "passion for justice" that prohibits one from ever accepting one's suffering and the legitimate indignation that one must learn to express but also to channel constructively into political philosophy and activism. In a speech delivered in Detroit in late 1964, Malcolm asserted that all revolutions worthy of the name had been struggles for land, and then he declared: "There's no such thing as a nonviolent revolution.... Revolution is bloody, revolution is hostile, revolution knows no compromise, revolution overturns and destroys everything that gets in its way."[38]

King's moral problem of when to exercise disobedience became, for Malcolm, the more intense question of when to exercise violent force while resisting injustice. It's crucial to see that both men were struggling to balance the claims of the ideal against those of the real. In Malcolm's case, that ideal was inherent in our very notion of politics, which, as Hannah Arendt has argued, is predicated on the belief that humans can resolve their differences without recourse to violence. For where violence begins, politics ends; where violence is necessary, democracy has failed. Yet the legitimate needs of particular people in a particular historical moment were just as important as those ideals. Black Americans were suffering injustice, and for them politics and democracy had failed. How, then, to reconcile their claims *in* history with ideals that stand *outside* history? Just as King had to explain how and when lawlessness was lawful, so Malcolm had to assert that violence was a legitimate expression of the political. The tension in Malcolm's answer was even more intense than that expressed by King's seeming oxymoron of "militant nonviolence." Malcolm was always careful not to advocate violence in the sense of urging black Americans to get revenge or terrorize whites. What he recommended rather was an *attitude* of controlled readiness to exercise violence in self-defense. As he told an audience in Cleveland in 1964:

> I don't mean go out and get violent, but at the same time you should never be nonviolent unless you run into some nonviolence. I'm nonviolent with those who are nonviolent with me. But when you drop that violence on me, then you've made me go insane, and I'm not responsible for what I do. And that's the way every Negro should get. Any time you know you're within the law, within your legal rights, within

your moral rights, in accord with justice, then die for what you believe in. But don't die alone. Let your dying be reciprocal. This is what is meant by equality. What is good for the goose is good for the gander.[39]

Malcolm's way of sustaining the tension between the real and the ideal was not to call for violence itself but to call for a certain posture: a readiness to strike *back* as long as one was "within the law." Like Douglass before him, he insisted that that black Americans be ready to fight and die in defense of their rights—to die fighting, in other words.[40]

Physically, then, the tension between acceptance and defiance was held in the stance of hair-trigger readiness to defend oneself and retaliate. Psychologically and rhetorically, it was held in Malcolm's brilliant use of the phrase "by any means necessary." These words affirmed the legitimacy of black violence in self-defense yet refrained from specifying exactly how much provocation might make it legitimate and precisely what forms it might legitimately take. When he announced, "*I'm not* advocating the breaking of any laws....*But* I say that our people will never be respected as human beings until we react as other intelligent human beings do," or when he said, "*This doesn't* mean that we should buy rifles and go out and initiate attacks indiscriminately against whites....*But* it does mean that we should get whatever is necessary to protect ourselves," his very syntax struck a balance like King's, Douglass's, and Murray's.[41] Malcolm was totally committed to working for social justice within history, yet he remained equally committed to a principle that stands outside and beyond history—the principle that for politics to exist at all, violence must be the option of last resort. He lived by this principle, yet he refused to name or announce it because he knew that doing so would constrain his options.

If the outbreak of violence marks the failure of democratic politics—if, as Hannah Arendt maintained, democracy is precisely the possibility of humans acting collaboratively and resolving their differences without recourse to violence—then any invocation or threat of violence is by definition antidemocratic. The question then becomes: how *near* to such a threat or invocation can a democratic actor move without sacrificing his or her democratic commitments? How tense can the relation become between a willingness to act in any way necessary to deal with certain concrete historical conditions of oppression, and a commitment to democratic politics that places moral and formal limits on how one may act? Malcolm's words and stance sustained that tension at an extraordinarily high pitch, higher even that King's "militant nonviolence." If faith is understood as a commitment to holding opposites in tension, then taking democratic politics right to that edge where violence might be required to save democracy was Malcolm's demonstration of his faith.

"But is this *faith*?" I hear some readers ask. "By 'faith' we mean believing in God, or believing that every word in the Bible is true." I would suggest that the true meaning of faith is not captured by these phrases, for they tell only half the story. To believe that every word in the Bible is true is an assertion of dogma; it becomes an expression of faith only when the believer also knows and admits that the warrant for this belief can never be given in this world. This is what we mean by saying that faith is "the evidence of things not seen." Faith is not faith if it can *behold* its object; faith is unreasonable and surpasses reason precisely because it is a claim that we can live in the world we see and be guided by the unseen even if we cannot reason our way from here to there. Faith always spans, or hold in tension, these seemingly incommensurable realms of the sacred and the profane. Douglass believed that the contingency thinking and standpoint knowing of a slave could be combined with an allegiance to the eternal principles of natural, or higher, law. King believed that he could be faithful to the moral law of the universe and to the corrupt laws of humankind if his resistance to these laws was also a submission to them. Malcolm knew that the eruption of violence would mean the end of politics; but he was not willing to forswear the use of violence if the threat of it served a political purpose.[42]

Let me put the matter more concretely: King and Malcolm, just like religious fundamentalists or Christian conservatives today, took their important political positions not because a value-free process of ratiocination had led them there but because their values and principles compelled them to. And because the truth of these values and principles were *not* self-evident to all, they had to hold to their truths as an exercise of faith. Yet unlike the faith that many religious fundamentalists profess, King's and Malcolm's faith expressed itself as a *tension*, or as a set of mutually reinforcing tensions. At a deep level, they were pulled in one direction by their belief that many black Americans who had suffered unjustly at the hands of whites had gained exceptional moral knowledge and moral authority; yet they were also pulled by their equally strong resolve to end that suffering no matter what moral and spiritual benefits it might have conferred on themselves and other black Americans. At another level, their faith-as-tension was caused by a conflict between their belief that a moral order had conferred this meaning upon black suffering and would ultimately end it, and their very strong doubts that any moral order worthy of the name would have permitted such suffering in the first place.

They experienced tension as they looked confidently toward the arrival of a better future that God had willed *and* they worked to hasten that arrival, since (in Martin Luther King's words) "human progress never rolls in on wheels of inevitability" (296). Finally, knowing as they did that white racists also claimed to know the will of God, they salted their faith with the awareness that all humans are fallible and that no one, including themselves, can know with absolute certainty who God is or what he wills. To say that they experienced their faith *with* this awareness is not quite correct. Rather, they knew that lacking such awareness, their beliefs would not be expressions of true faith.

Because Malcolm thought it necessary to downplay the suffering servant side and emphasize the striving for justice aspect of his faith, he seldom mentioned black suffering. But toward the end of *The Autobiography of Malcolm X*, he speaks in a way that places him squarely in the current of those who have sought to end black suffering while at the same time believing that black suffering has what Du Bois called "a message for the world." Asserting that white Americans and black Americans need to work at the same time, but separately, to end white racism, he says: "In our mutual sincerity we might be able to show a road to the salvation of America's very soul. It can only be salvaged if human rights and dignity, in full, are extended to black men."[43] Malcolm went on to say that he had "sometimes…dared to dream" that his "voice," which disturbed the white man's smugness, arrogance, and complacency, might therefore have "helped to save America from a grave, possibly even a final catastrophe" (434–35). And what did Malcolm feel authorized his voice? What did he feel gave it credibility?

> I believe it would be almost impossible to find anywhere in America a black man who has lived further down in the mud of human society than I have; or a black man who has been any more ignorant than I have; or a black man who has suffered more anguish than I have. But it is only after the deepest darkness that the greatest joy can come; it is only after slavery and prison that the sweetest appreciation of freedom can come. (437)

In Malcolm's view, then, it was the anguish he had suffered as a black man that enabled him to expose "the racist malignancy in America" (437) and thereby "show a road to the salvation of America's very soul" (434).

Seen in the light of their willingness to hold contraries in perpetual "tension," with each other, King and Malcolm had more in common than is often supposed. In "Notes Toward a Black Balancing of Love and Hatred," June Jordan makes precisely this point when she writes: "is it tragic and ridiculous to choose between Malcolm X and Dr. King: each of them hurled himself against a quite different aspect of our predicament, and both of them, literally, gave their lives to our ongoing struggle." And as her essay's title suggests, Jordan herself demonstrates such a willingness to balance contraries even as she argues that King and Malcolm did so.[44]

Reimagining Faith and Democratic Politics Now

In their different ways, all the figures whose words we have been reading here—Douglass, Du Bois, Cooper, Murray, Baldwin, King, and Malcolm—practiced a faith that strove toward the infinite while also respecting the pluralism inherent in individual experience and contingent historical conditions. Instead of imagining the transcendent and the worldly as either separated by an infinite expanse of empty time and space, or as one and the same thing, they saw them as always running parallel to each other and sometimes converging in a moment of action in the here and now. As Martin Luther King said in his Nobel Prize acceptance speech: "I refuse to accept the idea that the 'isness' of man's present nature makes him morally incapable of reaching up for the eternal 'oughtness' that forever confronts him."[45] Black theologian Nathan Wright Jr. likewise sought to honor the distinction between the historical and the eternal, the is and the ought, while also allowing for their convergence:

> Philosophically, life does not move upward toward the end of time. Time and eternity are not time sequences. Life does not historically improve as time goes on. There is always conflict, and never in the broadest sense is there "enduring peace." Time and eternity are like two horizontal though infinitely unequal lines, which are close enough to be in a kind of tension. Wherever the power of the eternal is appropriated and realized in human life, at such precise points the lines of time and eternity converge and become as one.... The sacred is anything which at any point in the time-eternity complex is God-empowered or God-possessed.[46]

I have tried to show how such an understanding of faith comports well with democracy's respect for diversity of belief and energizes citizens to take action on behalf of democracy.[47] When faith is a striving, when the infinite is unknowable, when all human representations of the truth are understood to be partial and incomplete—then faith actually promotes and encourages pluralism rather than threatening it. As Wright puts it: "Yet our religious life should enable us to bring into new and more creative focus things which otherwise we might not see and understand. Our religious life should enable us to see all reality in the light of Ultimate Reality.... Fundamentalism and intolerance are more than incidentally related.... There is an evident inherent basic flaw in any religious experience which cannot unloose and move beyond a deadly cultural bind or limitation."[48] Such a conception of faith suggests that the myriad parts of a democratic whole must work collaboratively to assemble their knowledge, and must respect what each person knows that no other person can know. They must commit themselves to actions decided in the light of eternal truths while knowing that their sight is necessarily dim and their grasp of such truths is necessarily uncertain. As Vincent Lloyd writes, "To acknowledge inherent, irreparable conflict and to continue to gamble—that is faith."[49] Citizens of a democracy should understand that "there will always be conflict" in a democracy as they bring their different perspectives and beliefs into the collaborative enterprise of collective self-government; yet they should also know that to mitigate the damage of such conflict, they must remember that "To no one type of mind is it given to perceive the totality of the Truth," and that while "absolute and eternal truth *is*, still truth must be infinite, and as incapable as infinite space, of being encompassed and confined by one age or nation, sect or country—much less by one little creature's finite brain." We hear such a disposition when John Lewis writes, "A free and open society—a democracy—is by definition an eternal work-in-progress. As someone once said, democracy is an ongoing conversation. It will always be altering, shaping, and defining itself for the better. This is the way we move forward, by responding to problem after problem, step-by-step."[50] We also hear it in Malcolm X's letter to his wife, Betty: "Despite my firm convictions, I have always been a man who tries to face facts, and to accept the reality of life as new experience and new knowledge unfolds it. I have always kept an open mind, which is necessary to the flexibility that must go hand in hand with every form of intelligent search for truth."[51]

To be sure, this disposition is hardly original with or unique to black Americans. Joseph Schumpeter argued that one must "realize the relative validity of one's convictions and yet stand for them unflinchingly." Richard Rorty called for us to become "liberal ironists," persons who combine "commitment with a sense of the contingency of their own commitment." Justice Learned Hand famously declared, "The spirit of liberty is the spirit which is not too sure that it is right; the spirit of liberty is the spirit which seeks to understand the minds of other men and women." But the voices of the black Americans I have been discussing add an inflection—not unlike what Eddie Glaude calls "a shade of blue"—to this fundamentally liberal and pragmatist orientation. What they have known firsthand and take more seriously is the costs such a spirit exacts: inevitable conflict and the existential pain of "striving." They testify that the faith "that is not too sure that it is right" is born out of a need to make sense of suffering, and that the doubts it experiences are therefore always anguished doubts. If such faith requires (or is) a sense of irony, it is a much more tragic sense of irony than Rorty's work knows or conveys. Nor is it just the spirit of liberty that is at stake in their reflections, but the more vulnerable and socially situated belief in individual human dignity. Faith as it moves through the words and deeds of these black Americans both inspires democratic action and accommodates an infinite democratic pluralism. In stark contrast to the liberal tradition and its "wall of separation," it does so not by ruling religious faith out of bounds but by locating an infinite and unknowable transcendence at the very heart of democratic theory and practice.[52]

6

"The Moment We're In"

THE DEMOCRATIC IMAGINATION OF BARACK OBAMA

THE NATURE OF Barack Obama's core political philosophy has been vigorously debated ever since he gained national visibility in 2004. The mystery of who Obama *really* is and what he *really* believes achieved frenzied intensity over the course of his first term, and it has barely subsided since his November 2012 reelection. One conservative pundit described him in April 2009, in the *National Review*, as "a left-wing culture warrior" who "transmogrifies his principled opponents into straw-man ideologues while preening about his own humble pragmatism. For him, bipartisanship is defined as shutting up and getting in line." But Peter Beinart has argued that "When it comes to culture, Obama doesn't have a public agenda; he has a public anti-agenda. He wants to remove culture from the political debate." William Kristol, writing in the *Weekly Standard*, has more than once embraced Obama as a fellow neoconservative. Gil Troy, writing in the *L.A. Progressive*, has praised Obama as "a liberal nationalist," while black intellectual Adolph Reed in May 2008 dismissed Obama in *The Progressive* as "a vacuous opportunist" and "a good performer with an ear for how to make white liberals like him." In April 2011, on an MSNBC panel discussion, Cornel West called him "the black mascot of Wall Street oligarchs." As Mitchell Aboulafia sums up this confusion: "Obama is making a lot of people, including traditional liberals, uncomfortable, and this discomfort in part turns on his unwillingness to inhabit given ideological boxes."[1] Is he a progressive? a liberal? a pragmatist? a neoconservative? At the close of this book on black American thought and public philosophy, it seems fitting to consider Obama's relation to the thinkers I have discussed.

To date, even the best studies of Obama's politics and political thought have paid insufficient attention to black American sources of his thinking and outlook. (The notable exceptions here are Gene Andrew Jarrett's chapter on Obama in *Representing the Race* and David Remnick's *The Bridge*; Jarrett convincingly demonstrates the subtle influences Malcolm X in particular might have had on Obama, and Remnick places Obama's *Dreams from My Father* squarely within the tradition of black autobiography.)² For example, James T. Kloppenberg's superb intellectual biography *Reading Obama* identifies "three distinct" traditions that have shaped Obama's political mind and policies. One is "the history of American democracy." A second is "the philosophy of pragmatism." The third is "the intellectual upheavals that occurred on American campuses during the two decades" (1970s and 1980s) Obama spent in college and law school.³ What is strikingly absent from Kloppenberg's account—and from so much of the voluminous commentary on Obama produced since 1994—is any sustained consideration of the ways Obama may have been shaped by black American political thought about democracy. Kloppenberg is certainly right that Obama was exposed to and influenced by various forms of civic republicanism and pragmatism when he was a student. But he offers no evidence that Obama himself actually read James or Dewey, while Obama has explicitly written that in high school he "gathered up books from the library—Baldwin, Ellison, Hughes, Wright, Du Bois. At night I would close the door to my room, telling my grandparents I had homework to do, and there I would sit and wrestle with words, locked in suddenly desperate argument, trying to reconcile the world as I'd found it with the terms of my birth."⁴ A brief, but even more telling indication of the depth of Obama's engagement with black art and thought about democracy appears in the epilogue to *Dreams from My Father*: "*We hold these truths to be self-evident.* In these words, I hear the spirit of Douglass and Delany, as well as Jefferson and Lincoln; the struggles of Martin and Malcolm and unheralded marchers bringing these words to life" (437).

What I find so remarkable about both passages, especially the second, is their unmistakable registering of the spirit of "antagonistic cooperation" that characterizes so much black American reflection on democracy. When Obama read the black writers he mentions, he felt immediately that he had to "wrestle" with them. And by the time he wrote *Dreams from My Father* (published in 1994), he had learned that black thought about democracy has usually been seen as a tradition woven of the two strands he takes such care to specify in the second quotation: Douglass *and* Delany, King *and* Malcolm. Note, too, his belief that the "struggles" of black Americans have brought the words of the Declaration "to life"—an insight he has surely gained by way of reading Martin Luther King, and perhaps Du Bois and Thurgood Marshall. (Kloppenberg mentions Marshall only once, yet Elena Kagan, Martha Minow, and Cass Sunstein—all of whom figure prominently in *Reading Obama*— have in common the experience of clerking for Marshall when he was on the Supreme Court.) And we can find Obama expressing his awareness of the dialectical nature of black political thought quite explicitly in his 1988 essay "Why Organize?": "From W.E.B. Du Bois to Booker T. Washington to Marcus Garvey to Malcolm X to Martin Luther King, this internal debate has raged between integration and nationalism, between accommodation and militancy, between sit-down strikes and boardroom negotiations. The lines between these strategies have never been simply drawn, and the most successful black leadership has recognized the need to bridge these seemingly divergent approaches."[5]

In *Not Even Past*, historian Thomas Sugrue writes that Obama is here recognizing "the fundamental pragmatism that animated the long black freedom struggle: few activists were ideologically pure."[6] But "pragmatism" (and its implied opposition to "purity") does not quite do justice to the orientation of these thinkers. When Obama describes Du Bois, Washington, Garvey, Malcolm X, and Martin Luther King in terms of the familiar binaries— "integration"/"nationalism," "accommodation"/"militancy"—and then goes on to say that the "lines between" them "have never been simply drawn," he is pointing toward a relation that is more complex than "pragmatism" or "compromise" suggest. For as we have seen, when black political thought is conceived as consisting of *both* these strands intertwining and supporting each other, the distinction between pragmatism and idealism, compromise and purity becomes much less sharp. For these black thinkers, "accommodation" is not always opposed to, or an alternative to "militancy"; it can mean instead a fierce affirmation of some of "the culture's principles" that the culture itself violates—respect others, refrain from violence if possible, love thy neighbor as thyself, and resort to violence only if necessary (to name just a few). King was not simply being pragmatic or compromising when he advocated "militant nonviolence"; he was conceptually fusing these two categories. Likewise, when Malcolm X identified himself and other black Americans with the founders "who were tired of tyranny and oppression and exploitation and the brutality," he was not just espousing "integration" with or "accommodation" to American norms that had already been established. He was also reinterpreting the past in the light of the present, rendering the founders black, not just troping blacks as white founders. To use Sheldon Wolin's terms, he was fusing continuity and innovation. To regard such fusion merely as pragmatism, or as a compromise of pure principle, is clearly wrong. Yet it's the trap we'll fall into if we take these binary terms too seriously.[7]

So perhaps Obama won't fit into the "ideological boxes" we are most familiar with—liberalism, progressivism, conservatism, neoliberalism, neoconservatism—because he has been shaped in part by the constellation of black thought I have been discussing in this book.[8] But can we therefore conclude that Obama's "new kind of politics" is best understood as expressing what US public philosophy would look like if it absorbed some of the black American perspectives we have been tracing here? Not quite.

Commitment to Perpetual Tension

As a writer and a thinker, Obama does indeed have affinities with a number of the figures I've been discussing, especially insofar as he explicitly commits himself to sustaining "a perpetual tension" between competing and antagonistic perspectives. In his books and speeches, Obama frequently analyzes issues using terms like "tension" and "balance" and recommending that we seek to reconcile the irreconcilable, by which he often means what so many other black writers and activists have meant: not melting the terms of polarities into one another, but developing our own ability to hold them both equally in our minds. In *The Audacity of Hope*, for example, he writes that "finding the right balance between our competing values is difficult. Tensions arise not because we have steered a wrong course, but simply because we live in a complex and contradictory world" (56). He suggests that such tensions are endemic to democracy and that our task as citizens is to learn to live with them: "In a country as diverse as ours, there will always be passionate arguments about how we draw the line when it comes to government action. That is how our democracy works" (57). What he admires about Lincoln, he writes, is that for him "it was never a matter of abandoning conviction for the sake of expediency. Rather, it was a matter of maintaining within himself the balance between contradictory ideals—that we must talk and reach for common understandings, precisely because all of us are imperfect and can never act with the certainty that God is on our side; and yet at times we must act nonetheless, as if we are certain, protected from error only by providence" (*Audacity*, 98). While in law school, Obama worked with legal scholar Lawrence Tribe on an article that urges a flexible approach to constitutional interpretation, one that calls to mind the thinking of Frederick Douglass.

In his Nobel Prize acceptance speech, similarly, Obama claimed that "part of our challenge is reconciling these two seemingly irreconcilable truths—that war is sometimes necessary, and war at some level is an expression of human folly." In the same speech, he said that "within America, there has long been a tension between those who describe themselves as realists or idealists—a tension that suggests a stark choice between the narrow pursuit of interests or an endless campaign to impose our values around the world. I reject these choices." What he meant by rejecting these choices, of course, was that he refused to see them *as* choices: the task before us, he suggests, is not to pick one or the other option but to hold both perspectives simultaneously, as philosophically inconsistent as that might seem. And in his 2010 speech on immigration reform, Obama in similar fashion sketched two opposing arguments and then offered his own: we must get "past the false debates that divide the country rather than bring it together....Now, once we get past the two poles of this debate, it becomes possible to shape a practical, common-sense approach that reflects our heritage and our values."[9]

Hope—Not Indignation and Conflict

Just here, however, in his belief that these positions are "false," we glimpse another side of Obama, one who believes that the challenge of democratic citizenship is not to sustain oppositions in collaborative antagonism but to dissolve them in the alembic of what he calls "unity." Obama's fervent belief in the possibility of unity has driven his political vision from its beginnings to the present moment. As he wrote in *The Audacity of Hope*, "the vast majority of Americans—Republican, Democrat, and independent—are weary of the dead zone that politics has become, in which narrow interests vie for advantage and ideological minorities seek to impose their own versions of the absolute truth....Perhaps more than any other time in our recent history, we need a new kind of politics, one that can excavate and build upon those shared understandings that pull us together as Americans" (9).

As we have seen, although the impulse to move beyond what is "narrow" to a broader field for democratic politics was strongly felt by many black thinkers and activists, they typically had little to say about "unity," and they had minimal interest in a politics that can "pull us together." They have sought inclusion, but they have emphasized that democratic politics are essentially and unavoidably conflictual. Recall Anna Julia Cooper's words: "Progressive peace in a nation is the result of conflict; and conflict, such as is healthy, stimulating, and progressive, is produced through the co-existence of radically opposing or racially different elements."

Unsurprisingly, in pursuing unity through compromise Obama has demonstrated little appreciation for indignation as a necessary and potentially powerful democratic emotion. Doubtless we must take into account here the widespread white American cultural prohibition that virtually forbids black men or women from showing anger. During the long course of the 2008 campaign, Obama was repeatedly warned by allies not to appear angry and chastised by conservative pundits for being so. Rush Limbaugh was typical of the latter: "I think Obama is largely misunderstood by a lot of people.... We're finding out that this guy's got a chip on his shoulder. He's angry at this country. He's not proud of it.... Let's face it, President Obama's black, and I think he's got a chip on his shoulder." As James Hannaham summarized Obama's dilemma in *Salon*: "So Obama is damned if he performs his black anger too fiercely—that would give biased people the impression that he's an 'angry black man' or worse, an extremist, and therefore unelectable. But now he has to face criticism from the left because he's not performing his anger—a specifically black, unreal variety of anger, remember—in the correct measure."[10]

Yet if Baldwin and the other figures we have been reading are correct, the prohibition against public display of political anger does not target only black Americans like Obama. On the contrary, a much wider fear of anger has been woven into various US public philosophies—including liberalism, civic republicanism, and communitarianism—for a long time. This fear is understandable: democracy does require that citizens be able to control their anger. But as we have seen, from the spectrum of emotions that fall under the term "anger," we should isolate one that we have been calling "indignation"—specifically the indignation that arises in response to assaults upon one's dignity. The black writers I have discussed in this book suggest that this particular anger should be seen for what it is and then transformed into a productive political emotion. Their writings also suggest that our failure to recognize the nature and value of indignation conceals from us the vulnerable and relational nature of our dignity. It also disposes us to experience our legitimate and valuable indignation as self-destructive and dangerous *ressentiment*.

I don't think Obama conceals his indignation only because he knows that too many white Americans would read it as "black" and then condemn it. Rather, he seems to have substituted for it another energy—hope. In his Ebenezer Baptist Church speech, speaking before an audience that would have welcomed at least some hint of indignation, he declared:

> But I also know this: nothing in this country worthwhile has ever happened except somebody somewhere decided to hope. That's how this

country was founded because a group of patriots decided they were going to take on the British Empire. Nobody was putting their money on them. That's how slaves and abolitionists resisted that evil system. That's how a new President was able to chart a course to insure that this nation would no longer remain half slave and half free. That's how the greatest generation defeated Fascism and overcame a Great Depression. That's how women won the right to vote. That's how workers won the right to organize. That's how young people and old people and middle-aged folks were willing to walk instead of ride the bus, and folks came down on Freedom Rides.

To this, many of the black writers we have been reading would reply: *No, no, and again no.* The Tea Party patriots of the eighteenth century were fired by indignation more than by hope. The same was true of most abolitionists in the 1850s; and my father's generation went unhesitatingly to war because they were enraged by the Japanese attack on Pearl Harbor, not because they already had hopes of victory. Obama is probably right that hope is an essential democratic emotion, but often he seems to think that it is sufficient, and that anger of *any* kind is destructive of democratic life.

Obama's strategy of conflict avoidance—or minimization at least—may have disposed him to seek national unity even at the expense of many black Americans whose votes were required for his election and reelection. For "unity," as a number of black intellectuals have pointed out, is too often pursued under the banner of color-blind universalism. Frederick Harris argues, for example, that "Proponents of 'race-neutral' universalism fail to acknowledge that policies that help everyone...are not enough to correct the deep-rooted persistence of racial inequality."[11] Harris traces Obama's public philosophy back to Bayard Rustin's essay "From Protest to Politics: The Future of the Civil Rights Movement," published in 1969. Repudiating Malcolm X's (and the late Du Bois's) call for independent black institutions and independent black politics focusing on the priorities of black Americans, Rustin advocated a "coalition" strategy. As Harris points out, this moment was a reprise of a long history of debate between advocates of assimilationist and black nationalist approaches to black politics in the United States; by turning away from what St. Louis congressman William Clay in 1972 called "the new politics of confrontation," Harris argues, black political leaders including Obama have short-changed their black constituents.

Harris's critique raises the much larger question of whether a public philosophy can in practice be "black and more than black"—since there is clearly a danger that, seeking to build coalitions that are *more than black*, such a strategy will wind up erasing the *black* itself. Indeed, this danger becomes especially clear when we take full account of the degree to which antiblack racism is being adopted by Asian, Latino, and other immigrants. As Thomas Sugrue writes (summarizing research conducted in Los Angeles by Lawrence Bobo and Camille Charles): "newly arriving Asian and Latin American immigrants—while they have a complicated relationship with the white majority—quickly define themselves as 'not black.' They are attracted to predominantly white neighborhoods and, like whites, view the presence of even a modest number of blacks as a sign that a neighborhood is troubled or in decline."[12] In short, we face the ironic possibility that, whatever the inspiring words and actions of black activists from Delany to Malcolm might mean in theory, in practice they will be warmly embraced to build a coalition of Americans who are united in their hostility to black Americans.

Yet as Douglass, Du Bois, Cooper, and Baldwin would argue, the danger to black politics does not lie in universalism per se but in the way it is imagined. All of them vigilantly espoused a universalism that is ever mindful of the particular. All of them insisted that conflict—a "politics of confrontation"—is an essential aspect of successful democratic practice. To the degree that what Harris calls the new "politics of [black] respectability" has failed to advance the real interests of most black Americans, the blame lies not with its commitment to enlargement per se but to the fantasy of enlargement without conflict. The thinkers I have focused on insist that enlargement and conflict are two sides of the same coin. To quote Anna Julia Cooper once again: "peace in a nation is the result of conflict." And of course the figures in this book would also urge us to consider that the best bulwark against spreading racism is a profound rethinking of our public philosophy, one that puts dignity on a level with freedom and equality; such a public philosophy would encourage citizens to admit to and accept the vulnerability of each person's dignity, thereby committing to nurturing and recognizing dignity with and for one another.

The Art of Citizenship

Perhaps because he was once a community organizer, Obama seems to share with Charles Chesnutt and some other black thinkers the view that democratic politics are necessarily personal politics. His behavior at least suggests that he feels that democratic leaders have a responsibility to model civic behavior that scrupulously respects the dignity of others. In David Remnick's account of Obama's election to the presidency of the *Harvard Law Review*, the crucial factor was Obama's relative popularity among conservative students. According to one of them: "At that point, the choice was among the liberals, and I recall that en masse the conservative vote swung over to Barack. There was a general sense that he didn't think we were evil people, only misguided people, and he would credit us for good faith and intelligence."[13]

Obama's refusal to "demonize" his opponents, and his determination to express respect for the patriotism of Republicans who have opposed him tooth and nail, are examples of the ways he consistently shoulders this responsibility to conduct politics through relationships. And when he wishes that he "could reach those voters directly," we hear his belief that personal, face-to-face encounters are where democracy really comes into being and flourishes. We hear this belief also when Obama speaks about the importance of "empathy" to democratic citizenship. In his speech at the Ebenezer Baptist Church commemorating King, for example, he spoke of the nation's "empathy deficit": "I'm talking about an empathy deficit, the inability to recognize ourselves in one another, to understand that we are our brother's keeper and our sister's keeper, that in the words of Dr. King, 'We are all tied together in a single garment of destiny.' " In the same speech, Obama also touched on the importance of "recognition." He quoted an "old black man" saying, "I am here because of Ashley. I am here because of this young girl, and the fact that she's willing to fight for what she believes in," and then he drew the lesson: "Now, by itself, that single moment of recognition between that young white girl and that old black man, that's not enough to change a country. By itself, it's not enough to give health care to the sick or jobs to the jobless or education to our children, but it is where we begin."

Moreover, when speaking of the value of empathy and recognition to democracy, Obama sometimes even registers the crucial complexities that Chesnutt, Larsen, and Baldwin perceived and articulated. "Of course, true unity cannot be so easily purchased," he observes in the same speech. "It starts with a change in attitudes. It starts with changing our hearts, and changing our minds, broadening our spirit. It's not easy to stand in somebody else's shoes. It's not easy to see past our own differences. We've all encountered this in our own lives." In Obama's phrase "broadening our spirit," we hear distinct echoes of all the figures I have discussed. We catch echoes of Larsen and of Baldwin especially when he acknowledges that "It's not easy to stand in somebody else's shoes. It's not easy to see past our own differences." But in a move that indicates just how difficult Obama's moment is, he goes on to say that our differences have been exaggerated, and that as a nation we have more in common than we often suppose.

Worldly Citizenship

Like Du Bois, Douglass, Baldwin, and many other black American writers and intellectuals, Obama has spent significant time living abroad and seeing the United States from the international perspective such experience provides. And like a number of them, he seems to believe in a modified version of the myth of American exceptionalism: the United States is indeed special because it has a unique historical commitment to democratic ideals, but this does not mean that the United States has a proprietary relation to those ideals or a "mission" to promote them around the globe. In his Nobel Prize acceptance speech, he remarks:

> Whatever mistakes we have made, the plain fact is this: The United States of America has helped underwrite global security for more than six decades with the blood of our citizens and the strength of our arms. The service and sacrifice of our men and women in uniform has promoted peace and prosperity from Germany to Korea, and enabled democracy to take hold in places like the Balkans. We have borne this burden not because we seek to impose our will.

Aside from his mention of "mistakes," these words sounds much like the mainstream tradition of American exceptionalism. But Obama gives this a subtle, unmistakably worldly twist when he goes on to say: "We have done so out of enlightened self-interest—because we seek a better future for our children and grandchildren, and we believe that their lives will be better if others' children and grandchildren can live in freedom and prosperity." Here Obama is most obviously trying to span the poles of the debate over realism versus idealism in US foreign policy: the United States does not act in the world for purely idealistic reasons; rather, it promotes its ideals in part because this is a practical, realistic thing to do. At the same time, however, he is quietly reinterpreting the idea of American exceptionalism, taking it out of its mythical frame and locating it in a more grounded, and honest, history.

In his 2009 West Point speech, Obama drew another subtle distinction between standard American exceptionalism and his own version of it when he used the phrase "claimed by people" instead of, say, "adopted by" or "given to" them:

> But this nation was founded upon a different notion. We believe "that all men are created equal, that they are endowed by their Creator with

certain unalienable rights, that among these are life, liberty and the pursuit of happiness." And that truth has bound us together, a nation populated by people from around the globe, enduring hardship and achieving greatness as one people. And that belief is as true today as it was 200 years ago. It is a belief that has been *claimed by people* of every race and religion in every region of the world.[14]

Obama's phrasing is subtly but importantly different from, say, President George W. Bush's words in his 2003 State of the Union Address: "Our Founders dedicated this country to the cause of human dignity—the rights of every person and the possibilities of every life. This conviction *leads us into* the world to help the afflicted, and defend the peace, and confound the designs of evil men." It is even more strikingly different from the wording of Bush's 2004 address:

> America is a Nation with a mission, and that mission comes from our most basic beliefs. We have no desire to dominate, no ambitions of empire. Our aim is a democratic peace—a peace founded upon the dignity and rights of every man and woman. America acts in this cause with friends and allies at our side, yet we understand our special calling: This great Republic will lead the cause of freedom.[15]

There is a crucial distinction between other countries and people in other countries *claiming* for themselves the belief that "all men are created equal end endowed with certain inalienable rights" and the United States believing that it has a "mission" or "special calling" to lead the rest of the world in "the cause of freedom." And where Bush took for granted that the United States was already a stellar upholder of these beliefs, Obama followed in the footsteps of many other black thinkers by stating instead that the United States has some work to do:

> And so a fundamental part of our strategy for our security has to be America's support for those universal rights that formed the creed of our founding. And we will promote these values above all by living them—through our fidelity to the rule of law and our Constitution, even when it's hard; even when we're being attacked; even when we're in the midst of war.

Faith and Democratic Pluralism

Finally, Obama has been cautious and ambiguous in expressing what he thinks about the place of faith in a democratic culture, but on the whole he subscribes to a vision that closely resembles that of Du Bois, Cooper, and the other figures in this book. On the one hand, he firmly criticizes "liberals who dismiss religion in the public square as inherently irrational or intolerant, insisting on a caricature of religious Americans that paints them as fanatical, or thinking that the very word 'Christian' describes one's political opponents, not people of faith."[16] Indeed, he has gone out of his way to insist that religious beliefs have sometimes played an important role in pushing US democracy toward justice for all of its citizens: "[I]t has not always been the pragmatist, the voice of reason, or the force of compromise, that has created the conditions for liberty. The hard cold facts remind me that it was unbending idealists...who recognized power would concede nothing without a fight. It was the wild-eyed prophecies of John Brown, his willingness to spill blood and not just words on behalf of his visions, that helped force the issue of a nation half slave and half free" (*Audacity*, 97). Yet at the same time, Obama's idealism (like that of the other figures I have focused on) has a sharp sense of its fallibility, as when he writes: "I must admit that I may have been infected with society's prejudices and predilections and attributed them to God; that Jesus' call to love one another might demand a different conclusion; and that in years hence I may be seen as someone who was on the wrong side of history. I don't believe such doubts make me a bad Christian. I believe they make me human, limited in my understandings of God's purpose and therefore prone to sin" (*Audacity*, 223–24).

Kloppenberg argues that Obama's understanding of the place of faith in a pluralistic, democratic society is essentially that of John Rawls, and I think he's correct. He points out, for example, that Obama "comes close to paraphrasing the language of [Rawls's] *Political Liberalism*" when he says, "What our deliberative, pluralistic democracy does demand is that the religiously motivated translate their concerns into universal, rather than religion-specific, values....If I want others to listen to me, then I have to explain why abortion violates some principle that is accessible to people of all faiths including those with no faith at all" (219). As we have seen, many black Americans who have reflected on democracy do indeed believe that there are "universal" truths, and that some of these are given expression in our founding documents. But most of the figures in this constellation of black thought would be profoundly skeptical of the translation process Obama calls for. Their route to pluralism does *not* lie through the mythical place where religion-specific values take universal form and where "people of all faiths, including people with no faith" can miraculously see these values the same way. It lies instead through the collective recognition of our fallibility, our sense that these truths are by definition beyond what any person or historical moment can fully and finally articulate. Although Obama does acknowledge his own fallibility, he seems unaware that it offers a fundamentally different—and better—strategy than translation for reconciling faith with democratic pluralism. This is unfortunate. As Charlton Copeland writes at the conclusion of his thoughtful analysis of Obama's faith politics: "Because of the possibility that there is something valuable in the voices of religiously motivated citizens that is lost in translation, and because there exists within at least some religious traditions resources for the development of virtues that support engagement in a plural democratic culture, we can only hope that Barack Obama will lend his distinct, untranslated voice to this conversation."[17]

Obama is surely correct when he says that if progressives "truly hope to speak to people where they're at—to communicate our hopes and values in a way that's relevant to their own—then...we cannot abandon the field of religious discourse."[18] And like a number of other black activists, he emphasizes that faith is not merely a support for struggle or a means to an end: it is, rather, the impulse from which the struggle arises and the energy that sustains it: "In the history of these struggles [for freedom and human rights], I was able to see faith as more than just a comfort to the weary or a hedge against death; rather, it was an active, palpable agent in the world" (*Audacity*, 207). Yet from the perspective of some of the writers we have been reading, Obama may not be stating the case clearly enough here: faith for them was indeed an "agent," but it was also a state of perplexity and doubt, always aware of its own contingency and fallibility.

The Moment We're In

Of course, in assessing Obama's political words and deeds in the light of the black thought I have described in this book, we must always bear in mind that his positions reflect his analysis of political realities, not his theory of democracy. His rootedness in a standpoint, in his time and place, predisposes him to be especially sensitive to the temporal frame of democratic action: this moment, this now. As Manning Marable points out, in the famous speech on race in Philadelphia, Obama did not repudiate Reverend Jeremiah Wright's anger so much as argue that this was not the *right time* for its expression. Indeed, he walked a very fine line: "Obama reminded white

Americans that 'so many of the disparities that exist in the African-American community today can be directly traced to inequalities passed on from an earlier generation that suffered under the brutal legacy of slavery' and Jim Crow segregation. But he also acknowledged the anger and alienation of poor and working-class whites, people who do not live especially privileged lives, and who feel unfairly victimized by policies like affirmative action. Obama criticized Reverend Wright's statements as 'not only wrong but divisive, at a time when we need unity; racially charged at a time when we need to come together to solve a set of monumental problems…that are neither black or white or Latino or Asian, but rather problems that confront us all.'"[19]

Obama has made quite clear why he believes that political conflict today is *not* "healthy, stimulating, and progressive" but degraded, distracting, and destructive. He believes that the decline of political discourse in our time has both exaggerated and trivialized our conflicts, leading many of us to wonder whether they are in fact "radically opposing" or just Punch and Judy puppets acting out a false drama controlled by a single pair of hands behind the scenes. Obama long ago came to the conclusion that "politics could be different, and that the voters wanted something different; that they were tired of distortion, name-calling, and sound-bite solutions to complicated problems; that if I could reach those voters directly, frame the issues as I felt them, explain the choices in as truthful a fashion as I knew how, then the people's instincts for fair play and common sense would bring them around" (*Audacity*, 17–18). This is why he has committed himself to fundamentally re-imagining, or reframing, our current democratic politics. This is why, as Gene Andrew Jarrett observes, Obama's account of US history "recasts social conflict as the growing pains of a promising nation."[20]

Whether or not we agree with his assessment and strategy, we should explore their deep sources. In *The Audacity of Hope*, Obama explicitly argues that the old alignments, the old sides, no longer represent the on-the-ground political needs of the people or, for that matter, their deepest political differences. Responding to those who have argued that the Democratic Party should adopt the Republicans' no-holds-barred approach to democratic politics, he writes: "Ultimately…I believe any attempt by Democrats to pursue a more sharply partisan and ideological strategy misapprehends the moment we're in. I am convinced that whenever we exaggerate or demonize, oversimplify or overstate our case, we lose. Whenever we dumb down the political debate, we lose" (*Audacity*, 39–40). This commitment to reframing raises an unprecedented question about presidential leadership. To my knowledge, no president before Obama has sought to lead in quite this way. Obama's is a bolder political commitment, as radical in its own way—*more* radical, I would say—than the politics proposed and practiced by many self-styled radicals on both the left and the right.

However, after witnessing the first term of his presidency, one is compelled to ask whether his posture really *is* leadership. Even if it makes conceptual sense, does it make political sense? Americans want to know what a president "stands for," and many now perceive him as not standing for anything because standing for a "new way of doing politics" is just too abstract. Leaders by definition lead in a particular direction; they lead the march toward an objective—toward more jobs, for example. Political leaders choose sides, and they fight for one side against the other.

Whether Obama turns out to be right or wrong, I suspect that the figures we have focused on in this book would understand his approach to democratic politics—but in the last analysis reject it. They would understand and empathize because, as we have seen, they were so profoundly aware that truly effective democratic politics requires us to reimagine democracy's borders and to keep rethinking who or what is represented in our policies and in our debates so we can also perceive who or what is being left out. Obama's willingness to reject the givens and to reimagine the very framework of politics is an expression of this black radical perspective. On the other hand, most of the black American writers and activists we have heard in this book would be sharply critical of Obama's unselfconscious use of a binary to structure his analysis of the present moment. Obama writes:

> For it's precisely the pursuit of ideological purity, the rigid orthodoxy and the sheer predictability of our current political debate, that keeps us from finding new ways to meet the challenges we face as a nation. It's what keeps us locked in "either/or" thinking.... What's needed is a broad majority of Americans—Democrats, Republicans, and independents of goodwill—who are reengaged in the project of national renewal, and who see their own self-interest as inextricably linked to the interests of others. (39–40)

Here, again, we catch distinct echoes of Douglass, Cooper, and Du Bois when Obama contrasts rigidity with flexibility, and narrow partisanship with a broad majority; we hear it, too, when Obama rejects "'either/or' thinking" and defines "self-interest" as being "linked to the interests of others." Unfortunately, however, some "either/or" thinking is at work in Obama's own words. He claims that Americans face a choice: they can either "exaggerate" and "demonize" *or* transcend the fray by being reasonable and moderate; they can either "oversimplify" and "overstate," or they can pull together in a vast embrace of national unity, overcoming their differences in a "common dream" (*Audacity*, 40). What's missing here is the possibility that some conflicts are inevitable, and that some partisan positions are much more defensible than others and require us to *fight* for them. What's left out as well is the possibility that passionate and aggressive partisan politics need not oversimplify and overstate, or demonize and exaggerate.

Where, then, does Obama stand with regard to the figures we have been reading in this book? He seems farthest from them when we contrast his pursuit of unity with their appreciation of indignation and the "collaborative antagonism" of democracy. He seems closest to them in his pursuit of enlargement, his willingness to sustain irreconcilables in tension with each other, and in his understanding of the partiality and fallibility of all forms of faith. Above all, in adapting to the exigencies of the present moment, he is faithful to these figures' radical realism—their understanding of themselves as situated citizens and activists. The black writers, thinkers, and activists we have been reading never wished to develop a self-consistent *theory* of democracy. Guided only by what Douglass called "a fixed principle of honesty," they undertook an improvisational, open-ended re-creation of democracy. They did not presume to stand outside experience, nor to hold their actions accountable to any political philosophy.

Today, many of those on the left especially might learn from them how to practice a politics of realism rather than holding Obama to a standard of ideological purity and consistency that no working politician could hope to meet.[21] They were deeply committed to acting in the present moment, yet they sought new ways of imagining democracy; they could feel themselves to be chained to the "ringbolt" of eternal truths, yet they knew that the meaning of these truths must be continually revised in the light of history's demands. What Obama most deeply shares with Douglass, Cooper, Du Bois, Baldwin, Ellison, King, and Malcolm is just this: his willingness to imagine a new kind of politics shaped by a particular understanding of the moment we're in.

A Coda for My Colleagues

FUSING CRITIQUE AND VISION

THE ARGUMENT OF this book has been straightforward: that some black American thinkers offer insights into the theory and practice of democracy around which to build a new and more effective public philosophy for the twenty-first century. In searching for a word to describe what these insights have done and might yet do for democracy, I have rejected "renewal" because it suggests a return to and dusting off of what US democracy has always already been. Even the word "reconstruction," which comes to hand with Du Bois's blessings, often implies something like "renovation." But the insights into US democracy that I find in the works of some black American writers and activists were actually gained from a standpoint not available to most white Americans. These figures observed from the perspective of those who have lived and thought as raced bodies within conditions of a radical unfreedom which white Americans have never experienced. (Du Bois called these conditions the "ground of the disadvantage.")[1]

Conversely, the tradition of thought and theorizing about democracy with which we are most familiar—whether it flows from Aristotle, Machiavelli, Hobbes, Rousseau, Locke, Hegel, Jefferson, Hamilton, Marx, Croly, Dewey, Rawls, or Ranciere—has been penned by persons who could and did take their existential and even political freedom for granted. With the exception of Dewey, all of these also mistakenly assumed that their thinking was autonomous and independent of their body. For any of them to see what freedom and democracy might look like from the standpoint of the ineluctably embodied and unfree would be to see the far side of the moon. Neither renewal nor reconstruction nor reimagining—no version of "re" anything—quite does justice to the original and particular that is inherent in this standpoint. And it was from this standpoint, and with full self-awareness of it, that Frederick Douglass declared: "There are times in the experience of almost every community when the humblest member thereof may properly presume to teach."[2]

Taken seriously, these words suggest that citizens of a democracy should learn to be attentive to what the "humblest" among them has to say. They must continually learn and relearn what their democracy is and how they should practice democratic citizenship. The reasons US citizens should do so are not hard to find. For one thing, as the voices in this book have repeatedly testified, US democracy was flawed from the outset. Slavery was written into the Constitution. So was gender inequality. For another, even if by some miracle the nation's founding documents had been perfect in all respects, the mere passage of time would eventually require citizens to change them. Democracy, as John Lewis has observed, is a "work in progress." Because the world changes, our public philosophy of democracy must change. Because our political principles live in history, we must respond to history by reinterpreting or reimagining their meaning. Finally, a majoritarian democracy always has winners and losers, and there is always a great danger that the winners will form a permanent league against the losers. "The hard truth of democracy," writes Danielle Allen, "is that some citizens are always giving things up for others. Only vigorous forms of citizenship can give a polity the resources to deal with the inevitable problem of sacrifice."[3] Therefore, to preserve their democracy, all citizens must cultivate the practice of listening to what comes from the losing side, since that is where the most powerfully democratic energies emerge. These energies revive democracy for all citizens. Robin D. G. Kelley has put it this way: "the marginal and excluded have done the most to make democracy work in America." And they do not merely achieve democracy as it has always been conceived; they produce democracy in new and hitherto unimagined forms: "Social movements generate new knowledge, new theories, new questions. The most radical ideas often grow out of a concrete intellectual engagement with the problems of aggrieved populations confronting systems of oppression."[4]

Americans have always suspected—and often repressed—these truths about democracy's origins and instability. In Benjamin Hale's 1835 textbook, *Familiar Conversations upon the Constitution of the United States Designed for the Use of Common Schools*, a father tries to impart this notion to his son. When he asks his son what he knows about the Constitution, the boy answers (as many radical conservatives would answer today): "I know it was to make people think and act alike." To this the father replies: "You are very nearly correct, my son; all people, you know are naturally prone to error, and oftentimes disposed to think differently from their friends on the same subject;—hence, you see, it was necessary to have some fixed law, by which to be governed, in order to promote harmony and good feeling, and for this purpose the Constitution was made." The distinction here is subtle but crucial: it is between a document that enforces uniformity and a document that tries to reconcile and harmonize inevitable differences. Later, the father and son discuss the process by which the purportedly "fixed law" of the Constitution might be changed by amendment. Once again, the boy expresses a juvenile wish for a settled order in which consensus has been established on a permanent basis: "I don't see how [the Constitution] can be altered for the better," he declares. To which the father replies with a gentleness that cannot conceal the unsettling flux of the democratic order: "There is scarcely a production of any kind, my child, but what may be improved in some shape."[5]

Most black Americans living in the United States at the time that book was published would have needed no such instruction as Hale offered his readers. They knew firsthand just how much US democracy needed to be improved, and some believed that black Americans would take the lead in bringing about such improvement. Consider, for example, a speech titled "The Destiny of the People of Color," delivered in January 1841 by Dr. James McCune Smith, the nation's first black physician and a noted abolitionist and intellectual. To many in his mainly black audience, the destiny of black Americans in the United States looked grim. In his own state of New York, black Americans had had their voting rights curtailed since 1827. South of the Mason-Dixon line, the slavery system was stronger than ever. And throughout the North the popularity of the American Colonization Society suggested that the probable future of free blacks would be unending suppression by white racism, voluntary emigration, or forced expatriation and resettlement on the western shores of Africa.

Smith offered a remarkable prediction. Contrasting the destiny of enslaved black Americans with the history of the once-enslaved Jews who had been led by Moses out of Pharaoh's Egypt, Smith asserted that the distinctive purpose of America's people of color was to remain in the land of their bondage in order to "bring liberty to" and "purify" it: "By remaining upon the scene of our oppression, we...proclaim to the oppressed few, 'Ubi patria, ibi libertas,' Where our country is, there shall Liberty dwell!.... One law then, at least, we are by our position destined to exhibit; and that is that the enslaved should remain upon the soil, and amid the institutions which enthrall them in order to bring liberty to the one by purifying the other."[6]

Smith went on to explain that this liberation and purification of the United States would occur primarily through what he called black "oratory."

That word had a much wider range of signification in the mid-nineteenth century than it does today, with one of its meanings connoting something like "public philosophy"—the rhetoric, the beliefs, and the terminology through which citizens understand the meaning of their democracy. Smith argued that "since oratory can only spring from honest efforts on behalf of the RIGHT, such will of necessity arise amid our struggle—no holiday speeches in which shall be uttered eloquent falsehoods, garnished untruths, and hollow boastings of a state of things which exist only in the imagination; but on the contrary, we shall utter the earnest pleadings of down trodden humanity seeking security from wrongs too long inflicted, no longer to be endured" (59). He suggested, in short, that the true oratory produced by black advocates of black Americans' rights would renovate the republic and make real its democratic principles.[7]

That black Americans could have anything of note to contribute to a public philosophy of democracy would have struck many of Smith's white contemporaries as most unlikely; after all, the vast majority of black Americans were enslaved, and those who were technically "free" were barred by custom and legislation from most of the benefits of democratic citizenship. What could black Americans know about democracy that could be of any use to enfranchised white citizens? As we have seen, Frederick Douglass mocked such skepticism in his autobiography, *My Bondage and My Freedom*, where he reports that his "American friends looked at [him] with astonishment" when he told them of his plans to become an editor: "A slave, brought up in the very depths of ignorance, assuming to instruct the highly civilized people of the north in the principles of liberty, justice, and humanity! The thing looked absurd!" Indeed it did—to them.[8]

I want to conclude this book by observing something important about the nature of the instruction Douglass and Smith had in mind, and that all of the figures I discuss here undertook: It was a fusion of critical analysis and vision. It was committed to working within history, and it was, in that sense, rigorously historicist; yet at the same time it drew inspiration and guidance from ideas, principles, and visions that were understood to be outside history, either because they were eternal or because they beckoned from a future not yet achieved and not yet in history. As Bernard Boxhill has succinctly put it: "Black American philosophy and activism has as its final goal the fulfillment of the hope that is inherent in true democracy—not a despair for the consequences of the contradictions and absurdities that yet must be fully overcome."[9]

The two core insights into democracy that appear repeatedly in the words and writings I have focused on are themselves a fusion of critique and vision. The first, as we have seen, is a radical skepticism toward representation itself: no one thing or idea person can really "stand for" or represent another. To use the terms of a position political theorists will associate with Jacques Ranciere, but which certainly antedates him: no part should be mistaken for, or claim to be, the whole. As we have seen Du Bois put the matter: "To no one type of mind is it given to discern the totality of the Truth." This insight quickly constellated itself with a second: that democracy is about conflict and struggle—a never-ending struggle of enlargement, through which what has claimed to be *all* of the whole is pressured to recognize itself as being, in fact, merely a *part* of it. And Cooper reminds us: "Progressive peace in a nation is the result of conflict; and conflict, such as is healthy, stimulating, and progressive, is produced through the co-existence of radically opposing or racially different elements." To use the term preferred by political theorists today: this vision of democracy is *agonistic*.

Consider for a moment the relation of these two insights to critique and vision. The black thinkers I focus on were skeptical of representation for a plainly historical, down-to-earth, empirical reason: they themselves and all other black Americans had been denied representation. Whites claiming to be the whole of the democratic polis had pushed blacks out. Only a determined war of critique—critique aimed at exposing the blindness that sustained and the hypocrisies that characterized whites' imagination of the whole—could crack that structure open and allow enlargement. This is why, as Gene Andrew Jarrett has argued, "African-American literature has been a tool of social change, addressing or redressing the attitudes of readers and stimulating social action" insofar as it has sought corrected and fuller representation of black Americans.[10] Yet at the same time, imagination, or vision, was equally indispensable. The very history that had consolidated itself as a seemingly permanent structure of domination and injustice did not within itself provide the resources required to bring it to an end. The ideology constructed to sustain that structure had assiduously made unthinkable and unrepresentable everything that threatened it, and these remainders could be retrieved only by going outside or around history, by imagining possibilities that had been forgotten or had not yet been born. Imagination is by definition both skeptical of representation *and* a means of re-presentation; this is what Wolin means when he says that it strives toward a "corrected fullness."[11]

Yet as I write, many colleagues in my home discipline of literary and cultural studies have come to believe that imagination is just a myth or fantasy. Because an earlier generation of critics writing seventy years ago seemed to depoliticize the work of criticism by banishing history from it, my generation has committed itself to bringing history back in. Many of us are now convinced that we can think only what our history has made possible, and that the very word *imagination* is therefore naive, misleading, and even dangerous—promising as it seems to an escape from history that simply is not possible. Consequently, literary and cultural studies today are energized by a largely—almost exclusively—critical energy. For thirty or more years now, these fields have been motivated mainly by an obligation to critique the world as it is, to question authority, to demystify ideology, and to train students in critical thinking. All this is well and good. All this is indispensable.

But what about imagination? What about vision? Can we deny that behind each and every one of our critiques stands a vision of a better alternative that we hold to implicitly—and seldom make explicit? Isn't it true that every demystification of what *has* been is meaningful only because it serves the possibility of what might *yet* be? What will be the long-run effect of teaching generation after generation of students to see through the veil of ideology to the ugly injustices it hides—if we do not also inspire them to seek some better future, something that has not-yet-been, something that lies outside history? And how can we and our students struggle to achieve that vision if we are not motivated by a sincere conviction that our beliefs and principles are right? Recall Anna Julia Cooper's argument that the struggle against injustice cannot be waged "in a primarily skeptical spirit. At such times most of all, do men need to be anchored to what they *feel* to be eternal verities."[12]

Surely there's a challenge here to our dictum that we must "always historicize" when we take it to mean—as we usually do—that we must *only* historicize. We make this mistake, I believe, because we strive for a kind of logical consistency that is fine thing in itself, but that is also the "hobgoblin" Emerson warned against when it becomes a rigid orthodoxy we can't shake free of. The figures in this book would urge us instead to hold the contraries of the historical and the nonhistorical in tension with each other. Douglass, as we have seen, addressed this problem head-on, arguing that true consistency is not mathematical but ethical. And Cooper likewise addressed our worry that faith in possibilities outside of history would instantly turn us into narrow-minded, antipluralistic fanatics: "I do not mean by faith the holding of correct views and unimpeachable opinions on mooted questions, merely; nor do I understand it to be the ability to forge cast-iron formulas and dub them TRUTH. For while I do not deny that absolute and eternal truth *is*,—still truth must be infinite, and as incapable as infinite space, of being encompassed and confined by one age or nation, sect or country—much less by one little creature's finite brain."

Only imagination and vision allow us to apprehend and stand in relation to what is larger than—and cannot be grasped or confined by—our little, finite brains. Political theorists have few qualms about bodying forth their visions in frankly normative arguments. Why are we in cultural and literary studies so reluctant to do likewise and make explicit our own visionary commitments? If imagination is indispensable to the practice of democratic citizenship and to political theory, can it be any *less* to those who take works of the imagination to be their primary objects of study?[13]

The voices in this book knew well that democracy requires critical thinking, for critique is an expression of the conflict that is inevitable within, and indispensable to, democracy. Yet they also knew that critique alone is not enough. They knew that we must do more than exhaustively research this democracy's many failings and shortcomings. This "more" is a radical openness to what is implied by the contingency of our own standpoint: that there is always something that we do not yet know, and that we should know, but that we have no means to know as yet. Our only approach to it, therefore, is through our imagination. As Danielle Allen writes, "democratic peoples need metaphors to make 'the people, the body of which they are a part, conceivable to themselves.... Metaphors, no less than institutions, are vehicles for the imagination, and indeed are central to securing 'the people' for democratic life. In short, citizens can explain their role in democracy only by expending significant conceptual and imaginative labor to make themselves a part of an invisible whole."[14]

There are tongues in trees, sermons in stone, and books in the running brooks! declared Frederick Douglass. When we hear these words today, we are astonished by their commitment to metaphor—and our first impulse is to think that they are *only* or excessively metaphorical. But as he observed from the vantage point he occupied, Douglass knew well that *all* words are metaphors, placeholders, stepping stones. Freedom. Equality. Dignity. Democracy: all these words are as metaphorical as Douglass's, their meaning to be given substance and precision only by more metaphors, and so on and so on in infinite linguistic regress. Poets understand this. So do activists. One day we may all stand in a democracy where citizens know to sustain each others' dignity, not just to respect each others' rights; to be citizens of their world, not just their nation; and to hold to a conception of faith that strengthens pluralism instead of undercutting it. But to get there, we will have to become poets as well as critics, practicing vision as well as critique.

Notes

INTRODUCTION

1. W. E. B. Du Bois, *A World Search for Democracy* (unpublished manuscript), 1. In W. E. B. Du Bois Papers, W. E. B. Du Bois Library, University of Massachusetts, p. 1. Du Bois's hopes for the self-reforming possibilities of US democracy had at this time ebbed almost to their lowest point. Compare, for example, his optimism in 1915, when he described the new journal the *Crisis* as a fulfillment of "the great ideal of establishing in the United States a dignified and authoritative organ of public opinion which should stand for the fundamental principles of American democracy.'" Quoted in George Hutchinson, *The Harlem Renaissance in Black and White* (Cambridge: Harvard University Press, 1995), 145.
2. W. E. B. Du Bois, *The Souls of Black Folk* (New York: Penguin, 1989), 11.
3. This may the moment to underscore that I am writing neither a comprehensive history nor a systematic theory of this body of black democratic thought. Nor do I mean to imply that this thought is never "radical" in the Marxist sense of that word. On the contrary, I have profited greatly from, among other scholars, Cedric Robinson and Robin D. G. Kelley. But I do not believe that at this moment in US history that kind of black radicalism can gain much traction in US politics, much less that it can help give a progressive shape to US public philosophy in ways that counter the efforts of the radical Right. I am well aware also that most of the individual black thinkers I discuss here—e.g., Douglass, Du Bois, Baldwin, and Malcolm X—radically changed their minds more than once about the nature and prospects of US democracy. So when I quote their words as they bear upon a particular problem of democracy, I do not mean to imply that those words are representative of the entirety of their views over the course of their careers. To argue that what Du Bois said at a particular moment about democracy is especially useful today is not to claim that that moment is especially representative of his thinking.

4. It is certainly true that, as Bernard Boxhill (among many others) has written, "The history of African American thought can be divided onto two traditions—the assimilationist and the separatist" (119). We should bear in mind, however, that this schema is a heuristic; as Boxhill's phrase "can be divided" indicates, we are often talking about a single field of thought that has two poles—poles which many black thinkers hold in tension with each other, or move back and forth between, rather than committing absolutely to one or the other. As Eric J. Sundquist writes, we should attend rather to "the relationship of two conflicting yet coalescing cultural traditions—'American' and 'African,' to use for the moment an inadequate shorthand—that together have produced a sustained tradition of the most significant literature of race in America"—and not just of "race" but, as this book will argue, of black democratic political thought as well. "Two Traditions of African American Practical Philosophy," *Philosophical Forum* 24, nos. 1–3 (1992-93), 119; Eric J. Sundquist, *To Wake the Nations: Race in the Making of American Literature* (Cambridge: Harvard University Press, 1993), 6.

5. "Racial liberalism, or white liberalism, is the actual liberalism that has been historically dominant since modernity: a liberal theory whose terms originally restricted full personhood to whites (or, more accurate, white men) and relegated nonwhites to an inferior category, so that its schedule of rights and prescriptions for justice were all color-coded." Charles W. Mills, "Racial Liberalism," *PMLA* 123, no. 5 (2008), 1382. Mills's analysis of the covert racial underpinnings of liberal thought, including both the contractarian and communitarian poles thereof, follows from his analysis of "the racial contract."

6. Richard Iton, *In Search of the Black Fantastic: Politics and Popular Culture in the Post-Civil Rights Era* (New York: Oxford University Press, 2008), 31, 32, and *passim*.

7. African American political thought can be seen as pursuing two complementary lines of inquiry. One is concerned primarily with what political theorist Robert Gooding-Williams calls "black politics," which he defines as any answer to the question, "What kind of politics should African Americans conduct to counter white supremacy?" The second grows out of the first. As African American thought has analyzed the reasons and the means by which blacks have been oppressed by white racism and excluded from US democracy, it has developed a systemic analysis of the failures of the dominant political and social structures per se. As philosopher Charles Mills writes, black political thought and philosophy are also "a (partially) internalist [immanent] critique of the dominant culture by those who accept many of the culture's principles but are excluded from them. In large measure, this critique has involved telling white people things that they do not know and do not want to know, the main one being that...the local reality in which whites are at home is only a non-representative part of the larger whole." Mills's last point is the one from which this book begins. Robert Gooding-Williams, *In the Shadow of Du Bois: Afro-Modern Political Thought in America* (Cambridge: Harvard University Press, 2009), 1. Charles W. Mills, *Blackness Visible: Essays on Philosophy and Race* (Ithaca, N.Y.: Cornell University Press, 1998), 5–6.

8. Leonard Harris, ed., *Philosophy Born of Struggle: Anthology of Afro-American Philosophy from 1917* (Dubuque, Iowa: Kendall Publishers, 1983). Patricia Hill Collins, "Learning from the Outsider Within: The Sociological Significance of Black Feminist Thought," *Social Problems* 33, no. 6 (1986), S16; George Yancy, "African-American Philosophy: Through the Lens of Socio-Existential Struggle," *Philosophy & Social Criticism* 37, no. 5 (2011), 552. Bernard Boxhill formulated an early version of this view of black American philosophy, one that emphasized its commitment to human rather than system-centered nature and its commitment to change. See "Frederick Douglass: The Black Philosopher in the United States: A Commentary," in Leonard Harris, ed., *Philosophy Born of Struggle*, 1–8.

9. Frederick Douglass, *Life and Times*, in *Autobiographies* (New York: Library of America, 1994), 978.

10. To readers who may worry that I am misappropriating an essentially radical tradition of critical thought to serve the center, I emphasize again that the thinkers in this book didn't want merely to occupy the old center, they wanted to imagine a new one. They are radical in their own way, even if it is not instantly recognizable to conventional political theory.

11. Danielle S. Allen, *Talking to Strangers: Anxieties of Citizenship since "Brown v Board of Education"* (Chicago: University of Chicago Press, 2004); Lawrie Balfour, *The Evidence of Things Not Said: James Baldwin and the Promise of American Democracy* (Ithaca, N.Y.: Cornell University Press, 2001) and *Democracy's Reconstruction: Thinking Politically with W.E.B. Du Bois* (New York: Oxford University Press, 2011); Gregg Crane, *Race, Citizenship, and Law in American Literature* (Cambridge: Cambridge University Press, 2002); Jason Frank, *Constituent Moments: Enacting the People in Postrevolutionary America* (Durham: Duke University Press, 2010); Robert Gooding-Willliams, *Look, A Negro! Philosophical Essays on Race, Culture* (New York: Routledge, 2005) and *Shadow of Du Bois*; Richard H. King, *Civil Rights and the Idea of Freedom* (New York: Oxford University Press, 1992); Ross Posnock, *Color and Culture: Black Writers and the Making of the Modern Intellectual* (Cambridge: Harvard University Press, 1998); Adolph Reed, *W. E. B. Du Bois and American Political Thought* (New York: Oxford University Press, 1997); George Shulman, *American Prophecy: Race and Redemption in American Political Culture* (Minneapolis: University of Minnesota Press, 2008); Jack Turner, "Awakening to Race: Ralph Ellison and Democratic Individuality," *Political Theory* 36, no. 5 (2008), 655–82.

12. Sheldon Wolin, *Politics and Vision: Continuity and Vision in Western Political Thought* (Boston: Little, Brown, 1960), 20. Moreover, as Judith Butler writes (in her account of Ernesto Laclau and Chantal Mouffe's work), "democratic politics are constituted through exclusions that return to haunt the politics predicated on their absence. That haunting becomes politically effective precisely in so far as the return of the excluded forces an expansion and re-articulation of the basic premises [*sic*] of democracy itself." Precisely because the excluded comes back as a haunting, we apprehend it most vividly through our imagination. Judith Butler, Ernesto Laclau,

and Slavoj Žižek, *Contingency, Hegemony, Universality: Contemporary Dialogues on the Left* (London: Verso, 2000), 11.

13. Martin Luther King, Jr. *A Testament of Hope: The Essential Writings and Speeches of Martin Luther King,Jr.*, ed. James M. Washngton (New York: HarperCollins, 1991), 217–18. Frederick Douglas, *Life and Writings*, ed. Philip S. Foner (New York: International Publishers, 1950), vol. 1, 366. This emphasis on the present moment as the privileged site of interpretation of the past (rather than, as historicism would have it, a text's moment of production) becomes for obvious reasons a staple of African American political imagination.

14. Michael J. Sandel, *Democracy's Discontent: America in Search of a Public Philosophy* (Cambridge: Harvard University Press, 1996), 4. Sheldon Wolin's term is "public discourse": "In large measure, collective identity is created by and perpetuated through public discourse. Public discourse consists of the vocabulary, ideologies, symbols, images, memories, and myths that have come to form the ways we think and talk about our political life." Sheldon Wolin, *The Presence of the Past, Essays on the State and the Constitution* (Baltimore: Johns Hopkins University Press, 1989), 9.

15. I am thinking here of such works as Robert Putnam, *Bowling Alone* (New York: Simon and Schuster, 2000); Robert Bellah et al., *Habits of the Heart: Individualism and Commitment in American Life* (Berkeley: University of California Press, 1985); Neil Jumonville and Kevin Mattson, eds., *Liberalism for a New Century* (Berkeley: University of California Press, 2007); Thomas Frank, *What's the Matter with Kansas: How Conservatives Won the Heart of America* (New York: Metropolitan Books, 2004).

16. James Bevel in Henry Hampton and Steve Fayer, eds., *Voices of Freedom: An Oral History of the Civil Rights Movement from the 1950s through the 1980s* (New York: Bantam Books, 1990), 172.

17. Their thinking anticipates and, to a remarkable degree, instantiates the thinking of Axel Honneth. See, for example, "Integrity and Disrespect: Principles of a Conception of Morality Based on the Theory of Recognition," *Political Theory* 20, no. 2 (1992), 187–201.

18. Charles W. Chesnutt, *Stories, Novels, and Essays* (New York: Library of America, 2002), 386.

19. David Roediger, *The Wages of Whiteness: Race and the Making of the American Working Class* (London: Verso, 1991).

20. Judith Shklar, *Redeeming American Political Thought* (Chicago: University of Chicago Press, 1998), 127. For a succinct summary of the tensions between democratic nation-states and global interconnectedness, see also David Held, "Democracy and the International Order," in Daniele Archibugo and David Held, eds., *Cosmopolitan Democracy: An Agenda for a New World Order* (Cambridge: Polity Press, 1995), 96–120. The persistence of this vexing question is what leads political theorist Seyla Benhabib to conclude that "the relationship between the spread of cosmopolitan norms and democratic self-determination is

fraught, both theoretically and politically." Benhabib, *Another Cosmopolitanism* (New York: Oxford University Press, 2006), 17. This chapter will also be draw heavily upon Joshua Cohen, ed., *For Love of Country: Debating the Limits of Patriotism—Martha C. Nussbaum with Respondents* (Boston: Beacon Press, 1996), and William Connolly, *Neuropolitics: Thinking, Culture, Speed* (Minneapolis: University of Minnesota Press, 2002).

21. Unfortunately, progressives on the left have had little to say about this challenge that is truly of use to a new public philosophy. At the more radical edge of the left, intellectuals have been engaged for nearly twenty years in a forceful critique not just of US empire but of the very concept of the nation state itself. As historically correct and conceptually coherent as this work may be, it does little to prepare US citizens for a new role in a world of partnerships—at least not in the near future, not now.

22. James Weldon Johnson, *Along This Way* in *Writings* (New York: Library of America, 2004), 529.

23. Michelle Anne Stephens, *Black Empire: The Masculine Global Imaginary of Caribbean Intellectuals in the United States, 1914–1962* (Durham: Duke University Press, 2005), 131. Stephens's argument is that some black travelers from the Caribbean developed a global conception of black American literature; likewise, some traveling black writers and activists developed a global conception of democratic citizenship.

24. Among philosophers and political theorists, the publication of John Rawls's *A Theory of Justice* (1971) is generally taken to mark the moment when liberalism committed itself exclusively to procedure and turned its back on questions of character, virtue, and the good. Already, however, a critical attack on liberalism was well under way, coming from feminist intellectuals such as Susan Okin and Cather MacKinnon, from social scientists influenced by Tocqueville such as Robert N. Bellah and Robert Putnam, and from historians who were excavating the Atlantic republican tradition's influence on the founders, such as Bernard Bailyn, Gordon Wood, and James T. Kloppenberg. Kloppenberg himself provides an elegant account of this multipronged critique of liberalism in *Reading Obama: Dreams, Hope, and the American Political Tradition* (Princeton: Princeton University Press, 2010), 85–149; see Stephen L. Carter in "Liberalism's Religion Problem," *First Things* 121 (March 2002), 21–32.

25. Anna Julia Cooper, *The Voice of Anna Julia Cooper*, Charles Lemert and Esme Bhan, eds. (Lanham, Md.: Rowman and Littlefield, 1998), 193.

26. See, for example, E. J. Dionne, *Souled Out: Reclaiming Faith and Politics after the Religious Right* (Princeton: Princeton University Press, 2008); Jim Wallis, *God's Politics: Why the Right Gets It Wrong and the Left Doesn't Get It* (San Francisco: HarperCollins, 2005); Sally Steenland, ed., *Debating the Divine: Religion in 21st Century American Democracy*, published by the Center for American Progress, 2008, http://www.americanprogress.org/wpcontent/uploads/issues/2008/06/pdf/debating_the_divine.pdf.

27. Du Bois, "Strategy of the Negro Vote," *Crisis* 40 (June 1933), 706. As he wrote to publisher Alfred Harcourt in a letter in which he proposed his (never to be completed) *A World Search for Democracy*: "I want to emphasize the fact that the fundamental differences between governments today are not differences between Democracy, Fascism, and Communism, but differences as to how far and in what way governments are going to attack the problem of work and wages and the distribution of wealth." February 11, 1937, in Herbert Aptheker, ed., *The Correspondence of W.E.B. Du Bois* (Amherst: University of Massachusetts Press 1973–78), vol. 2, p. 137.

28. Michael Hanchard, "Contours of Black Political Thought: An Introduction and Perspective," *Political Theory* 38, no. 4 (2009), 511.

29. In other words, I believe that black American political thought taken as a whole has within it more than one form of radicalism. The radicalism I discuss takes US constitutional democracy as its field of action and seeks not so much to overthrow it as to reinterpret it. It is *not* revolutionary if that means aiming to start over again from scratch, with a fundamentally different political order based on fundamentally different principles (as, for example, the Garrisonian abolitionists wished to do). But it is *radical* in the sense of aiming to shift the discussion of US democratic politics onto new ground. W. E. B. Du Bois, *The Souls of Black Folk* (New York: Penguin, 1989), 11; Williams, *Alchemy of Race and Rights*, 163; Thurgood Marshall, "Racial Justice and the Constitution: A View from the Bench," in John Hope Franklin and Genna Rae McNeil, eds., *African Americans and the Living Constitution* (Washington, D.C.: Smithsonian Institution Press, 1995), 317; Alain Locke, *The New Negro* (New York: Simon and Schuster, 1997), 7.

30. Toni Morrison, *Playing in the Dark: Whiteness and the Literary Imagination* (New York: Vintage Books, 1992). Morrison overturns the view that "traditional, canonical American literature is free of, uninformed and unshaped by the four-hundred year presence of Africans and then African Americans in the United States" (4–5). I am merely extending the reach of her argument from literature to public philosophy.

31. Quoted in The Rza, *The Tao of Wu* (New York: Riverhead Books, 2009), 147.

CHAPTER 1

1. Audre Lorde, "The Uses of Anger," *Women's Studies Quarterly* 9, no. 3 (1981), 7. Despite Lorde's forthright defense of black anger in 1981, serious discussion of it by political philosophers is rare.

2. Anne Valk and Leslie Brown, eds., *Living with Jim Crow: African American Women and Memories of the Segregated South* (New York: Palgrave Macmillan, 2010), 87.

3. Martha Nussbaum, *Hiding from Humanity: Disgust, Shame, and the Law* (Princeton: Princeton University Press, 2004), 99.

4. Douglass, *Autobiographies*, 343.

5. James Weldon Johnson, *Writings* (New York: Library of America, 2004), 281–82.

6. Pauli Murray, *Song in a Weary Throat: An American Pilgrimage* (New York: Harper and Row, 1987), 58.

7. Henry Bibb, *The Life and Times of Henry Bibb, An American Slave* (Madison: University of Wisconsin Press, 2001), 43.

8. William Craft, "Running a Thousand Miles for Freedom," in Arna Bontemps, ed., *Great Slave Narratives* (Boston: Beacon Press, 1969), 277.

9. James W. C. Pennington, *The Fugitive Blacksmith*, in Bontemps, *Great Slave Narratives*, 211.

10. James McCune Smith, introduction to *My Bondage and My Freedom*, in Douglass, *Autobiographies*, 127.

11. James Baldwin, "Stranger in the Village," in *Collected Essays*, 121.

12. Charles Mills makes the same point using different terms: "whites find it hard to understand the metaphysical *rage* and urgency permeating the non-Cartesian sums of those invisible sons and daughters who, since nobody knows their name, have to be the men who cry 'I am!' and the women who demand 'And ain't I a woman?'" (*Blackness Visible*, 9–10) (emphasis added)

13. W. E. B. Du Bois, *Souls of Black Folk*, in *Du Bois Reader*, 124. Malcolm X, *The Last Speeches*, Bruce Perry, ed. (New York: Pathfinder Books, 1989), 83.

14. Peter P. Hinks, ed., *David Walker's Appeal to the Colored Citizens of the World* (University Park: Pennsylvania State University Press, 2000), 12.

15. Denial of dignity is clearly distinguishable from domination, at least as that term has been understood (e.g., by Philip Pettit) as the ability to interfere with another on an arbitrary basis. When Olivia Cherry's employer pretends to forget her name, he is throwing no obstacle between her and her realization of her intentions. But he is certainly slighting her dignity. Likewise, when the police refuse to investigate adequately the death of Pauli Murray's father, they are reinforcing the attitude that black lives are less valuable than those of whites, and thus they are denying her father's dignity and that of her family and that of every other black American. Such denial may be an instrument, or means, of domination, but it is not conceptually identical to it. Philip Pettit, *Republicanism: A Theory of Freedom and Government* (Oxford: Oxford University Press, 1997).

16. As Charles Mills notes: "The denial of black existence is not individual, a refusal of recognition to one particular black for idiosyncratic reasons, but collective. It is not that blacks as a group do not exist because individual blacks do not exist, but rather than individual blacks do not exist because blacks as a group do not exist.... The refusal of this ontological elimination is an affirmation simultaneously of individual and group existence." This "refusal," I am suggesting, first comes into being as indignation, and what it affirms is dignity. Mills, *Blackness Visible*, 11.

17. Marilyn Richardson, ed., *Maria Stewart: America's First Black Woman Political Writer. Essays and Speeches* (Bloomington: Indiana University. Press, 1987), 56–57.

18. Anna Julia Cooper, *The Voice of Anna Julia Cooper*, 122, 128.

19. Ralph Ellison, *Going to the Territory* (New York: Vintage Books, 1995), 124.

20. Ellison, *Going to the Territory*, 7.

21. This self-oppositional quality is not quite captured by Du Bois's term "double-consciousness," for it is not so much a struggle between African and American

identities that are "fused in one black body" as it is a tension inherent in the struggle against white racism.

22. Du Bois, *The Souls of Black Folk* (Penguin ed.), 5.

23. Mark E. Button, "Accounting for Moral Blind Spots: From Oedipus to Democratic Epistemology," *Political Theory* 39, no. 6 (2011), 710.

24. Douglass, *Autobiographies*, 591.

25. Paul Giles, "Narrative Reversals and Power Exchanges: Frederick Douglass and British Culture," *American Literature* 73, no. 4 (2001), 785.

26. On Douglass representing himself as a self-made man in the tradition of Benjamin Franklin, see Joseph Fichtelberg, *The Complex Image: Faith and Method in American Autobiography* (Philadelphia: University of Pennsylvania Press, 1989), 148, 116–17.

27. Harriet Jacobs, *Incidents in the Life of a Slave Girl*, Jean Fagan Yellin, ed. (Cambridge: Harvard University Press, 1987), 9. All further page references will appear in the text.

28. In an illuminating reading of Jacobs's *Incidents*, literary scholar Saidya Hartman concludes that "Ultimately, what is revealed in the course of Linda's 'deliberate calculation' is that the very effort to 'liberate' the slave positions the self in a network of exchange underwritten by the extrications of constraint, property, and freedom." My suggestion is that more attention to Jacobs's indignation and dignity encourages a complementary, but less pessimistic, reading of this passage in her *Narrative*. Saidiya V. Hartman, *Scenes of Subjection: Terror, Slavery, and Self-Making in Nineteenth-Century America* (New York: Oxford University Press, 1997), 112. On Jacobs's impossible struggle to separate choice from compulsion, especially as these pertain to her sexuality, see also Claudia Tate, *Domestic Allegories of Political Desire: The Black Heroine's Text at the Turn of the Century* (New York: Oxford University Press, 1992), 27–32; Hazel Carby, *Reconstructing Womanhood: The Emergence of the Afro-American Woman Novelist* (New York: Oxford University Press, 1987), 49–61; P. Gabrielle Forman, "The Spoken and the Silenced in Incidents in the *Life of a Slave Girl* and *Our Nig*," *Callaloo* 13, no. 2 (1990), 313–24; John Ernest, *Resistance and Reformation in Nineteenth-Century African-American Literature: Brown, Wilson, Jacobs, Delaney, Douglass, and Harper* (Jackson: University Press of Mississippi, 1995), 98–108; Laura Doyle, *Freedom's Empire: Race and the Rise of the Novel in Atlantic Modernity, 1640–1940* (Durham: Duke University Press, 2008), 258–61.

29. Axel Honneth has provided a compelling theory of the social production of dignity that is congruent with the theory I am extrapolating from these texts and words of black Americans. See "Integrity and Disrespect: Principles of a Conception of Morality Based on the Theory of Recognition," *Political Theory* 20, no. 2 (1992), 187–201.

30. Orlando Patterson, *Slavery and Social Death: A Comparative Study* (Cambridge: Harvard University Press, 1982), 337–38.

31. Political theorist Sharon Krause has argued that "the ideal of intrinsic human dignity as a universal condition of persons could not produce [Douglass's] redemption on its own. The individual action was the key; without it, neither freedom nor self-respect was possible." For this reason, Krause argues, "Douglass's use of the term 'dignity' is more closely linked to honor than to the contemporary use of the word, which refers to the intrinsic worth of every human being." As I am hoping to show, Jacobs and even Douglass call into question this contemporary use of the word, urging us to embrace the paradox that dignity feels intrinsic yet is socially produced. Sharon Krause, *Liberalism with Honor* (Cambridge: Harvard University Press, 2002), 147.

32. See Gooding-Williams, *Shadow of Du Bois*, esp. 176–87. I entirely agree with Gooding-Williams that Douglass sought a "radical reconstruction" (191) of democracy and that he was "an exemplar of the possibility of re-founding and re-constructing the nation" (168). What I would emphasize, however, is that Douglass's commitment to democratic possibilities was strongly reinforced by his having to *transform* his indignation into such democratic reconstruction precisely because violent expression of it was not a viable strategy for black Americans at that time.

33. Yancy, "African-American Philosophy," 552.

34. As Axel Honneth argues: "the moral force within lived social reality that is responsible for development and progress is a struggle for recognition [of dignity]. This is a strong claim, one that sometimes seems to suggest a philosophy of history, and in order to give it a theoretically defensible form, evidence would have to be presented to the effect that the experience of disrespect represents the affective source of knowledge for social resistance and collective uprisings. But that . . . is not something I can directly prove here" ("Integrity and Disrespect," 143). The texts we have been reading here provide precisely the empirical validation Honneth's theory requires.

35. Pennington, *The Fugitive Blacksmith*, 211–12. My account of this passage from Pennington draws heavily on my earlier analysis in *By the Sweat of the Brow: Literature and Labor in Antebellum America* (Chicago: University of Chicago Press, 1993), 175–210. Still the most thorough discussion of self-respect and submission within slavery is John W. Blassingame's *The Slave Community: Plantation Life in the Antebellum South,* rev. ed. (New York: Oxford University Press, 1979), 284–322.

36. James Baldwin, *Collected Essays*, 25–26. All further references will be made in the text.

37. Ellison, *Going to the Territory*, 124.

38. William Ian Miller has suggested that "the mutuality of contempt is much of what pluralistic democracy is all about. What democracy has done is arm the lower with some of the contempts that only the high had available to them before." What distinguishes indignation from Miller's understanding of contempt is that indignation seems to provoke an awakening to the existence of one's dignity by way of a challenge to, or denial of, it. Indignation thus has the potential of becoming democratic

indignation and, in turn, action. By contrast, even Miller's "upward contempt" deflects attention from the vulnerability of one's dignity and hardens into static indifference. William Ian Miller, *The Anatomy of Disgust* (Cambridge: Harvard University Press, 1997), 234.

39. Katie G. Cannon and Carter Heyward, *Alienation and Anger: A Black and a White Woman's Struggle for Mutuality in an Unjust World* (Wellesley, Mass.: Stone Center, 1992), 8.

40. Martha Nussbaum, *Hiding from Humanity: Disgust, Shame, and the Law* (Princeton: Princeton University Press, 2004), 283.

41. Brown, *States of Injury*, 55–67.

42. Malcolm X, *Malcolm X Speaks*, George Breitman, ed. (New York: Grove Press, 1965), 107–8.

CHAPTER 2

1. Charles S. Johnson, *A Preface to Racial Understanding* (New York: Friendship Press, 1936), 185.

2. J. Saunders Redding, *On Being Negro in America* (New York: Charter Books, 1951), 9.

3. Lewis, *Walking with the Wind*, 486, 493.

4. Understanding racism in terms of race relations and interracial relationships sometimes overlooks the fact that racism is also structural and institutional—as Stokely Carmichael argued. Yet the converse is also true. It is important to bear in mind that antiracist struggle requires citizens of a democracy both to attack racist institutions (e.g., the War on Drugs, the proliferation of mandatory sentencing laws, and so on) and to overcome the interpersonal obstacles to interracial understanding and alliance-building.

5. Bonnie Honig, *Political Theory and the Displacement of Politics* (Ithaca: Cornell University Press, 1993).

6. (Emphasis added.) Quoted in Jonathon S. Kahn, *Divine Discontent: The Religious Imagination of W.E.B. Du Bois* (New York: Oxford University Press, 2009), 6.

7. Patterson, *Slavery and Social Death*, 100.

8. Steven Hahn, *A Nation under Our Feet: Black Political Struggles in the Rural South, from Slavery to the Great Migration* (Cambridge: Harvard University Press, 2003), 16–17.

9. The relation of race to class in the first decades of the twentieth century was complex, but there can be little doubt that the ideology of white racial superiority advanced the interests of those who stood to lose from interracial labor alliances.

10. Redding, *On Being Negro in America*, 113–14.

11. Jane Daily, *The Age of Jim Crow* (New York: W. W. Norton, 2009), 15. Further page references will appear in the text.

12. The southern strategy of resistance to the civil rights bill was to draw a distinction between civil rights and social rights. South Carolinian Robert B. Vance argued that "this bill goes further, and provides that colored children shall go into the same school with white children, mixing the colored children and the white children in the same schools. I submit to the committee whether that is not a social right instead of a civil right." Quoted by Paul Yandle, "Different Colored Currents of the Sea: Reconstruction North Carolina, Mutuality, and the Political Roots of Jim Crow, 1872–1875," in Paul. D. Escott, ed., *North Carolinians in the Era of the Civil War and Reconstruction* (Chapel Hill: University of North Carolina Press, 2008), 229. Yandle also points to the ways southern segregationists simultaneously acknowledged and denied relationships with blacks by claiming that segregation was a system of "mutual dependence" or "mutuality" (231, 233, 235).

13. John Stuart Mill, *On Liberty* (New Haven: Yale University Press, 2003), 141. However, as Nathaniel Adams Tobias Colemen has pointed out, Mill's assertion of such a right is strongly qualified by such phrases as "not to the oppression of his individuality" and "though not to parade the avoidance." See Coleman's unpublished "A Right to Avoid Blacks?" delivered to the Department of Philosophy, Pennsylvania State University, February 2013, and available online at http://www.academia.edu/2572656/A_right_to_avoid_blacks.

14. Pauli Murray, *Proud Shoes: The Story of an American Family* (New York: Harper and Row, 1956), 269.

15. Lewis Gordon in Bill E. Lawson and Frank M. Kirkland, eds., *Frederick Douglass: A Critical Reader* (Oxford: Blackwell, 1999), 222–23.

16. Charles W. Chesnutt, "The Future of the Negro" (1882) in Joseph R. McElrath Jr., Robert C. Leitz III, and Jesse S. Crisler, eds., *Charles W. Chesnutt: Essays and Speeches* (Stanford, Calif.: Stanford University Press, 1999), 29.

17. Chesnutt, "An Inside View of the Negro Question" (1886), in *Essays and Speeches*, 59. Further page citations will be given in the text.

18. Chesnutt, "A Multitude of Counselors" (1891), in *Essays and Speeches*, 82–83; emphasis added. Further page citations will be given in the text.

19. Chesnutt, "Liberty and the Franchise" (1899) in *Essays and Speeches*, 105; emphasis added.

20. Kenneth Warren, *What Was African-American Literature?* (Cambridge: Harvard University Press, 2011). On Chesnutt, see, see, for example, Dean McWilliams, *Charles W. Chesnutt and the Fictions of Race* (Athens: University of Georgia Press, 2002); Eric J. Sundquist, *To Wake the Nations: Race in the Making of American Literature* (Cambridge: Harvard University Press, 1993). Barack Obama, *Dreams from My Father: A Story of Race and Inheritance* (New York: Three Rivers Press, 1995), 294. These words come from Obama's account of his conversion experience in Reverend Jeremiah Wright's church. "Those stories—of survival, and freedom, and hope—became our story, my story; the blood that had spilled was our blood, the tears our tears; until this black church, on this bright day, seemed once more a vessel

carrying the story of a people into future generations and into a larger world. Our trials and triumphs became at once unique and universal, black and more than black." Critics who have investigated the dimension of critique in Chesnutt's work include Posnock, *Color and Culture*; and Stacey Margolis, *The Public Life of Privacy in Nineteenth-Century American Literature* (Durham: Duke University Press, 2005).

21. William L. Andrews, foreword to *The House behind the Cedars* (Athens: University of Georgia Press, 2000), xi.

22. Charles W. Chesnutt, *Stories, Novels, and Essays* (New York: Library of America, 2002), 352. Further page citations will be given in the text.

23. Margolis, *Public Life of Privacy*, 137. Despite our shared interest in privacy and the congruence of our conclusions, Margolis's persuasive reading of this novel runs a course—through a comparison of Chesnutt's work with British fictions of racial conversion—different from the one I have proposed here.

24. Terrence L. Johnson, *Tragic Soul-Life: W.E.B. Du Bois and Moral Crisis Facing American Democracy* (New York: Oxford University Press, 2012), 15, 6.

25. Chesnutt, Journal, May 29, 1880, cited by William Gleason in Joseph R. McElrath Jr., ed., *Critical Essays on Charles W. Chesnutt* (New York: G. K. Hall, 1999), 234.

26. McElrath, *Critical Essays*, 29, 30–31, 39, 50, 72.

27. McElrath, *Critical Essays*, 71, 68.

CHAPTER 3

1. Allen, *Talking to Strangers*. I will discuss Allen's work at greater length at the end of this chapter. For a more detailed version of my reading of *Passing*, see Nick Bromell, "Reading Democratically: Pedagogies of Difference and Practices of Listening in *The House of Mirth* and *Passing*," *American Literature* 81, no. 2 (2009), 281–303.

2. George Hutchinson, *The Harlem Renaissance in Black and White* (Cambridge: Harvard University Press, 1995), 206. Actually, Hutchinson is here paraphrasing the views of Mary Fleming Larrabee, a white critic who reviewed Nella Larsen's *Passing*, but I think we can take these words as an expression of his own judgment as well.

3. Elaine Ginsberg, "Introduction: The Politics of Passing," in Elaine Ginsberg, ed., *Passing and the Fictions of Identity* (Durham: Duke University Press, 1996), 2.

4. Larsen's *Passing* has given rise to an extraordinarily rich body of criticism that deals with the novel's treatment of identity: its nature, its performance, its suppression or repression. Recently, critics have also looked at the ways that, as Catherine Rottenberg writes, the phenomenon of passing "interrogates and problematizes the ontology of identity categories and their construction." Catherine Rottenberg, "*Passing*: Race, Identification, and Desire," *Criticism* 45, no. 4 (2003), 435.

5. Nella Larsen, *Quicksand and Passing* (New Brunswick, N.J.: Rutgers University Press, 1986), 149. All further page citations will be given in the text.

6. In a perceptive Lacanian reading of the novel, Nell Sullivan calls attention to Irene's (self-hating) racism, especially as it surfaces in her unconscious denigration of her black servant, Zulena. Nell Sullivan, "Nella Larsen's *Passing* and the Fading Subject," *African American Review* 32, no. 3 (1998), 376.

7. Bruce W. Wilshire, ed., *William James: The Essential Writings* (Albany: State University of New York Press, 1984), 58.

8. This was a commonly voiced complaint in Larsen's day. She may have read Robert Russa Moton's *What the Negro Thinks* (Garden City, N.Y.: Doubleday, Doran, 1929) in which he writes: "Perhaps no single phrase has been more frequently used in discussing the race problem in America than the familiar declaration, 'I know the Negro.'...Negroes have always met this remark with a certain faint, knowing smile" (1).

9. Cheryl Wall, "Passing for What? Aspects of Identity in Nella Larsen's Novels," *Black American Literature Forum* 20, nos. 1–2 (1986), 109. Wall's argument is that this novel represents the entwining of racial and sexual identity for black women. I think we can agree with such a reading of the novel while also exploring what it reveals about the complex dynamics of communication across and through differences of sexual and racial identity.

10. Young, *Inclusion and Democracy*, 83. See also Young's "Communication and the Other."

11. Tully, "Approaches to Recognition," 862. The article is a review essay, and he is referring specifically to Fred R. Dallmayr, *Achieving Our World: Toward a Global and Plural Democracy* (Lanham, Md.: Rowman and Littlefield, 2001).

12. Romand Coles, "Moving Democracy: Industrial Areas Foundation Social Movements and the Political Arts of Listening, Traveling, and Tabling," *Political Theory* 32, no. 5 (2004), 681–84.

13. Deborah McDowell, introduction to *Quicksand and Passing* (New Brunswick: Rutgers University Press, 1986), xxx; Claudia Tate, "Nella Larsen's *Passing*: A Problem of Interpretation," *Black American Literature Forum* 14, no. 4 (1980), 146.

14. This stubborn dilemma deeply troubles the optimism inherent in philosopher Donald Davidson's model of communication through passing theories. "All two people need, if they are to understand each other through speech," Davidson writes, "is the ability to converge on passing theories from utterance to utterance." Larsen's reply would be, *Well, yes and no.* Yes, they have no need of something "in common," nor do they require reliable markers that place and identify the other. But no, a certain difficulty is being elided here, since the "ability" to converge can be compromised both by failures on the listening side and by the fraught position of the one who must decide, from utterance to utterance, how much of her difference to bring into the conversation. How much passing does a passing theory require? How much can it sustain? These are the very difficult questions about communication through difference that this novel poses—and leaves unanswered. Davidson is quoted

in Richard Rorty, *Contingency, Irony, and Solidarity* (Cambridge: Cambridge University Press, 1989), 14.

15. Brandon Gordon, "Physical Sympathy: Hip and Sentimentalism in James Baldwin's *Another Country*," *Modern Fiction Studies* 57, no. 1 (2011), 89; Kevin Ohi, " 'I'm Not the Boy You Want': Sexuality, 'Race,' and Thwarted Revelation in Baldwin's *Another Country*," *African American Review* 33, no. 1 (1999), 264; Ernesto Javier Martinez, "Dying to Know: Identity and Self-Knowledge in Baldwin's *Another Country*," *PMLA* 124, no. 3 (2009), 783.

16. Susan Feldman, "Another Look at *Another Country*: Reconciling Baldwin's Racial and Sexual Politics," in D. Quentin Miller, ed., *Re-viewing James Baldwin* (Philadelphia: Temple University Press, 2000), 94.

17. James Baldwin, *Early Novels and Stories* (New York: Library of America, 1998), 425. All further page citations will be given in the text.

18. Thus, Michael F. Lynch is correct that "what concerns Baldwin primarily is the suffering that crosses racial lines," but he veers into unwarranted optimism when he concludes that "Baldwin's novel seeks and suggests a creative escape from, and victory over rage through the attainment of intimacy and love with another person." As Ohi argues, there is a great deal of seeking in the novel, but precious little "escape" or "victory." Michael F. Lynch, "Beyond Guilt and Innocence: Redemptive Suffering and Love in Baldwin's *Another Country*," *Obsidian II* 7, nos. 1–2 (1992), 1.

19. As George Hutchinson has observed in *The Harlem Renaissance in Black and White*, Sterling Brown and other black American writers associated with the Harlem Renaissance sought to show that "Lack of sympathy effects the erasure of otherness through caricature as surely as does the *premature* socially naïve leap to human 'universals' " (206).

20. Balfour, *Evidence of Things Not Seen*, 96.

21. Robert Tomlinson, " 'Payin' One's Dues': Expatriation as Personal Experience and Paradigm in the Works of James Baldwin," *African American Review* 33, no. 1 (1999), 138.

22. Ralph Waldo Emerson, *The Collected Works, vol. 2: Essays: First Series* (Cambridge: Harvard University Press, 1979), 30.

23. Walt Whitman, *Democratic Vistas*, in Michael Warner, ed., *The Portable Whitman* (New York: Penguin Books, 2004), 414; 415.

24. *The Portable Whitman*, 43.

25. Allen, *Talking to Strangers*, 156.

26. Quoted in Allen, *Talking to Strangers*, 185.

CHAPTER 4

1. *My Bondage and My Freedom*, 373. In his speeches in England and in his letters back to the United States, Douglass repeatedly emphasized this "transition"—the transformation he underwent as he experienced this mirroring back to him of his own

humanity in the looks of those who met him: "Eleven days and a half gone, and I have crossed three thousand miles of the perilous deep. Instead of a democratic government, I am under a monarchical government. Instead of the bright, blue sky of America, I am covered with the soft, grey fog of the Emerald Isle. I breathe, and lo! The chattel becomes a man. I look around in vain for someone who will question my equal humanity" (374).

2. Judith Shklar, *Redeeming American Political Thought* (Chicago: University of Chicago Press, 1998), 127. For a succinct summary of the tensions between democratic nation-states and global interconnectedness, see also David Held, "Democracy and the International Order," in Daniele Archibugo and David Held, eds., *Cosmopolitan Democracy: An Agenda for a New World Order* (Cambridge: Polity Press, 1995), 96–120. The persistence of this vexing question is what leads political theorist Seyla Benhabib to conclude that "the relationship between the spread of cosmopolitan norms and democratic self-determination is fraught, both theoretically and politically." Benhabib, *Another Cosmopolitanism*, 17.

3. Joshua Cohen, ed., *For Love of Country: Debating the Limits of Patriotism—Martha C. Nussbaum with Respondents* (Boston: Beacon Press, 1996), 6. All further page references will be made in the text.

4. *For Love of Country*, 30.

5. Balfour, *Democracy's Reconstruction*, 116. All further page references will appear in the text.

6. *For Love of Country*, 45, 47.

7. Bonnie Honig, *Democracy and the Foreigner* (Princeton: Princeton University Press, 2001), 105. Seyla Benhabib, *Another Cosmopolitanism*, 36.

8. Fionnghuala Sweeney, *Frederick Douglass and the Atlantic World* (Liverpool: Liverpool University Press, 2007), 2. In what follows, I am indebted to Russ Castronovo, who was the first critic to argue that the thrust of Douglass's writings during this first visit to Britain was to "contest the nation, to alienate its traditions and unsettle its hallowed doctrines so that descendants of the African diaspora [could] call—however uncertainly or uneasily—America home" (246). This is exactly right, and Castronovo sensitively understands that Douglass's ambivalence is not just incoherence. But when he claims that James McCune Smith's well-known statement that Douglass's second autobiography "is an American book, for Americans, in the fullest sense of the idea" "is...steeped in irony" (245), he misses something crucial: Smith was anything but ironic when he wrote "in the fullest sense of the idea." This move of enlarging is, as we have seen, characteristic of Du Bois and a number of other black American thinkers. A "fullest sense" of "the idea" of America is what Douglass—and many other African American writers—insisted upon. If there is an irony here, it lies in the fact Douglass put a transnational perspective to work in order to envision such national fullness. Russ Castronovo, "'As to Nation, I Belong to None': Ambivalence, Diaspora, and Frederick Douglass," *American Transcendental Quarterly* 9, no. 3 (1999), 245–60. See also Alan J. Rice and

Martin Crawford, eds., *Liberating Sojourn: Frederick Douglass and Transatlantic Reform* (Athens: University of Georgia Press, 1999).

9. *Life and Writings*, vol. i, p. 148.

10. *Life and Writings*, vol. I, p. 207..

11. *Frederick Douglass Papers*, Series One: vol. 2, p. 21. See also his speeches of May 11, 1847 in *Life and Writings*, 236, 237 and September 24, 1847 in *Frederick Douglass Papers*, Series One: vol II, p. 93.

12. *Life and Writings*, vol. i, p, 126, 149.

13. *Correspondence*, vol. i, p. 105.

14. *Frederick Douglass Papers*, Series One: vol. 2, pp. 60–61; emphasis added.

15. *Another Cosmopolitanism*, 50.

16. Nikhil Pal Singh, *Black Is a Country: Race and the Unfinished Struggle for Democracy* (Cambridge: Harvard University Press, 2004).

17. Johnson, *Writings*, 529. All further page references will be made in the text.

18. Brian Russell Roberts, "Passing into Diplomacy: U.S. Consul James Weldon Johnson and *The Autobiography of an Ex-Colored Man*," *Modern Fiction Studies*, 56, no. 2 (2010), 291. See also Etsuko Taketani, "The Cartography of the Black Pacific: James Weldon Johnson's *Along This Way*," *American Quarterly* 59, no. 1 (2007), 79–106; Alasdair MacIntyre, "The Indispensability of Political Theory" in *The Nature of Political Theory*, eds. David Miller and Larry Siedentop (Oxford: Clarendon Press, 1983), 24.

19. Deleuze is quoted by William Connolly, who writes (glossing this passage): "Thinking is often inspired by surprising encounters, either between new events and established thought-imbued conventions or between those conventions and something mute in the world that has not yet been translated (that is, lifted and altered) into the register of thought." Connolly, *Neuropolitics*, 98–99.

20. Walter Mignolo, "The Many Faces of Cosmo-polis: Border Thinking and Critical Cosmopolitanism," *Public Culture* 12, no. 3 (2000), 723.

21. Manning Marable, *Malcolm X: A Life of Reinvention* (New York: Viking, 2011), 302.

22. *Autobiography of Malcolm X* (New York: Ballantine Books, 1964), 391.

23. Anna Hartnell, *Rewriting Exodus: American Futures from Du Bois to Obama* (London: Pluto Press, 2011), 155.

24. Moreover, Malcolm's travels had also encouraged an entirely new hostility to capitalism. He stated in one public appearance, "It's impossible for a white person to believe in capitalism and not believe in racism." Although he never fully explained why be believed that capitalism logically entailed racism, he certainly was influenced by the time he had spent in several (theoretically) socialist nations in Africa after leaving Saudi Arabia. "All of the countries that are emerging today from under colonialism are turning toward socialism," he said. "I don't think it's an accident" (336). It's also plausible that Malcolm intuitively linked American capitalist ideology—in particular its obsession with individual material success at the expense of community welfare—to racism that promoted the interests of one group (race) at the expense of the well-being of the nation as a whole.

25. Quoted in Raymond Rodgers and Jimmie N. Rogers, "The Evolution of the Attitude of Malcolm X toward Whites," *Phylon* 44, no. 2 (1983), 108–9.

26. As Elizabeth Mazucci shows, by this time Malcolm had very likely come to see race itself "as a social construction—not a scientific fact." Elizabeth Mazucci, "Going Back: Interpreting Malcolm X's Transition from 'Black Asiatic' to 'Afro-American,'" in Manning Marable and Vanessa Agard-Jones, eds., *Transnational Blackness: Navigating the Global Color Line* (New York: Palgrave Macmillan, 2008), 258.

27. Quoted in Marable, 332.

28. OAAU Charter Statement available on-line at http://www.blackpeopleparty. com/3.html.

29. Dean E. Robinson has recently argued that "The most consequential feature of black nationalism in the United States has been not its radical critique of American politics and thought but *its inadvertent reproduction of them*." He notes in particular the ways "the main expressions of Black Power–era political and economic radicalism" critically and programmatically absorbed "the frameworks of cultural and political pluralism that defined the common sense of postwar American liberalism" (184–85). If this is so—and I find his argument convincing—then we might understand Malcolm X's democratic cosmopolitanism as in part an effort to move beyond the conceptual frameworks of both of the Nation of Islam *and* "postwar American liberalism." See "Black Power Nationalism as Ethnic Pluralism: Postwar Liberalism's Ethnic Paradigm in Black Radicalism," in Adolph Reed Jr. and Kenneth W. Warren, eds., *Renewing Black Intellectual History* (Boulder: Paradigm Publishers, 2010), 184–214. A fuller account of Robinson's argument can be found in his *Black Nationalism in American Politics and Thought* (Cambridge: Cambridge University Press, 2001).

30. *For Love of Country*, 52.

31. On this topic, as on the others I have discussed, Du Bois's thinking changed considerably over the course of his long career. Scholarly comment on it is likewise vast and varied. In what follows, I have tried to focus on a few see-through lines: Du Bois's sense that the world is politically interconnected, and that democratic justice cannot be achieved fully anywhere until it has been achieved everywhere; his commitment to enlargement and his (sometimes reluctant to be sure) awareness of the contingency of his own views. In addition to Singth, *Black is a Color* and Balfour, *Democracy's Reconstruction*, see especially Susan Gillman and Alys Eve Weinbaum, eds., *Next to the Color Line: Gender, Sexuality, and W.E.B. Du Bois* (Minneapolis: University of Minnesota Press, 2007); Paul Gilroy, *Postcolonial Melancholy* (New York: Columbia University Press, 2005), 33–38; Amy Kaplan, *The Anarchy of Empire in the Making of U.S. Culture* (Cambridge: Harvard University Press, 2002); Bill V. Mullen, W.E.B. Du Bois, "Dark Princess, and the Afro-Asian International," in Bill V. Mullen and James Smethurst, eds., *Left of the Color Line: Race, Radicalism, and Twentieth-Century Literature of the United*

States (Chapel Hill: University of North Carolina Press, 2003), 87–106; Penny M. Von Eschen, *Race Against Empire: Black Americans and Anticolonialism, 1937–1957* (Ithaca: Cornell University Press, 1997); Nicole A. Waligora-Davis, "Du Bois and the World Citizen" in *Sanctuary: African Americans and Empire* (New York: Oxford University Press, 2011), 22–43.

32. W. E. B. Du Bois, *The Autobiography of W.E.B. Du Bois: A Soliloquy on Viewing My Life from the Last Decade of Its First Century* (New York: Oxford University Press, 2007), 99.

33. *Du Bois Reader*, 47–48.

34. W.E.B. Du Bois, *Newspaper Columns*, Herbert Aptheker, ed. (White Plains, N.Y.: Kraus-Thomson Organization, 1986), vol. 1, p. 109 (Aug. 29, 1936).

35. Connolly, *Neuropolitics*, 195–96. In noting Connolly's affinities with the cosmopolitans of the black Americans I've been discussing, we should not overlook a significant difference—one that reflects, again, the comparatively secure social and political status he shares with Nussbaum. This security disposes him to discount the protections afforded by what he calls "single-entry universalism." When he writes that the task for cosmopolitan intellectuals is "to inspire more participants in each religious and metaphysical tradition to come to terms with its comparative contestability," his word "participants" fails to plumb the depths of their commitment to a tradition. To be sure, some aspects of it may indeed become visibly "contestable" to them; but other aspects may feel like indispensable guarantors of whatever margin of security they possess or aspire to possess. If Douglass, for example, were to read Connolly's argument, he would reply (I suspect) that truths such as "all men are created equal" are not at all contestable; but what *is* contestable is how we humans, beholding those truths from our contingent and particular historical locations, understand and articulate them. The distinction is subtle but crucial. Here we circle back to one of the central paradoxes, or inconsistencies, at the heart of this current of black American thought—its balanced commitments to both particularism *and* universalism.

36. Of course, as Balfour and Singh emphasize, the indispensable first step for *white* Americans is to acknowledge and reflect deeply upon the intertwined racial histories of the nation and the world. As we have seen, such abnegation of white American racial "innocence" is what James Baldwin, too, insisted on.

CHAPTER 5

1. Cooper, *Voice of Anna Julia Cooper*, 193.

2. As will become clear, I am not thinking here of the black American church taken as a whole (if such a thing even exists). Nor am I thinking primarily of what David L. Chappell calls the civil right's movement's black "nonviolent soldiers" who "were driven not my liberal faith in reason, but by older, seemingly more durable prejudices and superstitions that were rooted in Christian and Jewish myth." Although a

few of the figures I discuss (King, Murray, Lewis) were indeed believers of this sort, most were more secular in outlook yet were open-minded enough to realize that reason alone seldom prompts or sustains political struggle on behalf of democracy. David L. Chappell, *A Stone of Hope: Prophetic Religion and the Death of Jim Crow* (Chapel Hill: University of North Carolina Press, 2004), 3. However, Chappell's discussion of liberal's absolutist skepticism toward faith—and of those liberals like Reinhold Niebuhr who criticized this tendency—should be read by those of today's "progressive" leftists who think they have left liberalism far behind.

3. Just as it is difficult to find a vocabulary that adequately describes embodied and historically situated theorizing (because we wind up using words that reflect the very mind/body distinction such theorizing eschews), so it is nearly impossible to describe a certain stream of black American religious thought without likewise using words that reflect the immanence/transcendence and history/eternity binaries it rejects. Jonathon Kahn's term "pragmatic religious naturalism" comes close to capturing the spirit of this black religious thought; but even Kahn re-inscribes a dualism I believe Du Bois, Douglass, Cooper, and Malcolm X would all resist when he writes that "Pragmatic religious naturalists *use religion for ends* that have to do with exploring the angled perplexities of human finitude and not the wholeness of godly infinity" (13; emphases added). These figures' relation to religion is not as purely instrumental as Kahn's words imply. These figures find value in faith not only because it serves human political and historical ends that they and we are disposed to honor, but because they can effectively pursue those ends when (and only when) they admit to their own *dependence* on faith. Instrumentality obscures the humility and reverence entailed by "human finitude" that they considered to be indispensable. *Divine Discontent: The Religious Imagination of W.E.B. Du Bois* (New York: Oxford University Press, 2009)

4. Octavia V. Rogers Butler, *The House of Bondage, or, Charlotte Brooks and Other Slaves* (New York: Oxford University Press, 1988), 23, 31.

5. Lewis, *Walking with the Wind*, 63–64.

6. Douglass, *Autobiographies*, 278.

7. Douglass's enduring attachment to his faith is not hard to explain: Christianity helped many black Americans survive their enslavement, both individually and as communities. As Steven Hahn has put it: "If slave communities found quasi-institutional expression, it was most commonly in the religious congregations that they fashioned. In them, the varied threads of household, kinship, labor, gender, and leadership came to be joined with those of sensibility, ethics, aspiration, spirituality, and faith to create a social fabric both rich and varied, with many blends." Hahn, *Nation under Our Feet*, 43. Or, as Bettye Collier-Thomas writes: "In the slave community there was an 'invisible institution' hidden from whites, in which black men and women bonded and created a world in which the moral values of respect, cooperation, and compassion were central to group identity and survival." Bettye

Collier-Thomas, *Jesus, Jobs, and Justice: African-American Women and Religion* (New York: Alfred A. Knopf, 2010), 6.

8. Scholarly interpretation of Douglass's reading of the Constitution is varied and voluminous. In addition to Frank, *Constituent Moments*, see, especially, Waldo E. Martin, *The Mind of Frederick Douglass*, 31–40; David W. Blight, *Frederick Douglass' Civil War*, 30–35; Gregg D. Crane, *Race, Citizenship, and Law in American Literature* (Cambridge: Cambridge University Press, 2002), 104–30; Philip S. Foner, *Frederick Douglass* (New York: Citadel Press, 1964), 136–54; David. E. Schrader, "Natural Law in the Constitutional Thought of Fredrick Douglass," and Charles W. Mills, "Whose Fourth of July? Frederick Douglass and 'Original Intent,'" both in Lawson and Kirkland, eds., *Frederick Douglass: A Critical Reader*, 100–142; Hoang Gia Phan, *Bonds of Citizenship: Law and the Labors of Emancipation* (New York: New York University Press, 2013). Indispensable background is provided by William Wiecek, *The Sources of Antislavery Constitutionalism in America* (Ithaca: Cornell University Press, 1977).

9. Douglass, *Life and Writings*, vol. 2, pp. 149–50; emphasis added.

10. Douglass, *Life and Writings*, vol. 2, p. 157.

11. Wilson Jeremiah Moses, *Creative Conflict in African American Thought: Frederick Douglass, Alexander Crummell, Booker T. Washington, W.E.B. Du Bois, and Marcus Garvey* (Cambridge: Cambridge University Press, 2004), 48. Waldo E. Martin, *The Mind of Frederick Douglass* (Chapel Hill, NC: 1984), 33–34. David Blight likewise sees in the antebellum Douglass "a mind torn between moral principle and political action." David Blight, *Frederick Douglass' Civil War: Keeping Faith in Jubilee* (Baton Rouge: Louisiana State University Press, 1989), 36. After the Civil War, Blight suggests, Douglass became more able to sustain the "unresolved contradictions in his…thought" (195). By contrast, I would argue that Douglass learned to hold these in tension with each other as he broke with Garrison and came to understand himself occupying a standpoint from which the dichotomy of principle and action looked incoherent.

12. I intend this metaphor to call to mind Emerson's well-known sentences in "Self-Reliance" and thus to highlight the differences between these thinkers. Emerson writes: "The voyage of the best ship is a zigzag of a hundred tacks. See the line from a sufficient distance, and it straightens itself to the average tendency." For Emerson, the zigzag of apparent inconsistency reveals itself to be the reality of a straight line of consistency when we have removed ourselves to a "sufficient distance" from it; this move is entirely in tune with Emerson's transcendentalism and with his own personal experience of being "uplifted" in "infinite space." For Emerson, therefore, the best and truest thought can occur only in conditions of absolute freedom.

13. *Fredrick Douglass Papers, Series One; Speeches, Debates, and Interviews*, vol. 2: 1847–54, p. 368. All further page references will appear in the text.

14. Gregg Crane calls this style of thought a "cosmopolitan Constitutionalism" that reconciles the abstract potentiality of the Constitution with the inevitable

shortcomings of particular, historical interpretations of it: "Douglass came to recognize that, for individual moral aspiration to have effect, it must enter public discourse in such a way as to create a new moral consensus—as Emerson put it, "although the commands of the Conscience are *essentially* absolute, they are *historically* limitary." In attempting to achieve justice, we act on a moral impulse deriving, we believe, from eternal moral principles, but acknowledge at the same time that the implementation of that moral principle in consensual politics and law is temporal." Crane, *Race, Citizenship, and Law*, 109.

15. Shulman, *American Prophecy*, 17.

16. In a rather pessimistic reading of this speech, Charles W. Mills argues that Douglass was engaging in wishful thinking and that Justice Taney's historicist interpretation of the Constitution was more plausible. See "Whose Fourth of July? Frederick Douglass and 'Original Intent,'" in Lawson and Kirkland, *Frederick Douglass: A Critical Reader*, 100–142.

17. For a fuller discussion of these points and of Douglass's political philosophy more broadly, see Nick Bromell, "'A Voice from the Enslaved': The Origins of Frederick Douglass's Political Philosophy of Democracy," *American Literary History* 23, no. 4 (2011), 697–723. See also Nicholas Buccola, *The Political Thought of Frederick Douglass: In Pursuit of American Liberty* (New York: New York University Press, 2012); Peter C. Myers, *Frederick Douglass: Race and the Rebirth of American Liberalism* (Lawrence: University of Kansas Press, 2008). It is worth noting that, as Kenneth Warren has argued, toward the end of his life Douglass became positively hostile to political appeals made on the basis of religious belief rather than reason. This was because he saw the black church as retarding the advancement of blacks, not enabling it. Kenneth W. Warren, "Frederick Douglass's *Life and Times*: Progressive Rhetoric and the Problem of Constituency," in Eric Sundquist ed., *Frederick Douglass: New Literary and Historical Essays* (New York: Cambridge University Press, 1990), 253–70.

18. John Stauffer has noted the paradox: "For Douglass, representations of slavery brought feelings of freedom and degrees of power. But representations of freedom created in him a crisis of language and aesthetics." One explanation for this seeming paradox inheres, as Stauffer observes, in the genre of the slave narrative itself: it was designed to represent bondage, not freedom. A complementary explanation would point to Douglass's sense that his experience of enslavement had given him a certain philosophical authority different from that he has acquired as a free man. This would explain why, as Stauffer puts it, "Long after he had escaped from bondage in 1838, Douglass insisted that he was still a slave." John Stauffer, "Frederick Douglass and the Aesthetic of Freedom," *Raritan* 25, no. 1 (2005), 115, 114.

19. Du Bois, "The Church and Religion," *Crisis* 40 (October 1933), 720. The role that faith—or some appreciation of human imagination of transcendence—played in Du Bois's political thought has long been overlooked. Jonathon S. Kahn suggests that it was virtually silenced by such prominent scholars as Cornel West,

Adolph Reed, and David Levering Lewis. More recently, it has been getting the attention it deserves. In addition to Johnson, *Tragic Soul-Life* and Kahn, *Divine Discontent*, see especially Edward J. Blum, *W.E.B. Du Bois: American Prophet* (Philadelphia: University of Pennsylvania Press, 2007).

20. Du Bois, "Jefferson Davis as a Representative of Civilization," in *Du Bois Reader*, 243.

21. Du Bois, *Autobiography: A Soliloquy*, 92, 93.

22. Du Bois, *Souls of Black Folk*, in *Du Bois Reader*, 124. As Robert Gooding-Williams has argued, Du Bois would soon abandon this conception of the relation between leaders and the led—but his abandonment was not as complete and unequivocal as Gooding-Williams believes. To be sure, within the sphere of black politics, Du Bois did repeatedly enact a conception of leaders as rulers. But this was not the only sphere in which Du Bois moved and thought. In his political thought that addresses an imagined polity of blacks and whites and seeks to reimagine and reconstruct democracy, Du Bois returns often to what Gooding-Williams calls his "honest criticism model" (54).

23. Du Bois, *Darkwater*, in *Du Bois Reader*, 558.

24. Du Bois, *Autobiography: A Soliloquy*, 72, 98.

25. Du Bois, *Darkwater*, 555, 556, 561. Perhaps Du Bois's most eloquent expression of this vision of inclusion and democracy is spoken by one of the two main characters in his unfinished and unpublished novel, *A World Search for Democracy*. Democracy, she says, "is based on the widest recognition of human equality. It assumes that wisdom in government comes from the widest knowledge concerning the governed, a knowledge eventually so wide that it becomes in effect a pool of human experience to which all human beings contribute. Shut off one rill from this ocean of life and it becomes incomplete" (17).

26. Thomas Dumm, *Loneliness as a Way of Life* (Cambridge: Harvard University Press, 2008), 156.

27. Terrence Johnson also suggests that "Du Bois's political project is defined by a moral epistemic vocabulary that emerges from black suffering, sorrow, and hope." To this list I would add "indignation." *Tragic Soul-Life*, 40.

28. Gayraud S. Wilmore, "A Black Churchman's Response to the Black Manifesto" (1969), in Gayraud S. Wilmore and James H. Cone eds., *Black Theology: A Documentary History, 1966–1979* (Maryknoll, N.Y.: Orbis Books, 1979), 84.

29. Pauli Murray, "The Dilemma of the Minority Christian" (1974), in Bettye Collier-Thomas, ed., *Daughters of Thunder: Black Women Preachers and Their Sermons, 1850–1979* (San Francisco: Jossey-Bass, 1998), 261. All further page citations will be made in the text.

30. W.E.B. Du Bois, *The Correspondence of W.E.B. Du Bois*, Herbert Aptheker, ed. (Amherst: University of Massachusetts Press, 1973–78), vol. 2, p. 204.

31. Du Bois, "The Vision of Phillis the Blessed," in *Du Bois Reader*, 329.

32. My reading of Du Bois may bring to mind the work of Karl Barth, the twentieth-century theologian known for his insistence on the unknowability of God. I am aware

of no evidence that Du Bois himself read Barth. David Levering Lewis makes no mention of Barth in his biography. Yet Barth's book *Der Romerbrief*, published in 1919 and again in a revised edition in 1921, sent shock waves through the world of German theology, and Du Bois, attuned as he was to German intellectual life, may well have read about it. (His book *Darkwater: Voices from Behind the Veil*, from which many of the passages I have just discussed are drawn, was published in 1920.) In any case, J. Kameron Carter has written a fascinating essay on the "convergence" of Barth's *Der Romerbrief* and Du Bois's *Darkwater*, arguing that they both seek to undercut the religious and theological pretensions of European colonialism—what calls "Imperial God-Man." "An Unlikely Convergence: W.E.B. Du Bois, Karl Barth, and the Problem of Imperial God-Man," *CR: The New Centennial Review* 11, no. 3 (2012), 167–224.

33. "The Church and Religion," *Crisis* 40 (October 1933), 720.

34. For *Love of Country*, 102. My discussion of Du Bois's epistemology of suffering has been informed by Scarry's *The Body in Pain: The Making and Unmaking of the World* (New York: Oxford University Press, 1985).

35. Cooper, *Voice of Anna Julia Cooper*, 63. Her closing metaphor is ambiguous: is she contradicting herself and claiming that only black women can *represent* the whole race? or is she insisting, rather, that the whole race does not exist except when and where she is able to enter with her "undisputed dignity of womanhood?"

36. Collier-Thomas, *Jesus, Jobs, and Justice*, 26.

37. James M. Washington., ed., *A Testament of Hope: The Essential Writings of Martin Luther King, Jr.* (New York: HarperCollins 1991), 348. All further page references will be made in the text.

38. Malcolm X, "Message to the Grassroots," Detroit, November 9–10, 1963, in *Malcolm X Speaks*, 9.

39. Malcolm X, "The Ballot or the Bullet," Cleveland, April 3, 1964, in *Malcolm X Speaks*, 34–35.

40. Over and over, however, Malcolm had to rebut those who oversimplified his position and sought to portray him as "an advocate of violence." When interviewer Les Crane claimed, "You have made statements reported in the press about how the Negroes should go out and arm themselves, form militias," Malcolm was quick to correct him: "No, I said this: That in areas of this country where the government has proven its…inability or its unwillingness to protect the lives and property of our people, then it's only fair to expect us to do whatever is necessary to protect ourselves…. This doesn't mean that we should buy rifles and go out and initiate attacks indiscriminately against whites. But it does mean that we should get whatever is necessary to protect ourselves…where the governmental ability to protect us has broken down." Malcolm X, *The Last Speeches*, 83–84.

41. Les Crane interview in *Last Speeches*, 84, 85.

42. For a fuller discussion of faith and democratic politics, see Nick Bromell, "Faith-Based Politics: Walking with Wittgenstein and Malcolm X," *Raritan* 32, no. 3, (2013), 140–59.

43. Malcolm X, *The Autobiography of Malcolm X* (as told to Alex Haley) (New York: Ballantine Books, 1973), 434. All further page references will be made in the text.

44. As when she writes: "we should not choose between Bigger Thomas and Janie Starks; our lives are as big and manifold and as pained and happy as the two of them put together. We should equally emulate Black Protest and Black Affirmation, for we require both; one without the other is dangerous, and will leave us vulnerable to extinction of the body or the spirit" (89). "Notes Toward a Black Balancing of Love and Hatred," in *Civil Wars* (Boston: Beacon Press, 1981).

45. *Essential Writings*, 225.

46. Nathan Wright, "Black Power: A Religious Opportunity," in Wilmore and Cone, *Black Theology*, 60.

47. See also Troy Dustert's thoughtful argument that seeks the same end—a progressive politics less hostile to religious faith—but arrives at the very different conclusion that what's needed are sincerity, discipline, dialogic creativity, and forbearance. (These last two overlap, to some extent, with the "art of citizenship" discussed in chapter 3 and the sensitivity to standpoint and contingency discussed throughout this book.) *Beyond Political Liberalism: Toward a Post-Secular Ethics of Public Life* (Notre Dame, Ind.: University of Notre Dame Press, 2006).

48. Wright, "Black Power," 50.

49. Vincent Lloyd, *The Problem with Grace: Reconfiguring Political Theology* (Stanford, Calif.: Stanford University Press, 2011), 61. Lloyd's interest is in working out what he calls an "anti-supersessionist" understanding of faith, one he calls "faith as virtue"; his general account of such faith would describe as well the faith-as-disposition of the black American writers I focus on.

50. Lewis, *Walking with the Wind*, 494. Without judging, then, which is the more effectively pluralistic vision, I will point to two relative advantages of the one I have been limning here. First, it avoids the difficulties in Connolly's theory that he himself has pointed to: it does not court the problem of distinguishing saints from charlatans, and it is less likely to reintroduce the problem that progressive advancement is often indistinguishable from infinite delay. Second, the most effectively pluralistic feature of the black thought I've discussed is the way it locates itself in two frameworks simultaneously, a doubleness Douglass beautifully expressed in the title of his second autobiography: *My Bondage and My Freedom*. As much as Connolly seeks to break away from the Kantian tradition, what he shares with Kant is the underlying and usually unconscious assumption that he is *free to think*. By showing us the contingency of this assumption along with its contestability (who among us is, after all, really and unconditionally free to think?) and by exploring what philosophy becomes when one is *not* free to think, some black Americans add a missing dimension to philosophy, one that renders it perpetually alert and radically pluralistic. Along with its realistic recognition of the power of anger, of the need for relationships that confirm human dignity, and of the usefulness of a

cosmopolitan patriotism, the pluralism of this constellation of thought can make a crucial contribution to this country's public philosophy of democracy.

51. I also hear this willingness to sustain the tension between the idea and the real, the eternal and the historical, when Terrence Johnson writes: "I also believe consideration of political ideals is necessary in efforts designed to expand the boundaries of history. I hope, however, that the reader will hold a clear view of what stares us directly in the face as we contemplate the ideal. The context in which we struggle to forge an individual and collective self is built with the bones of our buried racial tragedies." *Tragic Soul-Life*, 180.

52. Richard Rorty, *Contingency, Irony, and Solidarity* (Cambridge: Cambridge University Press, 1989), 73–95; Joseph A. Schumpeter, *Capitalism, Socialism, and Democracy* (New York: Harpers, 1950), 243; quoted in Gerald Gunther, *Learned Hand: The Man and the Judge* (New York: Alfred A. Knopf, 1994), 549. By emphasizing the "tragic" and the "prophetic" dimensions of American pragmatism, Cornel West likewise gives a distinctively African-American inflection to this tradition. Cornel West, *The American Evasion of Philosophy: A Genealogy of Pragmatism* (Madison: The University of Wisconsin Press, 1989).

CHAPTER SIX

1. Available on-line. Jonah Goldberg: http://www.nationalreview.com/articles/227397/obamas-liberal-arrogance-will-be-his-undoing/jonah-goldberg; Kristol: http://www.realclearpolitics.com/video/2011/03/30/bill_kristol_obama_is_a_born-again_neo-con.html; Beinart: http://www.thedailybeast.com/articles/2009/01/26/the-end-of-the-culture-wars.html; Troy: https://www.laprogressive.com/president-obama-the-liberal-nationalist/; Reed: http://www.progressive.org/mag_reed0508; West: http://www.rawstory.com/rawreplay/2011/04/cornel-west-obama-is-another-black-mascot-of-wall-street-oligarchs/; Mitchell Aboulafia, *Transcendence* (Stanford, Calif.: Stanford University Press, 2010).

2. Jarrett, *Representing the Race*, 161–195; David Remnick, *The Bridge: The Life and Rise of Barack Obama* (New York: Vintage Books, 2011), 228–55.

3. Kloppenberg, *Reading Obama*, x–xiii.

4. Obama, *Dreams from My Father*, 85–86.

5. Barack Obama, "Why Organize? Problems and Promise in the Inner City," in *After Alinsky: Organizing in the 1990s*, ed. Peg Knoepfle (Springield, IL: Sangamon State University, 1990), 35–40.

6. Thomas J. Sugrue, *Not Even Past: Barack Obama and the Burden of Race* (Princeton: Princeton University Press, 2010), 25.

7. My reasoning here is an extrapolation from Charles Mills's discussion of the "*interconnection* between 'white' principles and black philosophy" in *Blackness Visible*, 5–6.

8. For a balanced appraisal of the Remnick and Kloppenberg biographies—and a judicious meditation on race and politics in "the age of Obama," see Richard H. King, "Becoming Black, Becoming President," *Patterns of Prejudice* 5, nos. 1–2 (2011), 62–85. As King writes, "Obama so impressed liberal legal theorist Laurence Tribe that Tribe enlisted the twenty-seven-year-old Obama's help in composing what became a well-known article, "The Curvature of Constitutional Space" (1989), in Obama's first year of law school. This article was, and is, calculated to drive constitutional "originalists" (what were the original intentions of the framers?) and "textualists" (what does the Constitution as a document say?) around the bend with its claim that the US Constitution must change, and is changed, by every important decision of the Court; practically every decision of the Court implicitly and sometimes explicitly re-orders the meaning of the whole document. Clearly, Obama belongs within contemporary liberal jurisprudence in stressing the flexibility of the Constitution as it confronts new legal-historical situations" (72).

9. Immigration reform speech is available online at http://www.whitehouse. gov/the-press-office/remarks-president-comprehensive-immigration-reform. Unpaginated.

10. Rush Limbaugh speaking with Greta Von Sustern on *On the Record*, Foxnews (Dec. 14, 2011), available online at http://www.foxnews.com/on-air/on-the-record/2011/12/15/limbaugh-obamas-chip-his-shoulder-phenomenon-not-romney-and-gops-fear-conservatives; James Hannaham, "Obama and the Rules for Angry Black Men," *Salon* (Sept. 28, 2008). Available online at http://www.salon. com/2008/09/18/angry_obama/.

11. Frederick C. Harris, *The Price of the Ticket: Barack Obama and the Rise and Decline of Black Politics* (New York: Oxford University Press, 2012), xii.

12. Sugrue, *Not Even Past*, 98.

13. Remnick, *The Bridge*, 207.

14. Emphasis added. Speech is available online at http://www.whitehouse.gov/the-press-office/remarks-president-address-nation-way-forward-afghanistan-and-pakistan.

15. The text of President Bush's 2003 State of the Union Address (Jan. 28, 2003) available online at http://www.washingtonpost.com/wpsrv/onpolitics/transcripts/bushtext_012803.html; the text of President Bush's 2004 State of the Union Address (Jan. 20, 2004) available online at http://www.washingtonpost.com/wp-srv/politics/transcripts/bushtext_012004.html.

16. Obama's 2006 "Speech on Faith and Politics" available online at http://www.nytimes.com/2006/06/28/us/politics/2006obamaspeech.html?pagewanted=all.

17. Kloppenberg, *Reading Obama*, 144; Charlton C. Copeland, "God-Talk in the Age of Obama: Theology and Religious Political Commitment," *University of Denver Law Review* 86 (2009), 29. Copeland criticizes Obama's "translation requirement" and suggests that it mirrors his appropriation of abolitionists and Martin Luther King Jr. to a tradition of progressive politics purged of specific faith commitments: "Obama's use of the abolitionist's narrative and his reference to Martin

Luther King, both draw upon and neglect the religious foundation and content of each of these movements for social justice" (13). Copeland himself is much closer to the figures I have discussed, for he argues that it is precisely in the recognition of universal human sinfulness (which Obama himself affirms) that "religiously motivated actors" can acquire a sense of their own fallibility that would dispose them to " enter the public space conscious of the fact that they do not have a property right to any particular revelation from God" (27).

18. Obama, "Speech on Faith and Politics" (2006).

19. Manning Marable, "Racializing Obama: The Enigma of Post-Black Politics and Leadership," *Souls* 11, no. 1 (2009); Obama's Philadelphia Speech on Race Jan. 17, 2009) available online (http://www.nytimes.com/2009/01/17/us/politics/17text obama.html?pagewanted=all&_r=0.

20. Jarrett, *Representing the Race*, 184.

21. As Lawrence R. Jacobs puts it: "The fundamental error of progressive historiography and harsh Obama criticism is, first, to equate accommodation to advance legislation with betrayal and, second, to neglect leverage as a tool for splitting elements of the ruling block and building coalitions. *The persistent tendency to link Obama's compromises with failure and betrayal reveals not devotion to principle but an immature understanding of the real workings of politics and an ahistorical conception of progress.*" Lawrence R. Jacobs, "Barack Obama and the Angry Left: The Fight for Progressive Realism," in *Obama at the Crossroads* (New York: Oxford University Press, 2012), 187.

CODA

1. Quoted in Balfour, *Evidence of Things Not Said*, 116.

2. Douglass, *My Bondage and My Freedom*, 390.

3. Danielle S. Allen, *Talking to Strangers*, 29.

4. Robin D. G. Kelley, *Freedom Dreams: The Black Radical Imagination* (Boston: Beacon Press, 2002), xi, 8.

5. Benjamin Hale, *Familiar Conversations upon the Constitution of the United States Designed for the Use of Common Schools* (Boston: E.P. Broaders, 1835), iv.

6. James McCune Smith, "The Destiny of the People of Color," in John Stauffer, ed., *The Works of James McCune Smith: Black Intellectual and Abolitionist* (New York: Oxford University Press, 2006), 51. Further page references will appear in the text.

7. To some in his audience, doubtless, Smith was being too optimistic. They would have been more likely to share the views of black abolitionist Martin Delany, who predicted a quite different destiny for black Americans. He argued that white Americans would never permit the development of a black leadership class, and that many blacks would do better to emigrate to the West Indies or South America. See Martin Delany, *The Condition, Elevation, Emigration, and Destiny of the Colored People of the United States, Politically Considered* (New York: Arno Press, 1968).

8. Douglass, *Life and Writings*, vol. 2, p. 132.

9. Bernard Boxhill, "Frederick Douglass: The Black Philosopher in the United States: A Commentary," in Leonard Harris, ed., *Philosophy Born of Struggle*, 8. Although James McCune Smith disparaged "things which exist only in the imagination" and favored instead things which arise from "our struggle," his speech itself was clearly a work of the imagination, since the "destiny" he envisioned for black Americans was still just that—a vision.

10. Jarrett, *Representing the Race*, 6.

11. "Most political thinkers have believed imagination to be a necessary element in theorizing because they have recognized that, in order to render political phenomena intellectually manageable, they must be presented in what we can call a 'corrected fullness.'... to act intelligently and nobly demand[s] a perspective wider than the immediate situation for which the action [is] intended.... This more comprehensive vision [is] provided by thinking about the political society in its corrected fullness, not as it is but as it might be." Wolin, *Politics and Vision*, 20.

12. In the course of writing this book, I found that I was hardly alone in feeling that we need to supplement our critical energies with explicit commitments to certain goods and values, and that the historicism we practice needs to become a more flexible and enabling disposition rather than an orthodoxy. See, for example: Bruno Latour, "Why Did Critique Run Out of Steam? From Matters of Fact to Matters of Concern," in *Critical Inquiry* 30, no. 2 (2004), 225-248; Chris Castiglia, "'A Democratic and Fraternal Humanism': The Cant of Pessimism and Newton Arvin's Queer Socialism," *American Literary History* 21, no. 1, (2009), 159-182; Stephen Best and Sharon Marcus, eds., "Surface Reading: An Introduction," *Representations* 108, no. 1 (2009), 1-21; Cindy Weinstein and Christopher Looby, eds. *American Literature's Aesthetic Dimensions* (New York: Columbia University Press, 2012); Nancy Bentley, ed., "In the Spirit of the Thing: Critique as Enchantment" in *J19*, Vol. 1, No. 1 (Spring 2013), 147–178.

13. Such disciplined reluctance may be why many of us sometimes feel that our professional journals and conferences have become a depressing and wearisome spectacle of scholars lining up to out-critique each other. As Chris Castiglia writes: "by making cynical disbelief the affective sign of muscular acuity and cosmopolitan high seriousness, [contemporary literary/cultural studies] forestalls the optimism that makes thinkable...local resistances or social alternatives. This last consequence is sadly ironic, because the optimistic faith that the world could be organized in better ways animates much of the best work in American literary studies....But we have closeted our hopes—vulnerable to critique and derision, fraught with imaginative responsibility—behind the harder-edged denunciations of critique." "'A Democratic Fraternal Humanism': The Cant of Pessimism and Newton Arvin's Queer Socialism," *American Literary History* 21, no. 1 (2009), 160.

14. Allen, *Talking to Strangers*, 16–17. To which I would add that the very invisibility of such a whole also requires one to have *faith* that it exists.

Index

Robinson, Dean E., 169n29

Roediger, David, 7

Rogers, Ben F., 119

Rogers, Octavia V., 105–106

Der Romerbrief (Barth), 174n32

Roosevelt, Franklin, 4

Rorty, Richard, 127–128

Rottenberg, Catherine, 164n4

Rousseau, Jean-Jacques, 101

Ruffin, Josephine St. Pierre, 121

Rustin, Bayard, 2, 135

Salon, 134

Sandel, Michael, 4

Scarry, Elaine, 120

Schumpeter, Joseph, 127

"Self-Reliance" (Emerson), 77, 88, 172n12

self-reliance ideologies, 34–35, 77–78, 91

separatist-assimilationist dichotomy, 2, 25–26, 93–97, 121–126, 131, 135, 154n4, 169n29

sexuality

  identity politics and, 6, 60, 69–76

  rape and, 23–24, 41–42

  social equality and, 40–46

Shklar, Judith, 7, 80

Shulman, George, 3, 111

Singh, Nikhil Pal, 85, 92–93, 98, 170n36

Sinha, Manisha, 20

Sixteenth Street Baptist Church, 5–6, 16

skepticism, 37, 40, 65, 104–106, 120, 140–141, 148–149

slavery. *See also* African Americans; democracy; dignity; history; indignation

  abolitionist movements and, 20, 79, 83–84, 108–112

  communicability of, 77–78

dignity and indignation and, 16–17, 21–22, 41–46, 97–98

faith's role with respect to, 9–10, 105–107

relationality and, 40–46

slave narrative tradition and, 18–19, 21–28, 41, 173n18

Smith, Gerrit, 109–110

Smith, James McCune, 17, 147–148, 167n8, 179n7

social equality (racial), 43, 48–49, 52–55, 163n12

The Souls of Black Folk (Du Bois), 20, 115, 169n24

Springarn, J. E., 88

standpoint theory. *See* ontological situatedness

"Statement of Basic Aims and Objectives" (Malcolm X), 96

Stauffer, John, 173n18

Stephens, Michelle, 8, 157n23

Stewart, Maria W., 1, 13–15, 17–21

storytelling, 100–101

suffering, 117–122, 125

Sugrue, Thomas, 131, 136

Sullivan, Nell, 165n6

Sundquist, Eric J., 154n4

Supreme Court (U. S.), 3, 48–50

Sweeney, Fionnghuala, 82

Tacitus, 22

Tate, Claudia, 67

Tea Party, 4, 36

temporality. *See also* African Americans; faith; ontological situatedness

  Baldwin and, 30, 68–69

  history and, 3–4, 105–112

  imagination and, 4, 92, 113–121

tension (term), 108–112, 124, 132–133, 136, 143, 176n50

A Theory of Justice (Rawls), 157n24

Tocqueville, Alexis de, 1, 77, 157n24